The German Nuclear Dilemma

CORNELL STUDIES IN SECURITY AFFAIRS

edited by Robert J. Art *and* Robert Jervis

The German Nuclear Dilemma

JEFFREY BOUTWELL

Cornell University Press

ITHACA AND LONDON

First published 1990 by Cornell University Press.

Library of Congress Cataloging-in-Publication Data

Boutwell, Jeffrey,
  The German nuclear dilemma / Jeffrey Boutwell.
    p.   cm. — (Cornell studies in security affairs)
  Includes bibliographical references.
  ISBN 0-8014-2402-X (alk. paper)
    1. Germany (West)—Military policy.   2. Nuclear weapons—Germany (West)
I. Title. II. Series.
UA710.B836   1990
355.8'25119'0943—dc20   89-46168

Printed in the United States of America

For
Stephen Barr Boutwell
1955–1989

Contents

Figures

Tables

Preface

In March 1958, a young Social Democratic representative from Hamburg, Helmut Schmidt, caused an uproar in the West German parliament during a debate over NATO nuclear weapons policy. The normally staid Bundestag erupted when Schmidt taunted the ruling Christian Democratic party of Konrad Adenauer with the epithet "rocket Christians" for supporting the deployment of new nuclear weapons in the Federal Republic. Adding insult to injury, Schmidt noted that many of those Christian Democrats who supported the nuclear deployments were the same politicians who had facilitated Hitler's rise to power twenty-five years earlier.

More than two decades later, Chancellor Helmut Schmidt was himself being vilified by hundreds of thousands of West Germans for being a prime architect of the 1979 NATO decision to deploy hundreds of new nuclear missiles capable of striking the Soviet Union. In 1958, Schmidt and the Social Democratic party (SPD) were in the vanguard of widespread public opposition to new nuclear weapons, but in the late 1970s the chancellor helped set in motion the deployment of intermediate-range nuclear forces (INF)—Pershing II and cruise missiles—which led in the early 1980s to the most intense antinuclear campaign in the Federal Republic of Germany (FRG) since the late 1950s.

Similar ironies have been evident in the nuclear weapons policies of the other major West German political party, the Union of Christian Democrats and Christian Socialists (CDU/CSU). In 1958, the government of Konrad Adenauer, and especially his minister of defense, Franz Josef Strauss, had forcefully overcome public opposition to gain the Bundestag's approval for the installation of new nuclear weapons on West German soil. In 1987, however, it was a Christian Democratic chancellor, Helmut Kohl, who bowed to public opinion in agreeing unilaterally to dismantle West Germany's force of seventy-two Pershing IA missiles to pave the way for a U.S.–Soviet treaty banning all INF systems. Moreover, other CDU/CSU leaders, including Franz Josef Strauss, were joining the Social Democrats in urging that arms control agreements be extended to cover shorter-range battlefield nuclear weapons as well, a step that other NATO partners feared would emasculate the Alliance's nuclear deterrent.

These vignettes of nuclear decision making in the Federal Republic symbolize the changes that have occurred in the postwar period in West Germany's relation to nuclear weapons. They do not, of course, tell the whole story. The domestic and external influences on SPD and CDU/CSU nuclear weapons policies from the 1950s to the 1980s, as well as the parties' internal decision-making processes, have been far more complex than these glimpses of Schmidt and Strauss suggest. In microcosm, however, they do point up the essential dilemma posed by nuclear weapons for West German security; that is, to what extent can a country that has unilaterally renounced an independent nuclear deterrent reconcile public ambivalence about these weapons of mass destruction with the need to rely on a superpower ally whose own interests quite often diverge from those of West Germany, which must balance Eastern and Western interests? In the words of Helmut Schmidt, nuclear weapons are a deterrent that, if ever used, "will not defend Europe, but destroy it."

While there has been continuity as well as change in Bonn's nuclear weapons policies since the 1950s, dramatic changes in the West German domestic political environment and in East–West relations present qualitatively new challenges to the FRG in its efforts to solve its nuclear dilemma. Not least, the rapid dismantling of Soviet control in Eastern Europe in late 1989, symbolized above all by the opening of the Berlin Wall on November 9, confronted West German policymakers with new uncertainties regarding European security. The prospect of a greatly reduced Soviet military threat, combined with the appearance of German reunification as a tangible, short-term political option, increased domestic pressures in the FRG regarding the utility of NATO's nuclear deterrent and the presence of thousands of nuclear weapons on German soil.

For most of the postwar period, the FRG has found more benefits than drawbacks in reliance on the U.S. nuclear guarantee. Whether these benefits will continue to outweigh the drawbacks will be a vitally important question for West German domestic politics and for European security in the 1990s and beyond.

My fascination with German history and politics extends back to grade school, when tales of Frederick the Great, the Napoleonic wars, and Bismarck made other subjects seem dull by comparison. Early on, I was hooked on the fascinating sweep of European history and the special role played by the Germans in continental and world affairs.

Over the years, I've accumulated quite a debt to numerous people who have helped foster my knowledge and, I hope, my understanding of German politics. As an undergraduate at Yale, I benefited from courses taught by Wolfgang Leonhard, Hans Gatzke, and Eva Balogh. A two-year detour through Chicago as a journalist was followed in 1976–77 by a stint in Berlin, where I studied German at the Goethe Institut and argued the merits of nuclear policy with many German colleagues. In 1977–78 I attended the London School of Economics and had the good fortune to have the always provocative Philip Windsor as a tutor.

My education in European political and military affairs continued the following year, when I worked as a staff assistant for Robert Hunter, Gregory Treverton, and Robert Putnam in the West European section of the National Security Council (NSC) in Washington.

Thus I found myself "present at the creation" of the INF issue: first in Berlin when German antinuclear sentiments began to emerge during the neutron bomb controversy; then in London when Helmut Schmidt gave his October 1977 speech at the International Institute for Strategic Studies; and finally at the NSC during the formulation of the United States' INF policy.

Among the many colleagues at MIT who deserve special thanks and gratitude are William Griffith, whose intellectual stimulation and wit were a steady companion. I am also grateful to George Rathjens, Jack Ruina, William Kaufmann, and Suzanne Berger for help and advice along the way. A special debt of gratitude is due Anne Grazewski for her special expertise in bureaucratic politics.

I would also like to thank colleagues at the Center for Science and International Affairs at Harvard University, including Gregory Treverton,

Paul Doty, Michael Nacht, and Steven Miller, for their support and criticism.

In Germany, Karl Kaiser and the Deutsche Gesellschaft für auswärtige Politik graciously provided an office, research materials, and contacts in the Bonn policy community. Others who helped in the FRG were Wilhelm Bruns of the Friedrich Ebert Stiftung, Wolfgang Pordzik of the Konrad Adenauer Stiftung, and colleagues at the Stiftung Wissenschaft und Politik (Ebenhausen), the Institut für Friedensforschung und Sicherheitspolitik (Hamburg), and the Aspen Institute Berlin.

For easing the burden of supporting a family throughout this venture, I am indebted to the Ford Foundation and two of its programs: International Security/Arms Control and Soviet/East European Area Studies and European Society and Western Security; to the U.S. Arms Control and Disarmament Agency and its Hubert H. Humphrey Fellowship Program; to the Deutsche Akademische Austausch Dienst; to the Institute for the Study of World Order and Harvard University's Center for European Studies; and to MIT's Center for International Studies.

The support and friendship of many colleagues at the American Academy of Arts and Sciences has been invaluable, in particular those of Frank Long, John Holdren, John Voss, Martha Snodgrass, Joel Orlen, and Edward Levi. Special thanks go to Annette Mann Bourne for graphics and editorial assistance and to Prudence Humphreys for typing assistance. Also, I'm indebted to Holly Bailey, Barbara Salazar and Allison Dodge of Cornell University Press for superb editorial work, and to Robert Art and Robert Jervis, co-editors of the Cornell Studies in Security Affairs.

Portions of chapters 1, 2, and 6 appeared in different form in the Spring 1983 issue of *International Security* and the Summer 1984 issue of *International Journal*; I thank MIT Press, publisher of *International Security*, and the Canadian Institute of International Affairs, publisher of *International Journal*, for permission to include the material in this volume.

From 1979 to 1988 I spoke at length about German security issues with more than three dozen West German government and party officials, military figures, academic analysts, journalists, and activists in the peace movement. I also benefited from extensive discussions with numerous American and NATO officials. No formal pattern was followed in these discussions; the aim was to draw upon the personal involvement of the individuals in the evolution of INF policy and to use their recollections as a check on published sources. I thank them all for their cooperation and candor.

Intellectually, my work owes much to Catherine McArdle Kelleher, and I would like to think that this book is an able successor to her *Germany and the Politics of Nuclear Weapons*. While neither Catherine nor any of the individuals noted above are responsible for its failings, they all deserve credit for whatever strengths it may possess.

Above all, I owe more than I can say to Suzan, David, and Sarah, who gave generously of love, support, and patience during the war of attrition that produced this volume.

JEFFREY BOUTWELL

Cambridge, Massachusetts

The German Nuclear Dilemma

Introduction

The issue of deploying theater nuclear weapons in Europe has had, for both the NATO Alliance and West Germany, a long and somewhat inglorious history. Since the first U.S. nuclear weapons arrived in Europe in the early 1950s, the perception of the Warsaw Pact's military superiority in central Europe has posed a vexing political problem, complicating both intra-Alliance and interbloc relations.

At least once each decade, West German domestic politics and the FRG's relations with its NATO allies have been strained by a major nuclear weapons issue. In the late 1950s, the issue was whether to provide the West German Bundeswehr with nuclear-capable artillery and aircraft, which led to massive public protest in the Federal Republic of Germany. In the 1960s, the Kennedy doctrine of Flexible Response, intertwined with the abortive Multi-Lateral Force (MLF) issue, produced strains between American and West German policymakers. In 1977–78, the neutron bomb controversy again sparked widespread public debate in the FRG and produced severe strains between Washington and Bonn when President Carter unilaterally canceled the project after having prodded Chancellor Schmidt to support it.

In the early 1980s, the Federal Republic again found itself in the middle of an important NATO nuclear weapons controversy, this time over intermediate-range nuclear forces (INF). At the now famous NATO ministerial meeting in Brussels in December 1979, the Alliance decided on a "double track" approach to counter what was perceived to be the pressing problem of a growing Soviet superiority in INF systems. Ostensibly, the NATO decision to produce and deploy Pershing II and cruise missiles while offering to negotiate limits on INF systems was a response to continued Soviet deployment of the SS-20 intermediate-range ballistic missile (IRBM). More important, however, were NATO perceptions that continued Soviet growth in strategic nuclear and conventional forces was leading to the "decoupling" of European security from that of the United States. Thus the Pershing and cruise missiles were seen as restoring the link between NATO's conventional and tactical nuclear capabilities and the strategic forces of the United States. Finally, there was the symbolic importance of the demonstration that the Alliance could reach political consensus on a contentious military issue.

At the time the NATO decision was made, the need for recouping Alliance solidarity was perhaps dominant, given the neutron bomb fiasco of 1977–78 and Europe's increasing doubts about the credibility of the U.S. strategic guarantee. Moreover, many members of the Alliance, while less than convinced about the military necessity of land-based INF, supported the 1979 decision as a demonstration of Alliance resolve in the face of an increasingly adventuristic Soviet foreign policy, a rationale that gained credence just a few weeks later with the Soviet invasion of Afghanistan.

Within little more than a year, however, a combination of factors, including the abeyance of the SALT process, deterioration in superpower détente, the defense and arms control policies of the Reagan administration, European antinuclear sentiments, and governmental instability in a number of NATO countries, had come together to threaten the Alliance consensus reached at Brussels.

Even more seriously, the upsurge of public opposition in Western Europe to the planned deployment of NATO's INF led many analysts to conclude that the continent was experiencing a wave of pacifist, neutralist, even anti-American sentiment that augured ill for the future of the Atlantic Alliance. Protest marches in European capitals that brought out hundreds of thousands of people, political party platforms calling for unilateral disarmament or the dismantling of American military bases, and the inability of European governments to meet NATO defense spending commitments were considered signs of greater accommodation to Soviet power and decreased faith in American leadership.

Once the first Pershings and cruise missiles were deployed in Europe in late 1983, however, the antinuclear sentiment began to wane. In 1985, following the rise to power of Mikhail Gorbachev, the

[2]

Soviets returned to Geneva to resume the INF negotiations, having walked out in 1983. Progress was slow at first, but picked up markedly in 1986–87, culminating in the signing of the INF Treaty during the Reagan–Gorbachev summit in Washington in December 1987.

Throughout the INF affair, as in earlier NATO nuclear weapons episodes, the Federal Republic occupied center stage along with the superpowers. For reasons of geography (the divided Germanies being the front-line states of NATO and the Warsaw Pact), history (the legacy of the Nazi past and the prohibitions against a German nuclear capability), and politics (West Germany, the most powerful European NATO partner, had to balance its commitment to Western values and security with its natural economic and social ties to Eastern Europe), the Federal Republic has had a particularly difficult role to play.

Moreover, it was the Federal Republic that provided much of the impetus for the NATO INF decision in the first place, as the governments in Bonn throughout the 1980s found themselves the focus of attention from domestic political forces, the NATO allies, the German Democratic Republic, and the superpowers over how to untangle the theater nuclear forces (TNF) dilemma. Indeed, the entire INF issue was often characterized as a battle for the hearts and minds of the citizens of the Federal Republic.

Adding to the nuclear dilemma as represented by INF were substantial changes taking place in the West German domestic political landscape. Even before the emergence of the INF issue in the late 1970s, the quarter-century dominance of the three main West German political parties—the Union of Christian Democrats and Christian Socialists (CDU/CSU), the Social Democratic party (SPD), and the Free Democratic party (FDP)—was being challenged by the emergence of an "antisystem" party, the Greens. When the INF debate spread across the country in the early 1980s, the Green party organization was in place to help nurture the rise of the peace movement (*Friedensbewegung*). By the same token, the political salience of the Euromissile issue proved to be a boon to the electoral fortunes of the Green party, which needed a national issue with which to propel itself into the Bundestag. Finally, the Greens and the peace movement furthered a leftward drift of the SPD which had been in progress for a number of years. Indeed, it was the radicalization of the SPD during the INF affair that contributed to the downfall of the Schmidt government in 1982 and to a weakening of the security consensus among the major West German political parties which had existed for much of the two previous decades.

THE WEST GERMAN SECURITY CONSENSUS

For most of the 1960s and 1970s, the major parties in the FRG sustained a broad-based consensus on the twin pillars of deterrence and détente as the basic tenets of West German security policy. Dating at least from the Grand Coalition between the CDU/CSU and the SPD in 1966, if not from the SPD's decision to support NATO (i.e., the Bad Godesberg program of 1959), this security consensus encompassed the moderates and left liberals in the SPD, the centrist FDP, and the dominant moderate conservative wing of the CDU. With the exception of the bitter ratification debates over Willy Brandt's Eastern treaties in the early 1970s, only the more doctrinaire socialist members of the SPD and right-wing conservatives in the CDU/CSU found themselves at odds with majority West German support for the twin goals of military security within NATO and détente with the East bloc.

In the 1980s, though, several developments seemed to signal an end to this consensus. The massive public demonstrations against the INF deployments, the rise of the Green party and a swing to the left on the part of the SPD, increased public questioning of NATO doctrine and of U.S. leadership, and uncertainty over the ramifications for German security of the INF Treaty have combined to produce growing unease and uncertainty in the FRG over where its security interests lie and how best to protect them.

For the first time since the 1950s, when the intertwined issues of West German rearmament and German reunification dominated the security debate, a wide range of proposals for safeguarding German security are being espoused. From the political left come calls for unilateral withdrawal from NATO (the Greens), or at least for withdrawal from NATO's military command (Oskar Lafontaine of the SPD). Moderates in both the SPD and CDU (Helmut Schmidt and Helmut Kohl) advocate a strengthening of the Franco-German military relationship as a hedge against vacillating U.S. policies. And from right-wing conservatives come renewed indications of support for a process that could lead to an independent European nuclear force, in concert with France and Britain, to take the place of the

[4]

perceived weakening of the U.S. commitment to NATO (Alfred Dregger of the CDU and the late Franz Josef Strauss of the CSU). Finally, from across the political spectrum various "nonprovocative defense" proposals for the restructuring of NATO forces are gaining a wider hearing with the German public, policy analysts, and military officials.

Much of the impetus for the fluid nature of the current German debate on security and the role of nuclear weapons comes, of course, from the rapidly changing nature of East–West relations brought about by new Soviet policies under Mikhail Gorbachev. Beginning in the mid-1980s, greater Soviet flexibility on arms control helped produce not only the INF Treaty but the prospect of deep cuts in strategic forces, a global ban on chemical weapons, and major reductions in NATO and Warsaw Pact conventional forces.

This process was then transformed in 1989 when massive demonstrations across Eastern Europe forced the indigenous Communist parties into power-sharing agreements with prodemocracy opposition groups. In the GDR, Erich Honecker fell from power and free elections were scheduled for March 1990. As East Germans streamed through the newly opened Berlin Wall, the issue of German reunification took on a life of its own, increasing the complexity of East-West relations.

Adding to this confusion have been growing structural changes in the makeup of West German party politics. Indeed, a central premise of this book is that there are two strong countervailing trends in West German domestic politics which will test the still existing, albeit fragile security consensus in the FRG in the 1990s and beyond.

The first is centripetal, acting to hold the security consensus together. For now, a majority of West Germans continue to look for moderate, centrist security policies from the government in Bonn. As was evident in the 1983 and 1987 elections, most West German voters are wary of radical new initiatives, whether from the left or the right, and are becoming extremely sophisticated in the use of the FRG's "two-vote" system (i.e., electoral ticket splitting) to ensure continuity in West German policy. Hence the increased support for the FDP in the 1987 election and the strengthened hand of Foreign Minister Hans-Dietrich Genscher in shaping West German policy.

The second trend, however, is centrifugal, and is based on a growing left–right polarization between the SPD and CDU/CSU

[5]

which could further strain the security consensus in the years ahead. Unlike the situation in the 1960s and 1970s, when the SPD and CDU/CSU competed for the "high middle ground" of the West German electorate and shared almost 90 percent of the vote between them, recent trends show both a greater left–right cleavage between the major parties and a decline in their total vote. A continued strong showing by the Greens at the national level, matched by a further drift to the left on the part of the SPD, could return the FRG to the type of polarized party politics that existed in the 1950s. Similarly, a strong showing by the radical right-wing Republican party in the December 1990 national election could fracture the security consensus completely.

Whatever the outcome of that election, the domestic politics of the West German security debate have been irrevocably altered by the tides of change that swept over Eastern Europe beginning in 1989. West German policy options have greatly expanded beyond the Cold War framework of defense and détente—that is, of carefully balancing its military alliance with the West and its *Ostpolitik*. Even if the reform process in Eastern Europe should fail, domestic pressures in the FRG would push West German policymakers into exploring new formulations for safeguarding the country's security. The FRG's traditional reliance on nuclear deterrence may be recast, modified, or altered entirely, but it will not conform to that of earlier decades.

FOREIGN POLICY AND DOMESTIC POLITICS

In analyzing the impact of changes in West German domestic politics on the FRG's nuclear dilemma in the 1970s and 1980s, I will concentrate on those points at which West German domestic considerations (whether bureaucratic, party, or from the polity at large) influenced governmental policy during the evolution of the INF issue. To be sure, any discussion of West German foreign policymaking must recognize the synergistic relationship of international and domestic trends. As Stanley Hoffmann noted, too often "theories of international politics seem to divide into opposite extremes," focusing either on the international system or on national decision making. In his view, theories of the former "have not yet examined carefully enough the weight with which the system presses on

[6]

various kinds of states at different times; theories of the latter type tend to be casual about the environment."[1]

What Hoffmann proposes, and what I try to provide in this book, is a bridge between the two. Accordingly, I will also survey the changes in the international environment in which West German foreign policy has been made in the post-war period, looking specifically at the INF issue from 1975 to 1989 and how those changes have altered the domestic decision-making maneuverability of West German policymakers. In turn, I will examine changes in the structure and process of West German domestic politics to see to what extent they have influenced the formulation of the Federal Republic's security policy. Indeed, the very nature of the INF issue as an example of West German decision making in a noncrisis situation over a decade and a half makes the issue a good case study for illuminating the interactive loop of foreign policy and domestic politics in the Federal Republic.[2]

In Chapter 1 I examine the "system dominance" the Adenauer government experienced in the 1950s, when both foreign and domestic policy reflected Germany's postwar occupation. The FRG's susceptibility to external influence greatly attenuated as the international system evolved from the confrontational politics of the Cold War to the détente of the 1970s,[3] which in turn produced substantial changes in the domestic bases of West Germany's postwar political order.

To a great extent, the domestic bases of Adenauer's foreign policy

1. Stanley Hoffmann, "Restraints and Choices in American Foreign Policy," *Daedalus* 9 (Fall 1962): 668.

2. My analysis of the interrelationship of West German domestic politics and foreign policymaking during the INF episode owes much to the following works: James N. Rosenau, *Domestic Sources of Foreign Policy* (New York: Free Press, 1967); Josef Joffe, "Society and Foreign Policy in the Federal Republic" (Ph.D. thesis, Harvard University, 1975); Rudolf Wildenmann, *Macht und Konsens der Innen- und Aussenpolitik* (Cologne: Westdeutscher Verlag, 1967); and Wolf-Dieter Narr, "Social Factors Affecting the Making of Foreign Policy," in Karl Kaiser and Roger Morgan, eds., *Britain and West Germany: Changing Societies and the Future of Foreign Policy* (London: Oxford University Press, 1971).

3. According to Wolfram Hanrieder, the FRG in the 1950s and 1960s exhibited the traits of a "penetrated system," a term applicable to those states whose decision makers are strongly influenced by external pressures and can achieve consensus among the broader policy elite only by accommodating themselves to those external forces. See his *West German Foreign Policy, 1949–1963* (Stanford: Stanford University Press, 1967). Ways in which the FRG conformed to and deviated from the norm of a penetrated system are treated more fully in chap. 1.

in the 1950s were conditioned by external factors: (1) security within the Western Alliance and the ability of the Federal Republic to forgo an independent defense policy; (2) a growing economic prosperity that helped legitimize the West German political system; and (3) Cold War anticommunism as a unifying ideology (in lieu of German nationalism) which facilitated the Federal Republic's reintegration into the West European political system.

By the 1970s, with the coming of both superpower and European détente, anticommunism was no longer a major domestic factor in shaping German security interests. Moreover, the increased importance of Bonn's Eastern policy (*Ostpolitik*) meant that West German defense policy had to be integrated with a foreign policy that looked both West and East. Also, a deteriorating global economy was introducing new strains into West German domestic politics and undercutting one of the major props of Bonn's foreign policy. Concomitant with these changes was a change in the international strategic environment: recognition of Soviet parity, along with a steady growth of Warsaw Pact capabilities, led to renewed doubts about the credibility of the U.S. nuclear guarantee, on which the Federal Republic is so dependent.

In Chapter 2 I analyze the effects of changes in the East–West security balance on the thinking of Helmut Schmidt, with particular attention to the chancellor's motivations for highlighting the INF issue in his now-famous speech at the International Institute for Strategic Studies, in October 1977. Given Schmidt's central role in shifting the INF issue from NATO's private agenda to the broader public agenda of the Western Alliance, it is worth examining in some detail the evolution of his thinking on security issues in general and on the German nuclear dilemma in particular.[4]

Once the INF issue did come out into the open and moved through the NATO decision-making process, West German domestic forces increasingly influenced the policies of the Schmidt government. Accordingly, Chapter 3 examines growing disquiet in Schmidt's Social Democratic party over INF and the neutron bomb, focusing in particular on debates at the party conferences in Hamburg (1977) and Berlin (1979).

The SPD party conference in Berlin was particularly important,

4. Especially important in this regard is Schmidt's concept of *Gleichgewicht* (best translated as "balance of forces") as a foreign policy strategy that encompassed far more than just East–West military parity. Among Schmidt's many writings, the most

occurring as it did just a week before NATO adopted the double-track INF decision at its December 1979 meeting in Brussels. Although Schmidt was able to overcome SPD opposition to INF in Berlin, the weeks and months following saw a greatly changed international situation (the Soviet invasion of Afghanistan, the demise of SALT II, the Reagan election, and deteriorating East–West relations). In Chapter 4 I analyze the effects of these external influences on the West German domestic debate, focusing on the rise of the peace movement and the Green party as well as on renewed internal rifts in the SPD. Growing domestic opposition to INF in the Federal Republic, while undoubtedly a source of pressure on the Schmidt government, also provided the chancellor with substantial leverage in shaping U.S. and NATO INF policy.

In Chapter 5 I examine how differences over security and economic policy between the SPD and its junior coalition partner, the FDP, led to the collapse of the Schmidt government in late 1982, and how the succeeding CDU/CSU government of Helmut Kohl handled the INF issue from 1982 to 1988. Despite growing fissures in the West German security consensus in this period, the CDU/CSU altered many of its attitudes on important components of FRG security (Ostpolitik, arms control), largely in deference to prevailing West German public opinion.

No analysis of the German nuclear dilemma, especially one that concentrates on West German domestic politics, can ignore the relationship of security issues to the *Deutschlandpolitik* (German policy) of the FRG and GDR. Given the sense of responsibility felt by successive West German governments for the welfare of those living in the GDR (a mandate written into the FRG Basic Law), it is not surprising that security and defense policy issues have assumed a greater role in the continuing dialogue between the two Germanies. Accordingly, Chapter 6 examines the effect of the INF issue on Deutschlandpolitik from 1980 to 1988, at the level of governmental policies and in the broader area of public attitudes toward the German nuclear dilemma.

In the final chapter I summarize the role played by various West German domestic forces during the INF episode and draw some conclusions as to the likely evolution of FRG security policy and the German nuclear dilemma in the years ahead.

---

important in this regard is *Strategie des Gleichgewichts: Deutsche Friedenspolitik und die Weltmächte* (Stuttgart: Seewald, 1969).

GERMAN NUCLEAR OPTIONS

With an acknowledged debt to the work of Catherine Kelleher and others on how West Germany sought to cope with its "strategic dilemma" in the 1950s and 1960s,[5] this analysis of the INF episode will illuminate both the continuity and the change in the German nuclear dilemma, and delineate the security and nuclear weapons options the Federal Republic might pursue in the years ahead.

Obviously, any West German decision to "go nuclear" would profoundly affect the country's relations both with its Western allies and with Eastern Europe and the Soviet Union. Nonetheless, in an extremely fluid European security environment where German reunification has become a distinct possibility, Germany's acquisition of an independent nuclear force cannot be ruled out. As was the case during the INF episode, of course, German policy will still be tightly constricted by political sensitivities, both domestic and external, concerning German control of nuclear weapons. During the 1980s, for example, both the Schmidt and Kohl governments sought to downplay Bonn's visibility, first by insisting on multilateral deployment of INF systems and the retention of sole U.S. control of those INF stationed in the Federal Republic, and later by unilaterally agreeing to dismantle West Germany's Pershing IA missiles to facilitate the U.S.–Soviet INF accord.

In other ways, however, the Federal Republic showed a new assertiveness in injecting itself into the nuclear affairs of the superpowers. As has been mentioned, the Schmidt government was largely responsible for setting the December 1979 decision in motion; indeed, there were times when the chancellor ironically noted that it was he who created the INF issue. At other points during the evolution of that issue, Chancellor Schmidt played a far more active role, both within the Alliance and between the superpowers, than had any of his predecessors during previous NATO nuclear weap-

5. The standard reference on the German nuclear dilemma continues to be Catherine McArdle Kelleher, *Germany and the Politics of Nuclear Weapons* (New York: Columbia University Press, 1975). For more on the origins of the FRG's nuclear dilemma, see Gerhard Wettig, *Entmilitarisierung und Wiederbewaffnung in Deutschland, 1943–1955* (Munich: R. Oldenbourg, 1967), and Hans Speier, *German Rearmament and Atomic War* (Evanston, Ill.: Row, Peterson, 1957).

ons decisions. From his campaign to get other European members of NATO to accept deployment of some INF systems to his visit to Moscow in 1980 to persuade the Soviets to begin INF arms control negotiations, Schmidt played the role of mediator and interpreter between the two blocs. Though Schmidt himself disdained the use of such labels, he and his government, especially the foreign minister, Hans-Dietrich Genscher, actively shaped the issues on the INF agenda.

This role for West Germany continued when the CDU/CSU came to power in 1982, despite the less assertive personality of Chancellor Helmut Kohl. Continuing as foreign minister, Genscher stressed the need for progress in INF arms control and stability in Bonn's Ostpolitik, while the new defense minister, Manfred Wörner, stressed the need for INF deployment in order to pressure the Soviets into negotiating seriously. In other areas as well, including closer Franco-German military coordination and proposals for extending the INF accord to include battlefield nuclear weapons, the Kohl government took the initiative to safeguard West Germany's security interests in a rapidly changing security environment.

Overall, this increased assertiveness in nuclear weapons issues has been only one facet of a greater West German assertiveness in foreign affairs generally. This willingness to pursue a more active foreign policy is traceable to many causes, including the country's political rehabilitation, its ability to use its relative economic well-being to further its security goals, a retraction of American power, and new opportunities provided by Soviet flexibility. Certainly the manner in which the FRG exercises this power in the years ahead will be of crucial importance. As Christoph Bertram wrote in the late 1970s, "this is, perhaps, the fundamental German question for the next decade: how to fill out the wide mantle of power and responsibility that the economic and political weight of the Federal Republic have bestowed upon it."[6] Writing at the same time, Karl Kaiser saw the central problem as one in which "the new reality of a German government actually using resource potential for political purposes . . . is sufficient to raise new questions and old spectres."[7]

Yet whatever the long-term evolution of West German security policy may be, the choices open to the Federal Republic in the 1990s

6. Christoph Bertram, "European Security and the German Problem," *International Security* 4 (Winter 1979/80): 114.

7. Karl Kaiser, "The New Ostpolitik," in Wolfram Hanrieder, ed., *West German Foreign Policy, 1949–1979* (Boulder, Colo.: Westview Press, 1980), p. 153.

will be nowhere near as clear-cut as they were earlier in the postwar period.

Since 1949 West Germany has pursued options, sometimes complementary, sometimes conflicting, in three broad foreign policy spheres: the Atlantic, the West European, and the Eastern. Yet the manner in which Bonn sought to exercise its options in those three spheres is far different today than it was in the 1950s and provides a very different context for examining how the Federal Republic might seek to deal with its nuclear dilemma. Moreover, as David Calleo has noted, by the late 1970s "each sphere had been developed as far as possible without foreclosing the others."[8] As we will see, the trade-offs inherent between dependence on the U.S./NATO security guarantee and Bonn's Ostpolitik led many to claim that the Federal Republic was either loosening its ties to the Atlantic Alliance or jeopardizing its Ostpolitik. An examination of the tightrope that West Germany had to walk during this process can tell us much about how Bonn might conduct its security policy in the future.

As it has evolved, then, the INF issue has been symptomatic of the increasing complexity of West German security policy and of the difficulty Bonn faces in pursuing options in its three foreign policy spheres. As well, the nuclear weapons debate in the Federal Republic points up two important domestic trends: a growing polarization of German party politics and an increase in various German nationalist sentiments.

In 1989 both of these trends were greatly influenced by the revolutionary developments in Eastern Europe and the prospect of German reunification. The question for the 1990s thus becomes: How will this recasting of the European security framework, if it continues, affect the German nuclear dilemma? Within the FRG, the Kohl government and the Social Democrats professed the continued importance of NATO for West German security. For others, however, the implications of a powerful reunited Germany in the center of Europe were far more ominous. As Arthur Schlesinger noted, "new German generations, feeling no personal guilt about Nazism, may well nurse a desire for national vindication. . . . Germany could have

8. David Calleo, *The German Problem Reconsidered: Germany and the World Order, 1870 to the Present* (New York: Cambridge University Press, 1978), p. 177. Calleo's book is one of the best for setting Federal Republic foreign policies in the larger context of German history.

by far the largest army in Europe west of Russia. With its technological skills, it may even acquire nuclear weapons."[9]

The probability of such a dire outcome depends greatly, of course, on the future course of the East European reform movements, on Mikhail Gorbachev's *perestroika*, and on efforts to reunite the two Germanies, as well as on Germany's role in the European Community (EC) and its relations with the United States. And this outcome is only one of many directions the German nuclear dilemma might take. In a period when traditional security concepts are on the verge of being entirely transformed, any predictions would take on the character of looking through a glass darkly. The most one can do is analyze previous German policy, both domestic and foreign, for indicators of how Bonn governments sought to retain maneuverability in all three German foreign policy spheres. How well the Schmidt and Kohl governments succeeded in that effort during the INF episode is the principal focus of this book. How well German governments manage this quest in the future will undoubtedly be one of the most important issues for European and East-West security in the 1990s and beyond.

9. Arthur M. Schlesinger, Jr., "Germany's Fate Will Determine Europe's," *Wall Street Journal*, December 21, 1989.

[1]

Evolution of the German
Nuclear Dilemma: 1949–1975

In many ways, the Federal Republic of Germany is truly a creation of the nuclear age. In August 1949, three months after the West German state was created, the Soviet Union detonated its first atomic weapon, joining the United States as a nuclear power. Even before the FRG gained full sovereignty, in May 1955, the first American nuclear weapons had been deployed on West German soil.

By the mid-1960s, the FRG was host to thousands of theater nuclear weapons, ranging from atomic demolition munitions (ADMs), designed for emplacement along its borders with East Germany and Czechoslovakia, to cruise missiles of sufficient range to strike the Soviet Union. Although the nuclear warheads themselves were controlled by the United States, the size of the NATO arsenal in West Germany putatively made the FRG the world's third largest nuclear power, with forces even greater than those of Britain and France.

Today the FRG continues to be the most densely nuclearized country in the world (see figure 1).[1] Although the NATO Alliance has reduced its nuclear forces in Western Europe in recent years, more than 2,500 nuclear warheads remain in the FRG, stored at dozens of sites traversing the country from the Baltic to the Alps. The combined NATO armies have several thousand nuclear-capable artillery pieces, as well as aircraft and naval vessels, based at hundreds of military installations in West Germany, with which to

1. For a detailed description of the nuclear weapons infrastructure in the FRG, see William Arkin and Richard Fieldhouse, *Nuclear Battlefields: Global Links in the Arms Race* (Cambridge, Mass.: Ballinger, 1985), pp. 101–116 and 236–245 especially.

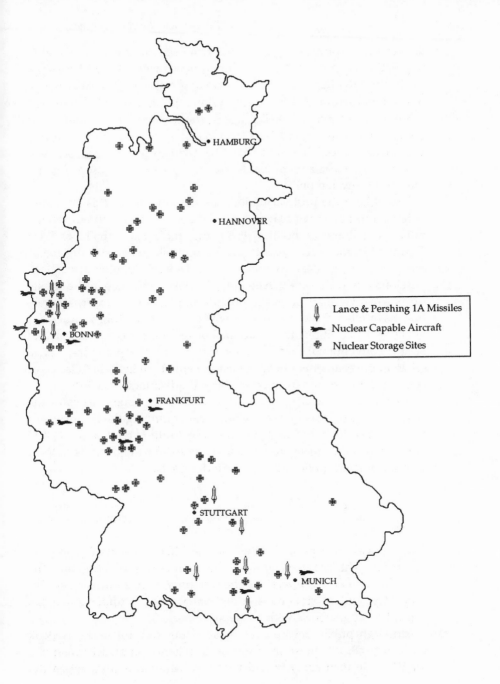

Figure 1. Deployment of nuclear weapons in West Germany, 1981. Adapted from "Atomrampe Deutschland," *Stern,* February 19, 1981, pp. 29–35.

deliver these warheads. In a country the size of Oregon but with a population equal to that of the United States west of the Mississippi River, the FRG has the most intricate and condensed nuclear weapons infrastructure in the world. When this is combined with the more than 1 million NATO troops (and dependents) and 4,000 military installations on West German soil, one can appreciate why a U.S. Army official has said that "by virtually every yardstick you care to use, Germany probably has the greatest imposed defense burden of any nation."[2]

Throughout the postwar period, the ramifications of this "imposed defense burden" have played a pivotal role in West German foreign policy and domestic politics. From the initial rearmament of West Germany in the early 1950s to the Euromissile debates of the 1980s, the politics of nuclear weapons in the Federal Republic have been passionate and divisive. Over time, however, changes in the make-up of West German domestic politics and the FRG's external situation have altered the manner in which nuclear weapons issues are debated. In addition, the "burden" of relying on U.S. nuclear and NATO conventional forces for security is one that successive West German governments not only have accepted willingly but also have been able to use for their own political advantage. Accordingly, in this chapter I look at the two major nuclear weapons issues of the 1950s and 1960s, the 1957–58 debate over equipping the Bundeswehr with nuclear delivery systems and the Multi-Lateral Force (MLF) issue of the early 1960s, to provide a context for the analysis of West German nuclear politics in the period 1975–89.

NATO Nuclear Strategy in the 1950s

The nuclear weapons debates that dominated West German politics in 1957–58 revolved around the twin issues of providing the West German armed forces, for the first time, with a nuclear delivery capability, and of stationing additional warheads under American control to be matched with those systems.[3]

Although public debate over these issues did not reach its peak until 1957–58, the question of increased reliance on nuclear weapons for West German security had been evolving since 1953, when the

2. Quoted in ibid, p. 101.
3. See Catherine McArdle Kelleher, *Germany and the Politics of Nuclear Weapons* (New York: Columbia University Press, 1975), esp. chap. 4.

first U.S. nuclear weapons arrived in the FRG. In October 1953, the same month that the 280-mm atomic cannons arrived in Europe, Eisenhower's National Security Council authorized the Joint Chiefs of Staff (JCS) to base their planning on the use of tactical and strategic nuclear weapons against conventional attacks, "where militarily advantageous."[4] A year later, the NATO supreme commander, Gen. Alfred Gruenther, was quoted to the effect that "we have determined that our strategy in the center [central Europe] requires the use of atomic weapons, whether the enemy uses them or not."[5]

Until 1955, these changes in NATO strategy had taken place largely out of the public eye. In March of that year, however, the dismissal of a West German defense official for criticizing NATO policy highlighted the increasing emphasis on nuclear weapons for the West German public.[6] This episode was followed in June by the wide publicity given to the NATO Carte Blanche exercise, in which the simulated use of 335 nuclear weapons over NATO territory resulted in the "death or incapacitation" of more than 5 million Germans.[7] Initial public indignation and horror over the results of the Carte Blanche exercise, only one month after the FRG had officially joined NATO, exacerbated the domestic debate over whether West German participation in the Atlantic Alliance would under-

4. For more on the evolution of U.S. nuclear strategy during this period, see David Alan Rosenberg, "The Origins of Overkill: Nuclear Weapons and American Strategy," *International Security* (Spring 1983): 29–32 especially. See also David C. Eliot, "Project Vista and Nuclear Weapons," *International Security* 11 (Summer 1986).

5. Robert Osgood, *NATO: The Entangling Alliance* (Chicago: University of Chicago Press, 1962), p. 109.

6. In March 1955, Col. Bogislaw von Bonin was dismissed from the Defense Ministry (known at the time as the Amt Blank) for criticizing Adenauer's rearmament plans and circulating his own plan, which called for the creation of "blocking units" (*Sperrverbände*) equipped with 8,000 antitank guns deployed in a thirty-mile-wide defensive zone along the inter-German border. See Hans Speier, *German Rearmament and Atomic War* (Evanston, Ill.: Row, Peterson, 1957). Von Bonin's scheme has much in common with current alternative defense strategies for NATO which stress nonprovocative defense.

7. Eleven NATO countries and 3,000 aircraft participated in the Carte Blanche exercise, which covered West Germany, Belgium, Holland, Luxembourg, and parts of France. Although designed to test NATO capabilities in the event a conventional conflict turned nuclear, the timing of the exercise seems to have been partly politically motivated, coming as it did just before the Geneva summit in July. As Gordon Craig has noted, perhaps "an impressive show of air strength on the very eve of the...summit would intimidate the Russians and make them more anxious to reach an accommodation with the West.... If this is true, the calculation was a bad one. The only people intimidated by Carte Blanche were the Germans." See his "NATO and the New German Army," in William Kaufmann, ed., *Military Policy and National Security,* 2d ed. (Port Washington, N.Y.: Kennikat Press, 1972), pp. 225–226.

cut the country's security and reduce the chances for eventual German reunification.

At the time, Chancellor Konrad Adenauer was opposed to the increased reliance on nuclear weapons and corresponding reductions in U.S. ground troops in Europe called for by the Massive Retaliation and New Look strategies of the Eisenhower administration.[8] In early 1956, as Adenauer was attempting to gain Bundestag passage of his government's conscription bill, which called for the raising of 500,000 West German troops by 1959, it was clear that NATO strategy was evolving toward increased emphasis on nuclear weapons and less reliance on conventional troops. Adenauer viewed the contribution of a half-million troops to NATO as demonstrating West Germany's good faith above all, but also as a bargaining counter the FRG could use with her Alliance partners. Yet less than a week after the conscription bill was passed, American press reports noted that the JCS was seeking an 800,000-man cut in U.S. armed forces and the reorientation of U.S. strategic planning to give primary emphasis to American nuclear retaliatory capabilities.[9] Spokesmen for the U.S. government denied that the so-called Radford Plan represented official policy; nonetheless, the fact that it was under consideration undercut the Adenauer government's justification regarding the need for a 500,000-man Bundeswehr to bolster NATO's conventional defense. To make matters worse, some U.S. spokesmen continued to stress the need for the full FRG troop contingent, even though the Americans (and the British) were talking of reducing their conventional forces, as the West German troops would be needed (in the words of one FRG politician) "to force the Soviet Union in the event of imminent attack so to concentrate its forces as to create the possibility of the use of atomic weapons."[10] In short, the twelve projected divisions of the Bundeswehr were now being described as a magnet that would concentrate Soviet forces so the latter could be targeted with nuclear weapons. Adenauer criticized these reported changes in NATO's deterrent strategy, especially as he had visited Eisenhower in Washington in June and had not been informed about them: "As to the debate that was started by the Americans about the relationship between conventional and nuclear weapons, I would like to stress that I regard shifting the principal emphasis to atomic weapons at the present time as a mistake. . . . I

8. See *Die Zeit*, July 7, 1955.
9. *New York Times*, July 13, 1956.
10. *Bundestag Record*, July 6, 1955, pp. 8777–8778.

am of the opinion that it is of special importance to localize small conflicts that may occur, and for this we need divisions with conventional weapons."[11]

It soon became apparent, however, that the Eisenhower administration was determined to increase NATO's tactical nuclear capability, although it did defer the substantial troop cuts called for in the Radford Plan. With Britain and France following Eisenhower's lead in emphasizing nuclear rather than conventional deterrence (the New Look strategy), Adenauer soon realized that continued criticism of the United States "would only alienate the one Alliance member whose benevolence had become all the more precious at a time when England and France seemed mesmerized by the apparent new pliancy of the Soviet Union."[12] Moreover, the FRG was on the verge of being deprived of any significant voice in the shaping of NATO nuclear policy if it continued to stress conventional deterrence. Therefore, Adenauer switched policy in September 1956 and came out in favor of equipping the Bundeswehr with what were euphemistically called "the most modern weapons." A few weeks later, this switch in West German policy became total when Franz Josef Strauss, an early and vocal advocate of nuclear deterrence, was made minister of defense.

Adenauer was able to use these changes in NATO strategy to justify delays in raising the 500,000-man Bundeswehr, delays that would have occurred anyway given manpower and economic difficulties in the FRG. Nonetheless, Adenauer had been forced to reinterpret the rearmament bargain between the FRG and its allies, that is, "the need to meet allies' demands for complete redemption of Germany's pledges regarding force levels in order to gain security and equality within the West." In doing so, Adenauer keenly felt "the vagaries of the American political process," which "confirmed his worst suspicions that abandonment or at least withdrawal was possible at any time."[13] For Adenauer, the Radford Plan had a neo-isolationist element that hinted at possible superpower collusion at the expense of West Germany. At a time when the growth of Soviet nuclear forces was producing the first signs of superpower nuclear stalemate, and when Khrushchev had begun the de-Stalinization process that would produce a thaw in East–West

11. *Government Bulletin*, August 21, 1956 (Bonn: Federal Information Office, 1956).
12. Josef Joffe, "Society and Foreign Policy in the Federal Republic" (Ph.D. thesis, Harvard University, 1975), p. 195.
13. Kelleher, *Germany and the Politics of Nuclear Weapons*, pp. 50–52.

relations, Adenauer was recognizing the inevitable divergence of American and West German interests.

THE 1957–1958 NUCLEAR WEAPONS DEBATE

Although the decision to "go nuclear" was made in October 1956, the Adenauer government did not present its armament plan for Bundestag approval until March 1958. With national elections coming up in the fall of 1957, and with the opposition SPD seeking to capitalize on growing public concern over NATO's nuclear strategy, Adenauer wanted to avoid having the issue injected into the election campaign. Moreover, operational planning within NATO regarding the deployment of nuclear delivery systems with European forces was proceeding slowly. Defense Minister Strauss joined his European colleagues in asking the Americans to expand nuclear weapons sharing agreements at the NATO Council meeting in December 1956, yet U.S. agreement was not forthcoming until the NATO Council session in December 1957, and the program itself, MC-70, was not adopted until April 1958. In the interim, however, West German military planners were developing plans for deploying new nuclear-capable aircraft and missiles, while Adenauer and Strauss continued to set forth the necessity of such deployments for West German military and political equality within the Alliance.

The spark that set off the widespread domestic opposition to these deployments occurred in April 1957 with the publication of the "Göttingen Appeal," a manifesto signed by eighteen prominent West German physicists. Declaring that they would refuse to "take any part in the production, testing or use of nuclear weapons," the physicists urged the Adenauer government to reject voluntarily "the possession of atomic weapons of any kind."[14] The SPD then pushed the issue in Bundestag debates in the spring of 1957 and in the period preceding the national election in November. Yet despite some polls showing that 64 percent of the public opposed arming the Bundeswehr with nuclear weapons (with 17 percent in favor and 19 percent undecided), the SPD was unable to capitalize on the issue

14. For an elaboration of the physicists' arguments (the physicists included Max Born, Otto Hahn, Werner Heisenberg, and Carl Friedrich von Weizsäcker), see *Politische Meinung*, May 1957, pp. 55–60.

electorally.[15] The 1957 election was a "stomach election," revolving primarily around economic issues, and Adenauer was also able to take advantage of the lackluster campaign style of his SPD opponent, Erich Ollenhauer.

In a domestic political environment dominated by the "double security complex" of economic and external stability, the quasi-Marxist economic and social policies of the SPD greatly limited its appeal. As in previous elections, the SPD was unable to win more than 33 percent of the vote. A younger elite within the party had begun to advocate that the SPD should broaden its appeal and shift from being a class party to a mass-based party (*Volkspartei*), yet this internal process of party reform was largely hidden from the West German electorate and bore no fruit until the Bad Godesberg party conference in November 1959. This younger elite, led by Fritz Erler, Carlo Schmid, Herbert Wehner, and Willy Brandt, argued that the SPD must move toward greater acceptance of the FRG's role in the Atlantic Alliance and unswerving support for the Bundeswehr. The 1957 election results—the CDU/CSU gained an absolute majority of the vote for the first (and only) time in the FRG—only provided additional arguments for these members of the *Gegenelite* (counterelite) that the party would continue to exist in "splendid isolation" if the SPD failed to move toward the moderate center and battle the CDU/CSU for the high middle ground of the West German electorate.[16]

Although Adenauer had been successful in keeping the nuclear weapons issue out of the 1957 election campaign, the December 1957 NATO conference in Paris, as well as the Sputnik launch and the Rapacki Plan for a nuclear-free zone in central Europe, refocused West German media attention on the issue. While the SPD tried

15. See Elisabeth Noelle and Erich Peter Neumann, eds., *The Germans: Public Opinion Polls, 1947–1966* (Allensbach: Institut für Demoskopie, 1967), p. 441. It appears that opposition to nuclear weapons did not necessarily stem from widespread fear of nuclear war; thus a February 1956 poll, asking whether the respondent felt that atomic bombs would be used in a future war, found only 33 percent saying yes, while 36 percent said no, 30 percent were undecided, and 1 percent said "it all depends." Furthermore, there was no clear-cut preference among the public for a particular defense strategy. An October 1956 poll found 31 percent of the respondents in favor of large conventional forces, 26 percent in favor of small forces equipped with nuclear weapons, 42 percent undecided, and 1 percent "didn't know." See ibid., pp. 441, 600.

16. Among the Gegenelite was a young parliamentarian from Hamburg, Helmut Schmidt. See Lothar Wilker, *Der Sicherheitspolitik der SPD* (Bonn–Bad Godesberg: Neue Gesellschaft, 1977), pp. 18–25.

to force a Bundestag debate on the government's policy before Adenauer's departure for the Paris NATO meeting, the chancellor was able to use his parliamentary majority to defer such a debate until after the NATO meeting.

At this 1957 conference the NATO heads of state concerned themselves primarily with American offers to deploy Thor and Jupiter IRBM/MRBMs on European soil as a counter to perceived Soviet advances in ICBM delivery capability.[17] As would happen during the INF debate two decades later, the U.S. IRBMs were touted as strengthening the coupling of European and American security and unifying the Alliance in the face of a new Soviet threat. The NATO SACEUR (Supreme Allied Commander, Europe), Gen. Lauris Norstad, believed as well that a growing Soviet intermediate-range nuclear threat also demanded an Alliance in-theater nuclear capability, and Norstad hoped that the Thors and Jupiters would eventually become part of an Alliance force that would make NATO a "fourth nuclear power."

Although the FRG was unwilling to deploy the IRBMs,[18] the Adenauer government was more receptive than other European governments regarding increased NATO deployment of short-range nuclear weapons. Following the NATO summit, which authorized General Norstad to draw up military requirements for these nuclear weapons (MC-70), Ollenhauer critized Adenauer for not following the example of Norway and Denmark in totally rejecting any basing of nuclear weapons on national soil. In the Bundestag debate on foreign policy on January 23, 1958, the SPD concentrated its arguments on how NATO nuclear weapons policy was foreclosing any chance of testing the Rapacki Plan.[19] When Strauss traveled to Washington the next month to discuss FRG acquisition of the Matador, a medium-range cruise missile that could be armed with either a conventional or nuclear warhead,[20] SPD leaders protested once

17. See especially Timothy Ireland, *Creating the Entangling Alliance: The Origins of the North Atlantic Treaty Organization* (Westport, Conn.: Greenwood Press, 1981).

18. Adenauer and Strauss feared that the first-strike capability of the Thor and Jupiter medium-range missiles would subject the FRG, and possibly West Berlin, to Soviet political pressure, while also undercutting the chancellor's argument that the Bundeswehr needed a nuclear capability purely for defensive purposes.

19. For a discussion of the January 23 Bundestag debate, see *Die Zeit*, January 30, 1958.

20. The Matador was deployed briefly in the late 1950s and was replaced by the Mace B, a cruise missile with a range of 1,300 miles and thus able to hit targets in the Soviet Union. As the Mace B was liquid-fueled and thus vulnerable to Soviet preemptive attack, it was replaced in 1964 by the Pershing 1, which, with a range of

again that Adenauer was showing no interest whatsoever in proposals for military disengagement in Europe, and especially in testing the Rapacki Plan, a new version of which had just been put forth by the Polish foreign minister.[21]

Finally, in March, Adenauer presented his nuclear weapons program to the Bundestag for approval. What followed was the bitterest parliamentary session in the short history of the FRG, characterized by vicious name-calling and by what one commentator, Theodore Eschenburg, described as "mouth anarchy."[22] In describing the general tone of the session, the historian Gordon Craig wrote that "speakers for the SPD . . . described the government's policy variously as an indulgence of Strauss' desire to play at soldiers, an indication of the Chancellor's subservience to John Foster Dulles, and a sign that the military caste was reasserting its dominance in German life. Speakers for the government tended to . . . regard oppositionists as pro-Communists and neutralists."[23] In the end, the government's resolution passed comfortably, and the SPD could only counter with a demand for Adenauer's resignation and the creation of a new government that would end West German participation in NATO nuclear weapons policy. Of course, any attempt to oust Adenauer through a vote of no confidence was futile, so the party now turned to an extraparliamentary course of action that had been evolving since January, when the Kampf dem Atomtod Committee had been formed.

THE KAMPF DEM ATOMTOD MOVEMENT

Prior to the Bundestag debates, on January 20, 1958, the SPD formally initiated the Kampf dem Atomtod (Fight Atomic Death) campaign, calling on party members to generate a "wave of resistance to atomic death" to block the government's plans for equipping

---

400 miles, could not target the USSR. See Ronald H. Huisken, "Cruise Missiles: Origins and Implications for Strategic Arms Control" (Ph.D. thesis, Australian National University, 1979).

21. For the text of the revised Rapacki Plan, see U.S. Congress, Senate, Committee on Foreign Relations, *Documents on Germany*, pp. 270–273.

22. See Eschenburg's article in *Die Zeit*, April 10, 1958, also, *Economist*, March 29, 1958.

23. Gordon Craig, "Germany and NATO: The Rearmament Debate, 1950–58," in Klaus Knorr, ed., *NATO and American Security* (Princeton: Princeton University Press, 1959), p. 245.

the Bundeswehr with nuclear weapons delivery systems and for stationing U.S. nuclear warheads to be matched with those systems.[24] Acting on Fritz Erler's feeling that it was time "to give public opinion a jolt," the SPD reached out to church leaders, trade unionists, scientists, literary figures, and others to form the Kampf dem Atomtod Committee. In its first public declaration, on March 10, the committee called on the government and Bundestag "not to participate in the atomic arms race but to support all efforts to create in Europe a zone free of atomic weapons as a contribution to détente."[25] Simultaneously, the SPD used its organizational resources to publish a plethora of broadsides, pamphlets, and films to educate the public on the dangers of nuclear weapons, while planning a series of mass demonstrations to pressure the Adenauer government.

Having helped mobilize public opinion, and with Bundestag approval of Adenauer's program having shut off SPD parliamentary opposition, the party now had to choose among several alternative courses in its fight to defeat what Helmut Schmidt referred to as "the rocket Christians" (that is, the CDU/CSU).[26] The party could try to make common cause with other mass organizations, such as the German Trade Union Federation (DGB), the churches, and various peace groups, to take the issue into the streets and factories. Yet, while public opinion seemed solidly behind the use of both public demonstrations and a general strike to press home the issue,[27] the SPD leadership realized that both courses of action had their dangers. Mass demonstrations could turn violent, and the party would be left open to the charge of having been manipulated by those elements in the peace movement who were promoting the

24. *Süddeutsche Zeitung*, January 31, 1958.

25. Karl Bauer, *Deutsche Verteidigungspolitik, 1945–1963: Dokumente und Kommentare* (Boppard: Boldt, 1964), p. 153.

26. Quoted in Gordon D. Drummond, *The German Social Democrats in Opposition, 1949–1960* (Norman: University of Oklahoma Press, 1982), p. 228.

27. In a February 1958 poll, 81 percent of the respondents opposed the installation of nuclear weapons launching platforms in the Federal Republic, while only 15 percent approved. Those opposed to equipping the Bundeswehr with nuclear delivery systems totaled 71 percent, those in favor, 21 percent. See Karl W. Deutsch and Lewis J. Edinger, *Germany Rejoins the Powers* (Stanford: Stanford University Press, 1959), p. 27. An April 1958 poll showed that 52 percent of the respondents thought a general strike would be justified "in order to prevent the Bundeswehr from being equipped with nuclear armaments," while 31 percent believed such a strike would not be justified, and 17 percent were undecided. See Noelle and Neumann, eds., *Germans*, p. 354.

interests of Moscow and East Berlin and who hoped to profit from violent street demonstrations. Because of the potent strain of anticommunism then running through West German society, the SPD shied away from direct alliance with anyone to its left, thus foreclosing, in Joffe's words, "not only a popular front [absent throughout German history, by contrast to the French] but also a sustained plebiscitary or grass roots struggle."[28]

The leadership of the SPD and the trade unions were equally cautious about using the general strike as a weapon against the Adenauer government.[29] Realizing that widespread strikes might conjure up visions of Weimar instability, the Trade Union Federation leadership contented itself with strong condemnations of nuclear weapons and exhortations to its 6 million members to protest such deployment in West Germany. Although some work stoppages did occur during the next few months, and several of the more radical trade union leaders did call for a general strike, the DGB decided to forgo endorsement of a general strike.[30]

In much the same way, the Protestant (Evangelical) church was confronted with the question how far to support the Kampf dem Atomtod movement in light of internal splits. For both the labor movement and the Evangelical church (EKD), the Third Reich had been a searing experience, and both groups had vowed after the war

---

28. Joffe, "Society and Foreign Policy," p. 216.

29. Although Ollenhauer at times declared that there was nothing illegitimate in a general strike, the SPD leader was reluctant to resort to one in support of the Kampf dem Atomtod; see *Frankfurter Allgemeine Zeitung*, March 28, 1958. Herbert Wehner was even more explicit, calling any talk of a general strike, "general nonsense"; see *Die Welt*, March 31, 1958.

30. The DGB's reluctance to throw its full weight behind the antinuclear campaign was due to historical, structural, and ideological factors. The historical reason was that, in order to become an effective voice for German labor, the DGB sought to avoid the political divisions that had weakened the Weimar labor movement. This aim required it to concentrate on economic issues rather than become sidetracked by issues not central to the welfare of the German labor movement. Structurally, the DGB's confederal organization, consisting of more than a dozen constituent unions, has usually resulted in a lowest common denominator strategy, so that the DGB can maximize its influence only when most of its member unions are in agreement. Indeed, this confederal structure is designed to tolerate ideological differences within the movement, especially on noneconomic issues. Ideologically, the DGB executive is predominantly Social Democratic, yet more than 20 percent of the rank-and-file members consistently vote Christian Democratic. See Gerard Braunthal, "West German Trade Unions and Disarmament," *Political Science Quarterly* 73 (Spring 1968); and Richard J. Willey, "Trade Unions and Political Parties in the Federal Republic," *Industrial and Labor Relations Review*, October 1974.

that they would never again remain passive in the face of disturbing political trends.[31]

In 1947, at the Evangelical church's first major postwar conference, the church leadership vowed to "assume the enormous and difficult duty of playing a much greater part than before in influencing public life and especially the political community."[32] Yet, as with the DGB, such action was to be taken independently of the political parties. In order to remain a distinct, moral force in West German politics, as well as to safeguard the church's internal unity, the EKD's entry into politics could not be overly partisan.

Although extreme political activism was also discouraged by the church leadership,[33] the EKD continued to be in the forefront of the disarmament and disengagement debates of 1957–58. In fact, the church even seemed to be on the verge of taking an organizational stand when, at the EKD synod in April 1958, Bishop Otto Dibelius, chairman of the EKD council, reversed himself and came out against Adenauer's policy. Dibelius based his position on the grounds that the mass destructiveness of nuclear weapons had invalidated the concept of a "just war." Dibelius seemed to be shifting toward a rejection of nuclear weapons on theological arguments that had long been advanced by Paster Martin Niemöller and the Lutheran pastor Helmut Gollwitzer (who became a leading figure in the peace movement of the early 1980s), both of whom argued that soldiers armed with atomic weapons "could not be considered in a state of grace."[34] While Dibelius did not go so far as to echo Niemöller's sentiments that it should be the duty "of a Christian soldier to

31. The quiescent role of the Protestant church during the Nazi period resulted in the postwar period in a "radically new concept of the church's role in society.... Though imperfectly realized, this ideal transformed German Protestantism into a generally progressive institution of post-war German life and one through which, despite internal restorative tendencies, political dissent could be expressed." See Frederic Spotts, *The Churches and Politics in Germany* (Middletown, Conn.: Wesleyan University Press, 1973), p. 12.

32. Ibid., p. 128.

33. The extent to which the Protestant church hierarchy would tolerate overt political activism was shown in the early 1950s when Gustav Heinemann (later to become president of the Federal Republic) and Pastor Martin Niemöller were removed from their positions of church leadership for advocating a national grass-roots campaign to block Adenauer's rearmament program. As Spotts notes, this repudiation of Heinemann and Niemöller by the EKD synod "in effect marked the formal rejection of any attempt to transform German protestantism into an active, partisan political force.... There would be no political crusades and no Protestant political army": ibid., p. 128.

34. Craig, "Germany and NATO," pp. 247–248.

betray the position of rocket ramps to the enemy rather than condone their use," he did seem to give new impetus to the church's involvement in the Kampf dem Atomtod movement.

In the end, however, more moderate elements in the church leadership, like those in the DGB and SPD, realized that a blanket condemnation of nuclear weapons by itself would not address the question what positive steps should be taken to ensure West Germany's security. In addition, many church members were uneasy about using the Gospel to oppose measures designed to protect the West against an avowed enemy of Christianity. Ultimately, the April 1958 synod was unable to agree to denounce nuclear weapons completely (although it did call for both Germanies to renounce such weapons), and had to be content with setting up a committee to study the problem.[35]

If the Protestant church was undergoing a crisis of conscience on how to respond to the nuclear weapons issue, the Catholic hierarchy suffered no such doubts. Staunchly pro-Adenauer and anticommunist, Joseph Cardinal Frings, archbishop of Cologne, invoked the authority of a recent papal affirmation concerning a nation's right to self-defense when he declared, "The Catholic Church does not advocate the outlawing of atomic and hydrogen bombs at the present time."[36] The Catholic leadership was also less troubled than its Protestant brethren in becoming actively engaged in partisan politics. Before the state election in North Rhine–Westphalia, in July 1958, the church published a pamphlet (*Christliche Friedenspolitik und atomare Aufrüstung*) that emphasized the need to combat the ruthless ideology of communism, fulfill Alliance defense commitments, and reject pernicious "better red than dead" sentiments. In June, just a month before the election, the five Catholic bishops in North Rhine–Westphalia came out openly in support of Adenauer and the CDU in their election pastoral message.[37]

35. Under the direction of Professor Carl Friedrich von Weizsäcker, later to be one of the leaders of the 1980s peace movement, the church committee met for several years, finally agreeing to disagree.

36. In a fit of historical absentmindedness, Cardinal Frings, who was in Tokyo at the time, made his comments in the one country that had experienced the devastation of nuclear weapons; see Spotts, *Churches and Politics in Germany*, p. 264.

37. Spotts has described the position of the Catholic church, as enunciated in its pamphlet *Christliche Friedenspolitik und atomare Aufrüstung*, as "mixing theology and politics so indistinguishably as to leave ambigious where Catholic moral philosophy ended and where the right of individual judgment in international affairs began." See his *Churches and Politics in Germany*, p. 266.

Having eschewed confrontational tactics, Ollenhauer and the SPD announced in April 1958 that the party would seek a national referendum (*Volksbefragung*) on the nuclear weapons issue. Carlo Schmid argued that such a referendum, which was submitted formally on April 24, was not intended as a binding plebiscite, but that the West German people nonetheless had the right to express themselves on Parliament's decision to "go nuclear." The use of such a poll in this case was especially relevant, the SPD stressed, because Adenauer himself during the recent election campaign had asserted that any decision on nuclear weapons would not be made for some time and that there would be "no experiments."

In response, government spokesmen accused the SPD of indulging in demagoguery and of seeking to circumvent the will of Parliament. Knowing its bill stood no chance of passage, the SPD then moved to seemingly more propitious territory, the state parliaments in the eleven *Länder* (provinces). Here as well, bills were submitted asking that regional surveys be taken at the state level. In those Länder where the SPD was in opposition, such as Bavaria, these requests were promptly voted down. In others, including North Rhine–Westphalia, where the SPD formed a coalition government, the local party leadership decided not to introduce the issue, given tenuous political relationships with their political partners. Only in two states where the SPD enjoyed an absolute majority, Hamburg and Bremen, did the party successfully pass legislation calling for officially sanctioned public opinion surveys.

At this point, Adenauer again sought refuge in the Constitutional Court, where he had been so successful in 1952 in turning aside SPD opposition to the European Defense Community. Arguing that the state governments had no right to interfere in issues of foreign policy and defense, which the Basic Law reserves to the national government, and that moreover the use of such polls contravened the concept of representative government, the Adenauer administration sought court injunctions against their use. Having granted such temporary injunctions in May, the court, on July 30, issued its decision, striking down the referendum laws previously passed in Hamburg and Bremen.

While the court was still deliberating, the SPD moved to its final political arena, the elections to be held in North Rhine–Westphalia on July 6. As with the Baden-Württemburg elections in 1952, the SPD hoped to use the election as a different form of referendum on the government's policy. Given that one-third of the West German electorate lived in North Rhine–Westphalia, the state election took on the appearance of what Carlo Schmid called a Bundestag by-election. The SPD's attempts at turning the election to the advantage of the Kampf dem Atomtod movement failed, however, when the CDU won more than 50 percent of the vote and thus gained an absolute majority in this traditional SPD stronghold for the first time. Along with the Constitutional Court's decision on July 30, the election results shut off the final "institutional" avenue open to the SPD. Given the party's reluctance to throw its full weight behind a grass-roots campaign, the Kampf dem Atomtod lost most of its momentum, lingering on in ineffectual protest for the next several months.

Finally, in November 1958, any remaining political utility to be had in opposing nuclear weapons vanished entirely when Nikita Khrushchev issued his Berlin ultimatum, which demanded that the Western powers negotiate a settlement of Berlin's status or vacate the city. This new crisis in East–West relations, and the vague nuclear threats issued by Khrushchev, only strengthened Adenauer's conviction that NATO and the Bundeswehr should be equipped with "the most modern weapons."[38]

SPD POLITICAL STRATEGY

At its height, in April and May of 1958, the Kampf dem Atomtod movement was able to bring hundreds of thousands of demonstrators into the streets to protest Adenauer's nuclear weapons policy. As we have seen, public opinion ran strongly against that policy, even to the extent of supporting a general strike to stop it. In analyzing why the SPD failed to capitalize on these public sentiments, and why the party chose the particular political tactics it did, we must take into account two factors of special importance: the internal reform movement in the party and the SPD's peculiar status in the West German political "correlation of forces."

In regard to the first issue, the SPD's nuclear weapons policy was only one part of a broader debate within the party on defense and foreign policy, which in turn was only one facet of the party's fundamental dilemma of trying to refashion an identity for itself in

38. For a fascinating account of Khrushchev's Berlin ultimatum and the role played by nuclear weapons in the crisis, see McGeorge Bundy, *Danger and Survival: Choices about the Bomb in the First Fifty Years* (New York: Random House, 1988), chap. 8.

the evolving socioeconomic structure of the Federal Republic. As we have seen, the reformist wing of the party had begun years earlier to stress that the SPD must shed its more doctrinaire Marxist tenets and move to the right if it was to have any chance of coming to power. By the time of the Stuttgart party conference in May 1958, these reformers had attained enough power within the party organization, even though Ollenhauer remained head of the party, to put forth their previously blocked *Grundsatzprogramm* (basic program). Especially after the party's poor showing in 1957, most observers assumed that the issue of party reform would be the dominant theme at Stuttgart, with the reformers at last able to move the party toward the moderate center of German politics. As it happened, the emergence of the nuclear weapons issue and the Kampf dem Atomtod movement somewhat preempted the reform issue. Yet it was never very far from the surface, and the debate between the party traditionalists and reformers on how the SPD should oppose the government epitomized their respective conceptions of the party itself.

At issue was both the political means to be used to oppose Adenauer and whether the party should be content merely to register that opposition or should go further and integrate its antinuclear stand into a politically viable security policy for Germany. On the whole, the party traditionalists were the more outspoken in their antinuclearism, yet less willing to advance security policies that might generate broader appeal outside the party. Some of the most doctrinaire members of the party, citing the pacifist, antimilitarist traditions of the SPD, argued that anything less than a full mobilization of the party's supporters against the government would be tantamount to betrayal of the party's ethos. To avoid repeating the mistakes of 1914, when SPD members of the Reichstag supported the Kaiser and voted for war credits, and those of 1933, when the party was ineffectual in blocking Hitler's rise to power, these party members advocated full use of the party's ultimate weapon, the general strike and mass protests.

In the end, sentiments in favor of carrying the battle into the streets were limited. While Ollenhauer called the nuclear weapons issue "a question of life and death" and noted that it had been years since the party had "gone into the streets for such a good cause and in such good company," he also admitted that "it is easy to talk about so-called extra-parliamentary actions" but "difficult to carry them out."[39] Despite criticism at the conference that the party would be left with no strategy at all should the state referendum tactic fail, Ollenhauer and the SPD Vorstand (executive committee) were content to put forth only a general resolution, committing the party to opposing nuclear weapons in the FRG and favoring greater efforts at disarmament and reunification.

In their speeches to the Stuttgart conference, Erler and Wehner emphasized the need for the party to come up with a constructive security policy of its own. Neither man went so far as to voice support for NATO or a strictly pro-West orientation for the FRG; indeed, their arguments in favor of an SPD security policy were predicated on the fact that "military security measures have to be brought into line with reunification efforts."[40] Yet both men also emphasized that these reunification efforts could not be implemented unless the SPD came to power in Bonn, and that the party stood no chance of gaining governmental responsibility unless it could convince the West German electorate that it had a workable plan for German security. Through this circuitous reasoning, Erler and Wehner began to nudge the party toward the acceptance of German participation in Western defense efforts which would occur at the party's Bad Godesberg conference eighteen months later.

For the SPD, the issue boiled down to whether the party should concentrate on inducing large scale societal transformation or whether the immediate aim should be the "conquest of state power."[41] Despite the attenuation of class divisions in the Federal Republic, however, the SPD was still subject to attempts by Adenauer to, in the words of Fritz Erler, "eject the Social Democrats and their supporters from the state."[42] Given the pervasive anticommunist sentiments aroused by the Cold War and Soviet subjugation of East

---

39. Quoted in Drummond, *German Social Democrats*, p. 234.

40. For more on the Stuttgart Party Congress of the SPD, see ibid., pp. 233–241.

41. The history of the SPD reveals long-standing tensions within the party on how the SPD should go about winning political power and influencing society. At the party congress in Erfurt in 1891, the moderates (Lassalleans) argued that a socialist revolution would best be implemented by working through democratic institutions. The Marxist wing of the party remained committed to a revolutionary struggle to win state power. Along with this debate on party ideology went a similar debate over organizational issues. Both issues would be similarly played out in the 1950s. For more on the historical development of the SPD, see Helga Grebing, *Geschichte der deutschen Arbeiterbewegung* (Munich: Deutscher Taschenbuch, 1979), pp. 108–120.

42. *Der Sozialist* (Hamburg), November 1958.

Germany, Adenauer was able to some extent to cast the SPD beyond the pale of political legitimacy.

This historical burden of still not being recognized as a legitimate player in the political system, despite the party's long tradition, severely handicapped the SPD in opposing Adenauer. While not all Germans accepted Adenauer's campaign of "guilt by association," in which the SPD was portrayed as serving the cause of Soviet communism, the SPD was nonetheless handicapped in having to prove itself almost "holier than thou" on questions of German security.

While the party took the first major step on this road with its adoption of the Bad Godesberg reforms in 1959, it was not until 1969 that there would be sufficient changes in both the party itself and the West German political environment (an emerging détente externally and the concomitant decrease of anticommunist sentiments domestically) to enable the party to win the chancellorship. Before Bad Godesberg, and especially during the Kampf dem Atomtod campaign, the SPD had to determine first to what extent it would make common cause with German communists and radicals to its left. This question was only one part of the larger issue of how far the party would go to ally itself with any nonsocialist faction in opposing Adenauer, which itself was but one facet of the fundamental question posed earlier: how would the party come to power—by transforming society from below or by capturing the state apparatus and implementing socialism from above?

To Erler and Wehner, this question had lost much of its relevance, given the diminution of class conflict in the Federal Republic. Where the reformist wing of the SPD had traditionally seen the party as a mass pressure group working from below, the reformers of the 1950s considered that, according to Douglas Chalmers, "the older questions of what power is adequate to carry out a social transformation have died out, and the discussion of means and ends turns around more technical questions concerning the position the party can hope to win in the German political system and the strategy it should adopt in order to win this position."[43] Or, as Erler said: "We are fighting not the state, but a false policy of the government and its majority. . . we are fighting not against the state, but for the state, and, in fact, not the state of the distant future, not the state only in a

43. Chalmers, *The Social Democratic Party of Germany* (New Haven: Yale University Press, 1964), p. 96.

reunified Germany, but the state in this Federal Republic, which we want to govern."[44]

Given such sentiments, the reformers viewed the nuclear weapons issue more from the perspective of long term strategy, of how the party could solidify its political respectability, than from that of short-range tactical considerations. Unlike some members of the party's left wing, who wanted to mobilize grass-roots sentiments against Adenauer—even if that meant collaboration with communists and radicals—Erler, Wehner, and the reformers were more concerned with firmly establishing the party's credibility vis-à-vis the interest groups and political elites in the FRG whose support the party would need to gain power.[45]

Throughout the nuclear weapons debate, then, as throughout the 1950s, the SPD was caught in a peculiar situation. The party attempted to maintain a socialist identity in a society in which class distinctions were softening, while also attempting to broaden its electoral appeal through a reexamination of its relationship with nonsocialist groups. Wehner especially emphasized the need for party members to establish contact with political groups not traditionally allied to the SPD, such as small business organizations, farmers, and professionals. For Wehner and others, the party's identity problem was not what the SPD really stood for, but what its opponents made it out to be. Wehner called this problem one of *"Goebbelschen Zerrbilder"* ("Goebbels' distorted images," referring to Hitler's propaganda chief), and noted how the CDU was attempting to identify the SPD with the East German ruling party, the Socialist Unity Party (SED). To combat these distortions, what was needed was a concerted effort to make "the members of the middle classes so aware of Social Democratic goals that the false images that are spread about us will, insofar as

44. Quoted in ibid., p. 102.

45. At the tactical level, this split within the party was epitomized by a struggle between Willy Brandt, newly elected party chairman in West Berlin, and the local party traditionalists led by former party chairman Franz Neumann over how much support the party organization should give the local Kampf dem Atomtod movement. At a special conference held on April 19, 1958, Neumann advocated full SPD support for massive street demonstrations and a plebiscite to oppose nuclear weapons. Brandt, fearing communist manipulation of street demonstrations, countered that the SPD should concentrate on formulating a disarmament policy in cooperation with the Federal Republic's allies. Brandt was able to carry his motion by only eight votes, yet this victory presaged the distancing of the SPD from the nationwide Kampf dem Atomtod movement following the SPD's poor showing in the July 1958 elections in North Rhine–Westphalia. See Drummond, *German Social Democrats*, pp. 227–228.

possible, lose their effect."[46] For Wehner, too great an identification between the SPD and the Kampf dem Atomtod movement was not the best way to banish such "false images."

Not surprisingly, this effort was opposed by party militants and bureaucrats who argued that the SPD, far from moderating its policies, must return to an emphasis on strengthening working class consciousness (*Klassenbewusstsein*). For many in the old guard, such as the leftist Marburg law professor Wolfgang Abendroth, the SPD was in danger of being conned into accepting a theory of class convergence which was being propagated by the CDU and the ruling elite. As Abendroth argued:

> A large section of the German workers have taken over the ideology of the classless character of the present society which was sponsored by the ruling classes ... and have not developed their own. So long as that is lacking, the workers can be manipulated through the usual advertising offensives.... [The SPD] must be the opinion-forming center and leading cadre of the employed in their political-social opposition to finance capital.[47]

Another fundamental problem for the SPD in the 1950s was the difficulty of presenting a socialist alternative to Adenauer in a domestic political climate dominated by anticommunism. As Wolf-Dieter Narr has pointed out, the Cold War climate of the period, in conjunction with the uncertainty over the political status of the two Germanies, led to a high correlation between external and internal concepts of security in German politics. The result was a "double security complex," in which the "internal and external anxiety about the whole status of the Federal Republic found not its resolution but its guiding behavioral norm in anti-communism."[48] Any attempt by the SPD to radicalize the nuclear weapons issue, especially without having a viable security policy of its own, would have only alienated most West German voters and kept the party isolated. As Narr has pointed out, the prevailing "ideological anti-communism narrowed down the political margin of maneuver," so that the SPD was forced to move closer to the CDU and gain respectability before it could hope to achieve power. In effect, the reformist wing of the SPD was

46. Quoted in Chalmers, *Social Democratic Party*, p. 111.
47. *Der Sozialdemokrat* (Frankfurt), November 1957.
48. Wolf-Dieter Narr, "Social Factors Affecting the Making of Foreign Policy," in Karl Kaiser and Roger Morgan, eds., *Britain and West Germany: Changing Societies and the Future of Foreign Policy* (London: Oxford University Press, 1971), pp. 113–114.

content to dissociate the party from the Kampf dem Atomtod movement in the service of longer range goals, recognizing as it did that "alternatives were, by the nature of the system, hardly feasible and retained, not accidentally, the form of powerless campaigns."[49]

Of course, Wehner, Erler and the others had to be careful not to alienate the traditional wing of the party with their pragmatism. Any worsening of the existing split within the party could jeopardize the reformers' attempts to steer the SPD in the direction of the Bad Godesberg platform. To ensure that the party's left wing would not bolt and create a splinter party, as it had done in 1917, the reformers sought to keep the party's participation in the Kampf dem Atomtod movement within acceptable political channels. While the use of such tactics as state referenda were themselves controversial and contravened the spirit if not the letter of the Basic Law, the reformers could argue that the party was at least limiting itself to working within the FRG's political institutions, as compared with the damage the party might suffer if it organized a general strike and engaged in radical street actions.[50]

Ultimately, then, the reformist leaders of the SPD sought to capitalize on the nuclear weapons issue by using it to promote their program within the party, as well as to engage in some bridge building with nonsocialist, democratic elements to their right. Their success in reorienting SPD policies became more fully apparent one year later, with the adoption of the moderate party program at the special Bad Godesberg party conference.[51]

In declaring its "allegiance to the defense of a free democratic order" and its support of the Bundeswehr, the SPD for the first time largely accepted West Germany's role in the Western Alliance. It is true that Erler and other moderates continued to stress the party's opposition to NATO reliance on nuclear weapons and its preference, in Erler's words, "for détente and reunification, and not a nuclear

49. Ibid., pp. 113–114.

50. Gordon Craig, for one, has argued that the SPD's attempt to take the issue to the people through referenda in the Länder showed an "utter disregard for the lessons of history [Weimar] and for the facts of constitutional law." See his "Germany and NATO," p. 246. However, the SPD leaders themselves thought such referenda bent the constitution far less than a general strike, about which Ollenhauer could say, "The Social Democrats are Democrats as a matter of principle, and the party will not do the [Christian Democratic] Union the favor to tread outside the bounds drawn by the Constitution" (quoted in Joffe, "Society and Foreign Policy," p. 216).

51. *Grundsatz Programm der Sozialdemokratische Partei Deutschlands: Beschlossen vom Ausserordentlichen Partei der SPD in Bad Godesberg, November 13–15, 1959* (Bonn: Vorstand der SPD, 1959), pp. 10–11 especially.

arms race." Yet Erler recognized that "success in the battle against nuclear weapons presupposes the possession of political power [and] a Bundestag majority," and that total SPD rejection of Western defense policies would continue to isolate the SPD politically.[52] Thus the Bad Godesberg program signaled a new approach on the part of the SPD for coping with Germany's nuclear dilemma, an approach that bore fruit in 1966 when the party joined the CDU/CSU in the Grand Coalition government.

NATO POLICY IN THE 1960S

With the acceptance by the SPD of the major tenets of West Germany's role in the Atlantic Alliance, the domestic public debate in the FRG regarding nuclear policy essentially subsided. Public dissatisfaction with NATO nuclear weapons policy did not disappear entirely, as evidenced by the Easter protest marches in the FRG, Britain, and elsewhere in the early 1960s. Yet the intensity of antinuclear sentiments during the Kampf dem Atomtod movement would not be seen again until the neutron bomb and INF episodes of the late 1970s and early 1980s. Rather, the focus of the nuclear debate shifted from weapons systems and nuclear deployments to NATO strategy and nuclear decision making within the Alliance, and the venue of these debates was not the public at large but the policy elites of the FRG and its NATO allies.

Discussions within the Alliance on the question of control sharing (i.e., European participation in the stockpiling, targeting, and use of nuclear warheads) had been going on since the late 1950s, spurred by the arrival of U.S. weapons on European soil and by the nascent British and French efforts to acquire independent nuclear forces. In the case of the Federal Republic, these issues were particularly important, symbolizing as they did the trade-offs facing the FRG in the pursuit of its Atlantic, European, and Eastern foreign policy goals.

An example of these trade-offs is the previously mentioned proposal by Gen. Lauris Norstad, the NATO SACEUR, for creating a separate NATO MRBM force. Although reluctant to deploy MRBMs on German soil, the Adenauer government nonetheless was willing

52. See Erler's memorandum "The SPD and Nuclearization of the Bundeswehr," excerpted in Mark Cioc's fine work, *Pax Atomica: The Nuclear Defense Debate in West Germany during the Adenauer Era* (New York: Columbia University Press, 1988), p. 155.

to support SACEUR-based proposals such as Norstad's in order to maximize the U.S. connection and minimize the political importance of the evolving British and French independent forces.

By the same token, however, the FRG did not want to foreclose the possibility of nuclear weapons cooperation with its European NATO allies. Adenauer's commitment to a Europeanist policy, symbolized by integrationist efforts that led to the creation of the Common Market and Euratom in 1956–57, was carried over into the security realm when Defense Minister Strauss began exploring with Italy the possibility of joint financial aid to the French nuclear weapons program in return for technological benefits. There was no question here of the FRG seeking a surreptitious route to acquiring its own nuclear weapons; the domestic and external constraints were just too formidable. These so-called F-I-G discussions also included plans for joint production of various dual-capable systems, yet both aspects of the program came to naught when de Gaulle returned to power in 1958 stressing the absolute independence of the French nuclear effort. Nonetheless, the FRG did take the lead in organizing European coproduction of other weapons systems (such as Hawk and Sidewinder missiles), and Strauss continued to work closely with his European counterparts in pressing the Eisenhower administration for the creation of a NATO nuclear force.

One particularly salient example of the tension between West Germany's Atlantic and European interests is worth mentioning here. Because the Paris and London accords of 1954 prevented it from acquiring long-range aircraft and missiles as well as "atomic, bacteriological and chemical" weapons, Bonn had to decide in the late 1950s between the U.S. F-104 Starfighter and the French Mirage III as the Luftwaffe's primary combat aircraft. West Germany had sound military and technical reasons, in addition to the desire to solidify its American connection, for its choice of the F-104. Yet it has been reported that some U.S. officials unofficially stressed as well that acquisition of the Starfighter would make it easier for the FRG to plead for greater access to and control over the U.S. nuclear weapons that would ultimately be matched with the aircraft.[53]

The F-104 and the other dual-capable weapons systems that the FRG was ordering from the United States in the late 1950s (see table 1) symbolized the growing importance of the control-sharing issue. Yet few of these systems had actually been deployed in early 1961,

53. Kelleher, *Germany and the Politics of Nuclear Weapons*, pp. 102–104.

Table 1. Bundeswehr tactical nuclear delivery systems, 1956–1960

Type	Function	Capability	Range * (miles)	Source *	Outcome by 1960 *
Air-defense missiles					
Nike-Hercules	Surface-to-air	Dual	75	Purchase from U.S.	Authorized
Hawk	Surface-to-air	Conventional	15	Pool production under U.S. license	Authorized
Sidewinder	Air-to-air	Conventional	2	Pool production under U.S. license	Authorized
Seacat	Sea-to-air	Conventional	Limited	Purchase from Britain	Authorized
Short-range vehicles					
203-mm howitzer	Surface-to-surface	Dual	Under 10	Purchase from U.S.	Authorized
Honest John missile	Surface-to-surface	Dual	12–15	Purchase from U.S.	Authorized
Sergeant missile	Surface-to-surface	Dual	75	Purchase from U.S.	Authorized
Davy Crockett cannon	Surface-to-surface	Dual	Under 5	Purchase from U.S.	Planned
Long-range vehicles					
Mace missile	Surface-to-surface	Dual	700 +	Purchase from U.S.	Authorized
Pershing missile	Surface-to-surface	Dual	300 +	Purchase from U.S.	Planned
Polaris missile	Sea-to-surface	Dual	500 +	Purchase from U.S.	Under consideration
Starfighter F-104 airplane	Fighter; strike	Dual	400 + (radius)	Purchase from U.S. and pool production under U.S. license	Authorized
Fiat G-91 airplane	Light strike; reconnaissance	Potentially dual	Limited	Pool production	Authorized

* Information possessed by German military authorities during 1956–1960.

SOURCE: Catherine McArdle Kelleher, *Germany and the Politics of Nuclear Weapons* (New York: Columbia University Press, 1975). Copyright © 1975 by Columbia University Press. Used by permission.

when the incoming Kennedy administration startled the Europeans by announcing its intention to conduct a wholescale review of NATO's nuclear and conventional strategy. The evolution of the Kennedy administration's Flexible Response strategy, entailing strengthened conventional force capabilities and greater options in the use of nuclear weapons, is a complex story and does not need retelling here.[54] It is sufficient to note that the shift in U.S. strategy, from Eisenhower's emphasis of early and massive use of nuclear weapons to deter Soviet aggression to the Kennedy/McNamara strategy of flexible response and escalation dominance, threatened to undermine the rationale of West German defense planning since 1955 and called into question the essence of Adenauer's original rearmament bargain. The chancellor feared that a switch in NATO strategy to meeting Soviet aggression with conventional forces and the concomitant U.S. effort to establish more clearly a firebreak between conventional and nuclear war would weaken the U.S. nuclear guarantee. Adenauer saw McNamara's attempt to get the Europeans to strengthen their conventional forces as a replay of the 1956 Radford Plan (i.e., signaling a drawdown of the U.S. military commitment in Europe) which would end up undermining the NATO deterrent and West German security.

This fear of a weakened U.S. commitment to the FRG was fueled as well by the Kennedy administration's handling of the Berlin Wall crisis and by new U.S. diplomatic and arms control initiatives towards the Soviets in 1961–62. The result was a heightening of the immediacy and importance for the FRG of the nuclear control-sharing issue. Just as important, the implications of the Soviet's growing capability to attack the continental United States directly for the credibility of the U.S. strategic guarantee made West German participation in the release and firing of NATO's nuclear weapons all the more vital. Yet this desire on the part of the Adenauer government ran counter to one of the central tenets of the new U.S. policy: secure command and control of nuclear forces. More than the Eisenhower administration, McNamara and others in the Kennedy administration would support such arrangements only if they met the criteria of secure control and responsiveness in a crisis and were content to let the Europeans take the initiative in proposing such schemes. In short, "the degree of disinclination if not direct

54. William W. Kaufmann, *The McNamara Strategy* (New York: Harper & Row, 1964).

unwillingness of Kennedy's Washington to proceed seriously with earlier American initiatives or vague new proposals was more than equalled by the intensity of Bonn's belief that the imperatives toward control-sharing were now stronger than ever."[55]

For some American officials, particularly in the State Department, the intensity of Bonn's efforts signaled a West German desire for ultimate national control of nuclear weapons. Catherine Kelleher, for one, has convincingly demonstrated that this was not the case; the domestic constraints and external realities were just too great.[56] Nonetheless, taking their cue from Kennedy and McNamara's concerns with the proliferation of national nuclear forces, officials such as Robert Bowie and Gerard Smith at the State Department argued that West Germany would soon be following France and Britain down the nuclear path. To head off such a possibility, Bowie, Smith and others proposed a "joint hardware–joint control" approach to NATO's nuclear dilemma, as compared with McNamara's preference for maintaining strict centralized control of nuclear weapons but allowing greater European input into the policy-decision process.

Subsequent attempts by Bowie and others to create a mixed-man, sea-based nuclear force (the multilateral force, or MLF) are well enough known that a short summary here will suffice.[57] The idea was an outgrowth of the 1960 Herter Plan, which had been proposed as an alternative to Norstad's MRBM force under SACEUR's control. As modified by Bowie, Smith, Henry Owen, and others, the creation of a multinational force of surface ships equipped with 100 MRBMs could supplement the five U.S. Polaris submarines assigned to NATO and thus give the Europeans a direct stake in the Alliance's nuclear deterrent. As we have seen, however, the MLF proposal conflicted with Kennedy's desire for secure, centralized control of all nuclear forces (e.g., the Polaris subs were kept under the control of SACLANT (Supreme Allied Commander, Atlantic) in Norfolk rather than SACEUR in Europe). Others in the American bureaucracy were opposed to the MLF for a variety of reasons, including similar concerns with centralized control (the Joint Chiefs), issues of sharing nuclear weapons information and technology (Atomic Energy Commission and some members of Congress), and concerns in the U.S. navy over dividing its nuclear role between submarines and surface

55. Kelleher, *Germany and the Politics of Nuclear Weapons*, p. 157.

56. See ibid., chap. 11 especially.

57. John Steinbruner, *The Cybernetic Theory of Decision* (Princeton: Princeton University Press, 1974).

ships (Adm. Hyman Rickover). That the MLF proposal survived as long as it did, until December 1964, when President Johnson shelved it, was due largely to the bureaucratic finesse of its proponents and the lack of depth of the opposition, as well as to the continuing interest of the FRG in some form of nuclear control sharing.

The MLF proponents in the United States and West German governments were handicapped by the steadfast commitment of the British and French to the pursuit of independent nuclear forces. This situation undercut one of their main arguments—that a multinational NATO force could realize McNamara's goal of preventing the prolif-eration of nuclear forces that to him were "dangerous, expensive, prone to obsolescence, and lacking in credibility as a deterrent."[58] Just as significant, neither the British nor the French were at all enthusiastic about the prospect of an MLF that assumed the charac-ter of a bilateral U.S.–FRG force. In the United Kingdom, the Labour Party's victory in the October 1964 election seemed to offer the MLF proponents some hope, given the lukewarm attitude of the previous Conservative government and Labour's seeming opposition to maintaining the independent British deterrent. Quite quickly, how-ever, Prime Minister Harold Wilson showed that he was no more supportive of the MLF idea than Harold MacMillan had been, and the Labour government continued development of national British nuclear forces.[59]

In France, the somewhat tolerant attitude of de Gaulle toward FRG participation in the MLF stiffened considerably in the second half of 1964. At a meeting in Bonn with the newly elected chancellor, Ludwig Erhard, in July 1964, de Gaulle made clear his misgivings about the Atlanticist thrust of West German policy under Erhard and Foreign Minister Gerhard Schröder, which the French president felt was undermining European integration efforts. This point was driv-en home to the Erhard government in October 1964 when the French government announced that it would block progress in the Kennedy Round of the GATT talks and possibly even boycott the Common Market if the FRG was not forthcoming on the issue of common grain prices. Five days later, on October 26, France announced it had reached agreement with the Soviet Union on a five-year trade

58. The quote, from McNamara's famous Ann Arbor commencement speech of 1962, reiterated publicly the position taken by the United States at the NATO meeting in Athens in May 1962. See *Department of State Bulletin*, July 6, 1982, p. 8.

59. See Lawrence Freedman, *Britain and Nuclear Weapons* (London: Macmillan, 1981), and Peter Malone, *The British Nuclear Deterrent* (London: Croom Helm, 1984).

pact. Finally, de Gaulle let it be known through reliable channels that the French were considering withdrawing from the NATO military command, a step ultimately taken in 1966.

This French assault on all three of Bonn's foreign policy spheres—the European, Eastern, and Atlantic—demonstrated de Gaulle's displeasure with what he saw as the increasingly bilateral (U.S.-FRG) character of the Alliance, symbolized in part by the MLF.[60] In private conversations, de Gaulle warned that Bonn's aspirations for a nuclear role in NATO would impede any chance of eventual German reunification. In public, the French president pointed to the dangers for European security of relying on an uncertain U.S. strategic guarantee.[61]

In fairness to the Erhard government, which persisted in its support of the MLF concept, de Gaulle refused to specify how the FRG might participate in the French nuclear force, beyond vague promises of providing "immediate protection" for West Germany. Moreover, it had always been clear that de Gaulle's definition of European integration presupposed French dominance, as was demonstrated by his veto of Britain's entry into the European Economic Community in 1963.

This did not prevent the Gaullists in the CDU, led by Adenauer and Strauss, from supporting de Gaulle and attacking Erhard's policies and leadership.[62] With Adenauer sharing de Gaulle's misgivings about the credibility of the U.S. strategic guarantee and Strauss unhappy over the lack of defense cooperation agreed to under the 1963 Franco-German agreement, Erhard faced serious opposition in his own party. Knowing that he would have to mollify the CDU/CSU Gaullists to win reelection in the September 1965 national election, Erhard was content to let the MLF issue slide when Johnson indefinitely postponed American consideration of it in December 1964.

When it came to the election, Erhard was reelected by a surprisingly comfortable margin. Yet his new government was still beset by divisions within the CDU/CSU and by disputes over economic policy with the junior coalition partner, the FDP. Ultimately, the

60. Wilfrid Kohl, *French Nuclear Diplomacy* (Princeton: Princeton University Press, 1971), and F. Roy Willis, *France, Germany, and the New Europe* (Stanford: Stanford University Press, 1965).
61. See, for example, a report of a major de Gaulle policy speech in Strasbourg, "De Gaulle Cautions Bonn on Becoming 'Auxiliary' of U.S.," *New York Times*, November 23, 1964, p. 1.
62. *Economist*, July 18, August 8, and September 24, 1964.

downfall of the Erhard government in November 1966 was caused by the resignation of the four FDP ministers in Erhard's cabinet over means to rectify a growing budget deficit.[63] Yet an important role was also played by those in the CDU/CSU who opposed Erhard's Atlantic orientation, as symbolized by the MLF issue. The "joint hardware–joint control" approach of the MLF was finally dead, to be replaced by the joint consultation approach that McNamara revived at a NATO meeting in May 1965 and that took shape as the Nuclear Planning Group (NPG) in 1966.

THE NONPROLIFERATION TREATY AND BONN'S EASTERN POLICY

Intra-Alliance discussions on the MLF in the first half of the 1960s were complicated considerably by the ongoing negotiations for a nuclear nonproliferation treaty (NPT) being held under the auspices of the United Nations in Geneva.[64] These negotiations, which traced their lineage to the 1946 Baruch Plan, were attempting to build on the success of the 1963 Limited Test Ban Treaty in preventing other countries from joining Britain (1952), France (1960), and later China (1964) in the nuclear weapons club. By 1964, the growing development of nuclear energy for civilian purposes as well as the prospect of nuclear sharing within the NATO Alliance had given the talks a new sense of urgency. Yet when President Johnson in January 1964 submitted a new plan to the United Nations for curbing the spread of nuclear weapons, the USSR responded that no such agreement was possible as long as the MLF proposal threatened to increase nuclear weapons sharing within NATO and possibly even to lead to direct West German national control of nuclear weapons.

In the FRG, neither the Adenauer nor the Erhard government was terribly pleased by what both regarded as the infringements on West German sovereignty of the Limited Test Ban Treaty and the proposed NPT. While disclaiming any aspirations for independent na-

63. By the standards of the 1970s, the West German economic downturn in 1966 seemed mild; nonetheless, the inflation rate of 3.5 percent was at a fifteen-year high, unemployment had risen markedly to 500,000, the foreign trade surplus was the lowest since 1952, and the West German GNP had contracted in real terms for the first time since 1949.

64. For a summary of the negotiations leading up to the NPT and the text of the treaty, see U.S. Arms Control and Disarmament Agency, *Arms Control and Disarmament Agreements* (Washington, D.C.: U.S. Government Printing Office, 1980), pp. 82–98.

tional control of nuclear weapons, FRG spokesmen maintained that such agreements could not be permitted to block NATO nuclear-sharing arrangements and must be accompanied by Soviet concessions on the issue of German reunification. As we have seen, this point had become particularly important by 1963, given West German fears that new U.S. diplomatic initiatives signaled a willingness for superpower arrangements at the expense of West German security interests.

When the NPT negotiations gained momentum during the summer of 1965, their relation to Erhard's support for the MLF became a principal campaign issue. The Johnson administration attempted to persuade Bonn that its new NPT proposal, issued on August 17, was phrased so that it would prohibit neither a NATO MLF scheme nor a European nuclear force, should one eventually come into being. For the moment, Erhard and Schröder were satisfied; not so Adenauer, Strauss, and the German Gaullists, who continued to argue that discriminatory measures that limited West German freedom of action and equality within NATO could well fracture the Alliance. Though Erhard's reelection in September dampened debate for a short period, centripetal pressures within the ruling CDU/CSU soon reappeared, leading to Erhard's resignation in late 1966. Negotiations on the NPT continued, but by the time they were completed in 1968, the domestic political makeup of the FRG had undergone a marked change with the coming to power of the Grand Coalition government of the CDU/CSU/SPD, where for the first time in the postwar period the Social Democrats found themselves sharing government power.

The inclusion of the SPD in the Grand Coalition in 1966, with Willy Brandt as the new foreign minister, was due in no small part to the party's acceptance of West Germany's role in NATO, which had been set in motion during the Kampf dem Atomtod debate and formally enunciated in the Bad Godesberg program of 1959. By the mid-1960s, the SPD was aided by its equal emphasis on defense and arms control measures, which was more in line with U.S. thinking than were the policy preferences of the CDU/CSU. Because the party was willing to go further than its new coalition partner in recognizing the security needs of both its Western and Eastern neighbors (as Fritz Erler put it, "security for Germany and security from Germany"), the SPD was more willing to support U.S. arms control efforts such as the test ban treaty and NPT, while also affirming the FRG's right to participate in NATO nuclear control-sharing proposals such as the MLF.[65]

To a limited extent, SPD leaders in the early 1960s did share CDU/CSU concerns that American détente and arms control policies could undermine German interests by formalizing the status quo in central Europe, increasing the legitimacy of the German Democratic Republic with no quid-pro-quo, and complicating an ultimate solution to the division of Germany. Where the SPD differed from the Adenauer and Erhard governments was in its belief that East–West arms control efforts could prove beneficial if they reduced political tensions to the point where diplomatic solutions to the German problem became more feasible. Thus from 1961 on, the SPD coupled its support for U.S. policy with calls for a more vigorous political, economic, and cultural policy toward Eastern Europe (Ostpolitik). When the party entered the government in 1966, Brandt replaced Schröder's "policy of small steps" with a more active Ostpolitik that included new trading agreements with several East European countries.[66]

Continued differences within the Grand Coalition, however, prevented the government from ratifying the NPT, which was signed in July 1968. Chancellor Kurt-Georg Kiesinger and others in the CDU/CSU (Adenauer died in 1967) criticized the NPT regime for hindering intra-Alliance nuclear cooperation, while Brandt and the SPD were prepared not only to sign the NPT but to renounce publicly any national nuclear options for the FRG. Brandt felt that West German adherence to the NPT was a necessary precondition for normalizing relations with Eastern Europe and would also undercut Soviet propaganda that the FRG was a revanchist power bent on acquiring nuclear weapons. Upon becoming chancellor in 1969, when the SPD won its first electoral victory in the postwar period, Brandt signed the NPT on behalf of the FRG and greatly accelerated the Ostpolitik he had begun as foreign minister. Nonetheless, the political linkage between the NPT and Ostpolitik, and continued CDU/CSU opposition to both, meant that Brandt and his successor, Helmut Schmidt, would have to wait until 1975, after Ostpolitik had

65. See Helga Haftendorn, *Security and Détente: Conflicting Priorities in German Defense Policy* (New York: Praeger, 1985), p. 111.

66. For a good account of the evolution of West Germany's Eastern policy in the 1960s, see Philip Windsor, *Germany and the Management of Détente* (New York: Praeger, 1971).

become an accepted part of West German foreign policy, to achieve formal West German ratification of the NPT.

SUMMARY: DOMESTIC POLITICS AND FOREIGN POLICY MAKING

In evaluating the particular mix of external pressures and domestic influences on the making of West German security policy in the postwar period, we may usefully think of a continuum, extending from complete autonomy at one end (the primacy of domestic politics) to complete dependence at the other (constraints imposed by the international system). Of course, policymaking rarely exhibits either extreme. Nonetheless, in the 1950s especially the Adenauer government found itself at the dependent end of the spectrum. Before West Germany gained national sovereignty in 1955, its policy was directly influenced by the dictates of the Allied occupying powers. Yet even after 1955, policymakers in Bonn were heavily constrained by the FRG's security dependence on the United States and its Western allies, as well as by its growing economic stake in West European integration.

Wolfram Hanrieder has described the FRG during this period as a "penetrated system," in which decision makers in Bonn were strongly influenced by external events and could achieve consensus among the broader policy elite only by accommodating themselves to these external pressures.[67] Although a useful description of West Germany's lack of political maneuverability, Hanrieder's concept does not go far enough in explaining the particular motivations for Adenauer's foreign policy. As the analysis of the debates over German rearmament and the Kampf dem Atomtod affair demonstrate, Adenauer's policy was a mixture of necessity and choice. While it is true that Bonn's options in the 1950s were extremely limited,[68] it is also true that Adenauer had little desire to pursue options other than those of military and economic security in the Western Alliance. Given the chancellor's concern that the Germans had to be "protected from themselves," plus his distaste for the "barbarous East," it is not

67. Wolfram Hanrieder, *West German Foreign Policy, 1949–1963* (Stanford: Stanford University Press, 1967), p. 230.
68. As Hans Speier put it, "Dr. Adenauer has often been hailed in the West as a great German statesman. Upon sober reflection, it appears rather that he steadfastly promoted a policy that was forced upon West Germany by its geographic location, by the anticommunist feelings of its population, and by the cold war." See Speier's *German Rearmament and Atomic War*, p. 10.

surprising that Adenauer gave absolute priority to his *Westpolitik* over vague and uncertain schemes for German reunification.[69]

To be sure, Adenauer had to have at least the tacit support of the West German public and political elites in order to carry out his policies. To a great extent, this support was provided by the anticommunist climate of the Cold War, the existence of a communist-controlled East Germany, and Narr's double security complex of military and economic security for the FRG as the primary considerations of the West German electorate. In addition, structural aspects of the West German political system (such as Adenauer's ability to dominate a foreign-policy bureaucracy that he largely created and the inability of the SPD to establish itself as a legitimate contender for political power until 1959) enabled Adenauer to push through even those policies that were opposed by a majority of the public. As long as Adenauer could demonstrate that his policies were ensuring West German security against possible Soviet aggression, as well as internal security in terms of domestic stability and economic well-being, then public concern with reunification, or the dangers of deploying nuclear weapons, was bound to remain an unredeemable political commodity for the SPD.

Thus Adenauer's foreign policy in the 1950s limited itself to two out of the three "natural" German spheres: relations with the United States (the Atlantic sphere) and relations with France and the other Western allies (the West European sphere). Into the 1960s, the main concern of successive West German governments was to avoid having to choose between these Atlantic and West European options. If Adenauer on the whole was oriented more toward France and West Europe, while his successor Ludwig Erhard was more of an Atlanticist, both chancellors recognized the complementarity of securing the Federal Republic economically and politically in Western Europe (i.e., the EEC, Euratom, and the Western European Union) and militarily in the Atlantic Alliance (NATO). As David Calleo has noted, both of these options were essentially federal in nature, in that West Germany willingly surrendered some autonomous decision-making power in return for external (military) and internal (economic) security.[70] While these options certainly provided for the

---

69. An apocryphal story has it that Adenauer, whenever he traveled by train from Frankfurt to Berlin, would pull down the shade when he crossed the Elbe River so he wouldn't have to look out across the "Asian steppes."

70. David Calleo, *The German Problem Reconsidered: Germany and the World Order, 1870 to the Present* (New York: Cambridge University Press, 1978).

protection of German interests, it was only with the pursuit of Bonn's third option, the Eastern option, in the late 1960s that a more independent foreign policy predicated on traditional German interests came into being.

Yet even here, West German policy at first was as much reactive to external events as it was predicated on domestic, national considerations. Even in the late 1960s, when West German economic strength, combined with an attenuation of U.S. power because of the Vietnam war, seemed to increase Bonn's maneuverability, "there remained . . . an unwillingness to admit the principle of an international role for Germany."[71] From the mid-1960s on, Bonn found itself lagging behind its two most important Western allies as international tensions eased and France and the United States began to pursue détente with the Soviet Union. It was only after Willy Brandt led the SPD to power in 1969 that the Federal Republic actively began to pursue an Eastern policy (Ostpolitik) in tandem with superpower détente. These two strands of détente—at the superpower level, primarily in the form of arms control agreements, and at the European level consisting of economic and humanitarian as well as security agreements—allowed Bonn to inch along the continuum toward greater articulation of domestic interests in its foreign policymaking.

In particular, West German ratification of the Moscow and Warsaw treaties in 1972, as well as the Berlin Four-Power Agreement that same year, were important for two reasons.[72] First, these treaties clarified long-standing ambiguities regarding Central European boundaries and thus reduced Bonn's dependence on its Western allies in dealings with the Soviets and Eastern Europe. Before the 1970s, West Germany had depended on the support of the United States and other allies for its refusal to recognize East Germany or to accept the territorial changes imposed by the Soviets following World War II. By ratifying the renunciation of force agreements with Poland and the Soviet Union (the Warsaw and Moscow treaties) and then recognizing the East German regime in 1974 (de facto if not de jure), West Germany no longer had to labor under the fears, prevalent in the 1950s and 1960s, that it might find itself isolated as the Western

71. William Wallace, "Old States and New Circumstances: The International Predicament of Britain, France, and Germany," in William Wallace and W. E. Paterson, eds., *Foreign Policy Making in Western Europe* (Westmead, U.K.: Saxon House, 1978), p. 41.

72. See Josef Joffe, "All Quiet on the Eastern Front," *Foreign Policy*, no. 37 (Winter 1979/80).

powers, and especially the United States, engaged in accommodation with the Soviets over the German question at the expense of Bonn.

Second, the very substance of Brandt's Ostpolitik, including increased trade with the East, greater contact between the peoples of East and West Germany, and the repatriation of ethnic Germans from the Soviet Union and Eastern Europe, gave Bonn new gains to be protected against any future breakdown in détente. For the first time in its twenty years of existence, the Federal Republic was attempting to balance its "national" foreign policy option with its West European and Atlantic "federal" options. As long as there was a confluence of superpower and European détente, which crested in 1972 with the interrelated Warsaw and Moscow treaties, the Berlin Four-Power Agreement, and the SALT I accords, the complementarity of interests between the United States and West Germany meant that possible conflicts of interest would remain latent.[73] Once these interests began to diverge, however, as they did in the mid-1970s with the beginning of American disillusionment with détente,[74] this new self-assertiveness on the part of the Federal Republic in protecting its Ostpolitik was bound to strain U.S.–West German relations. These diverging interests did not mean that Bonn was about to engage in either the *Schaukelpolitik* ("seesaw politics") of Bismarck or the Rapallo politics of Weimar. They did mean, however, that the

73. See Uwe Nerlich, "Washington and Bonn: Evolutionary Patterns in the Relations between the United States and the Federal Republic of Germany," in Karl Kaiser and Hans-Peter Schwarz, eds., *America and Western Europe*.

74. Polls taken in the early and mid-1970s among the U.S. and West German business and military elites show the high expectations surrounding détente in the United States. Among the Americans polled, 57.8 percent of the business elite and 39.6 percent of the military elite perceived a decreased military threat from the USSR, compared to only 8.7 percent of the West German elites. Similarly, while only 18.9 percent of the West German elites imagined that increased East–West economic cooperation would reduce East–West tensions, 61.5 percent of the U.S. business elite and 44.1 percent of the U.S. military elite considered "trade, technical cooperation and economic interdependence" to constitute the "most important approach to world peace." Even when we allow for differences in time frame (the U.S. polls were taken in 1973, the FRG polls in 1976) and in the way the questions were posed, there was a greater sense of optimism in the United States about the benefits of détente and accordingly a greater sense of betrayal when Soviet–American relations began to deteriorate because of Soviet actions in Angola, the Horn of Africa, and finally Afghanistan in the mid- to late 1970s. For the U.S. polls, see Bruce Russett and Elizabeth Hanson, *Interest and Ideology: The Foreign Policy Beliefs of American Businessmen* (San Francisco: W. H. Freeman, 1975), p. 271; for the West German polls, see Dietmar Schossler and Erich Weede, *West German Elite Views on National Security and Foreign Policy Issues* (Frankfurt: Athenaeum, 1978), p. 80.

Brandt government, unlike the Adenauer regime, would increasingly be faced with an inherent tension between its Western security policies on the one hand and its Ostpolitik on the other. No longer would a West German government have the luxury of subsuming security issues under larger political objectives, as Adenauer had done in the 1950s. Indeed, the very existence of foreign policy achievements in the East meant that the Soviets would enjoy, and seek to capitalize on, an increased leverage over West German policymaking.

Paradoxically, then, the détente of the 1970s increased the maneuverability of Bonn's foreign policy within the Western Alliance while it introduced new countervailing pressures from the USSR. At a second level, that of domestic politics, détente signaled an important change in the lingua franca of domestic debate over the direction of West German security policy. With the general easing of international tension following the Berlin crises of 1958–1961 and the Cuban missile crisis of 1962, and with both the United States and France initiating their own tentative steps toward rapprochement with the USSR, no longer was anticommunist sentiment a dominant theme of debates over the Federal Republic's foreign affairs.

To take one example: although the struggle over Bundestag ratification of the Eastern (Warsaw and Moscow) treaties, from 1970 to 1972, was as partisan and bitter as the nuclear weapons debates of the 1950s, and although the CDU/CSU opposition accused Brandt of playing into the hands of the Soviets, the fact remained that appealing to anticommunist sentiment in the Federal Republic was no longer an effective political weapon. For one thing, Brandt could emphasize, as he did, that his Ostpolitik had received the blessing of the Nixon administration and was being carried out in tandem with U.S.–Soviet détente. For another, public opinion in the FRG was no longer as reflexively anticommunist as it had been in the 1950s, especially in regard to the SPD. The evolution of the Social Democrats into a legitimate contender, and then holder, of political power had taken away the CDU's ability to indulge in the "guilt by association" accusations of the 1950s. The domestic debates in the early 1970s over Brandt's Ostpolitik no longer focused on whether the Social Democrats were "loyal" to the West German state, but concentrated on which party could best advance and protect German interests.

Conversely, however, the détente process in the early 1970s also meant that a process of decoupling was under way between the United States and the Federal Republic on two vital issues: the German question and the U.S. security guarantee to West Germany. Although the goal of reunification had been replaced by the evolutionary Ostpolitik of Brandt, the achievement of the Eastern treaties and the Berlin agreement had now, according to Uwe Nerlich, "reduced the compulsion for Washington to always consider Bonn's special problems in their deliberations—a factor which had determined the character of German–American relations for almost two decades."[75] If Bonn had now achieved a bit more autonomy in its relations with the Soviet Union, so had Washington. The Nixon administration could proclaim that the "era of confrontation" had been replaced by the "era of negotiation" without fear that a German chancellor would complain that the Americans were negotiating a deal with the Soviets at the expense of the FRG.

The increased maneuverability that détente afforded both the United States and the Federal Republic also extended to the issue of nuclear arms control, and by extension to the question of the U.S. strategic guarantee to West Germany. As Adenauer had foreseen in the late 1950s, following *Sputnik*, the approach of U.S.–Soviet strategic parity increased the risks of superpower accommodation at Europe's expense. In the intervening years, France and Britain had acquired their own independent nuclear deterrent as a hedge against such an eventuality, while NATO continued to wrestle with the problem of maintaining the credibility of the U.S. nuclear umbrella. As we noted earlier, the Alliance in the early 1960s subjected itself to the protracted confusion of the MLF episode, which was yet another attempt to couple the security of Europe with that of the United States. As John Steinbruner has pointed out, many of the arguments of those Americans who supported the MLF concept—that is, that the MLF would promote European integration and forestall the Germans' demands for their own independent deterrent—bore little resemblance to the real needs of West Germany in solidifying the U.S. nuclear guarantee.[76] Following the demise of the MLF in 1964, these needs were better met by deployment of longer-range nuclear weapons in West Germany and the creation of the Nuclear Planning Group, in which the Federal Republic and Italy were given equal status with the United States and the United Kingdom in the

75. Nerlich, "Washington and Bonn."
76. Steinbruner, *Cybernetic Theory of Decision*.

planning of NATO's nuclear strategy. In addition, an increased program of nuclear consultation, responsibility, and participation through the mechanisms of additional dual-key responsibility and expanded "programs of cooperation" (POC) served to create, in the words of a U.S. Senate report, "physical evidence of U.S. commitment which the FRG considered even more important than the proposed MLF arrangements."[77]

By the early 1970s, however, the U.S.–Soviet negotiations in SALT and the existence of Soviet parity in strategic nuclear forces were incubating yet another bout of Allied concern over the credibility of coupling. Up until the mid-1970s, such fears remained latent, owing to continued U.S. advantages in MIRV technology (and thus warheads), the United States' refusal to include its European "forward based systems" (FBS) in the SALT negotiations, and a decreased sense of the Soviet threat because of détente.

By 1977, however, the appearance of the SS-20, continued increases in Soviet conventional forces, and perceptions in West Germany that the United States might be willing to sacrifice European security concerns on the altar of SALT II brought into the open yet another round of intra-Alliance tension over the role of nuclear weapons in NATO strategy. As we shall see in Chapter 2, the neutron bomb and INF (intermediate-range nuclear force) issues dominated NATO deliberations in the late 1970s, throwing into sharp relief the vicissitudes of the German nuclear dilemma. In contrast to its stance in previous nuclear weapons controversies, however, the government in Bonn took a far more activist role in shaping the terms, if not the outcomes, of the neutron bomb and INF issues.

---

77. *SALT and the NATO Allies*, report prepared for the U.S. Senate Committee on Foreign Relations, Subcommittee on European Affairs, 1979, p. 2. "Dual-key" refers to the fact that, while the U.S. retains control of all NATO nuclear warheads, its NATO allies operate the delivery systems (artillery, aircraft) for these warheads, so that they have partial control over their use.

[2]

Helmut Schmidt and the Origins
of the INF Issue: 1975–1979

By 1975, NATO nuclear strategy, and with it the German nuclear dilemma, was on the verge of moving into a third and qualitatively new phase. The massive retaliation doctrine of the 1950s had given way to McNamara's flexible response strategy in the early 1960s. Although flexible response still survives (shakily) as official NATO doctrine today, a key component of that strategy, the role of NATO's theater nuclear weapons in Europe, underwent a profound transformation in the mid-1970s. And the prime stimulus behind that transformation was the West German government of Helmut Schmidt.

The period from the origins of flexible response in the early 1960s up through the mid-1970s has been aptly described as "the wilderness years," given that Alliance attention shifted away from the specifics of NATO nuclear forces to the broader arenas of East–West détente and arms control. The confluence in the late 1960s and early 1970s of U.S.–Soviet détente and West Germany's Ostpolitik shifted public attention from the East–West military competition to that of political accommodation. In the area of arms control, the foci of public attention were strategic nuclear forces (the SALT talks) and conventional forces in Europe (the Mutual and Balanced Force Reduction—MBFR—negotiations). The very fact that theater nuclear forces (TNF) were referred to during this period as "gray-area weapons" testified to their amorphous character. As Lawrence Freedman put it, TNF issues occupied a "position comparable to the Holy Ghost in the Christian trinity and [were] just about as difficult to explain."[1]

1. See Lawrence Freedman, "The Wilderness Years," in Jeffrey Boutwell, Paul Doty, and Gregory F. Treverton, eds., *The Nuclear Confrontation in Europe* (London: Croom Helm, 1975), p. 44.

It was not until the mid-1970s, when the blush of superpower détente began to fade, that NATO nuclear weapons reemerged from the wilderness. This renewed public attention and debate on NATO nuclear policy resulted from several factors.

Most important were the underlying tensions in NATO's flexible response strategy itself. From its very inception, flexible response was interpreted differently on the two sides of the Atlantic. Whereas many strategists in the United States emphasized the need for a "flexible" mix of conventional and, only if necessary, nuclear options, the Europeans continued to stress the importance of the "response" element; that is, NATO's nuclear forces and the U.S. strategic nuclear guarantee as the primary elements of deterrence. Throughout the 1960s, the European allies, and especially the Federal Republic, disagreed sharply with U.S. estimates of the Warsaw Pact conventional threat and, by extension, with American opinion that NATO had the ability to field a credible conventional deterrent.[2] Accordingly, the FRG and the United Kingdom in particular resisted the notion that flexible response implied a robust conventional deterrent, focusing instead on the principle of deliberate escalation to nuclear weapons to enhance deterrence.

Ultimately, then, NATO strategy embodied a tenuous compromise between the United States' desire for strengthened conventional forces to reduce the necessity of early use of NATO nuclear weapons and the European preference for continued reliance on the central role of nuclear weapons in deterring conflict in Europe. As Defense Secretary Robert McNamara noted at the time flexible response was adopted, "After years of effort, this is the most ambitious strategy we have been able to convince our allies to accept."[3]

Until the early 1970s, these interpretations of NATO doctrine were confined largely to policymakers and were overshadowed by the ongoing SALT and MBFR negotiations and other examples of East–West détente, such as the Berlin Quadripartite Agreement and the Helsinki Conference. Yet there were indications that the tensions

2. For a good review of the origins of and debate over flexible response in the 1960s, see Alain C. Enthoven and K. Wayne Smith, *How Much Is Enough? Shaping the Defense Program, 1961–1969* (New York: Harper & Row, 1972), and Jane Stromseth, "The Origins of Flexible Response: A Study of the Debate over NATO Strategy in the 1960s" (D. Phil. thesis, Oxford University, 1985).

3. Robert S. McNamara, "Draft Memorandum for the President, Subject: NATO Strategy and Force Structure," Department of Defense, January 16, 1968, p. 4, quoted in Jorg Baldauf, *How Big Is the Threat to Europe? Transatlantic Debates over the Balance of Forces*, Rand paper P 7372 (Santa Monica, Calif.: Rand Corp., October 1987).

inherent in flexible response were growing, as in the intra-Alliance debates over U.S. Defense Secretary James Schlesinger's review of conventional deterrence and the limited nuclear options strategy in 1973–74.[4]

In a secret speech to NATO's Defense Planning Committee in 1973, Schlesinger reiterated the McNamara line that conventional deterrence not only was within the Alliance's reach but had become all the more important in light of superpower parity in strategic weapons, as had been recently codified in the SALT I accords. Although Schlesinger was not advocating any changes in the flexible response doctrine or the giving up of the nuclear first-use option, the secretary did maintain that NATO's nuclear forces should be seen principally as "a direct deterrent to a nuclear attack by the Pact *and as a serious hedge* against a major breakdown in our conventional defense."[5] Once again, however, the FRG and the United Kingdom took the lead in criticizing U.S. threat estimates and the ability of the Alliance to deploy sufficient conventional forces to deter a Pact conventional attack. As Gen. Johannes Steinhoff, chairman of NATO's Military Committee, emphasized, "the troops available to NATO in Central Europe were *just about sufficient* to secure the continued credibility of the nuclear guarantee."[6] For the West Germans especially, a truly robust conventional deterrent was neither economically nor politically feasible, especially during a period when Bonn was seeking to improve its relations with its Eastern European neighbors.

All in all, the McNamara and Schlesinger episodes demonstrated the continuing intra-Alliance differences over the appropriate mix of conventional and nuclear forces in NATO strategy. As Jorg Baldauf noted, these tensions posed particular problems for the Federal Republic, going as they did to the heart of the German nuclear dilemma.[7]

On the one hand, Bonn policymakers were fearful that U.S. attempts to strengthen conventional deterrence represented a desire to reduce the salience of nuclear deterrence for NATO (and, by extension, the U.S. nuclear guarantee to West Germany). On the

4. This section on how NATO Europe reacted to the Schlesinger initiative on conventional forces is based largely on Baldauf, *How Big Is the Threat to Europe?*

5. James R. Schlesinger, *Principal Remarks at NATO Defense Planning Committee Ministerial Meeting, Brussels, June 7, 1973* (Washington, D.C.: Department of Defense 1973), pp. 3–4; emphasis added.

6. Steinhoff's remarks were made on television (Zweites Deutschen Fernsehen) and are quoted in Baldauf, *How Big Is the Threat to Europe?* pp. 16–17; emphasis added.

7. Baldauf, *How Big Is the Threat to Europe?* pp. 35–42 especially.

other hand, many Americans continued to advocate both a greater European contribution to NATO and withdrawal of U.S. troops from the continent (e.g., the Senate resolutions introduced by Mike Mansfield in 1969 and 1973). If the West Germans and other European allies subscribed to McNamara's and Schlesinger's view that conventional deterrence was within reach, their concurrence might fuel arguments for a reduction of American force in Europe. Either way, a process could be started that would lead to a gradual decoupling of the United States from the defense of the FRG and Western Europe.

Finally, many Europeans shied from relying primarily on conventional forces, given that conventional deterrence had broken down twice in the previous fifty years, with disastrous results, above all for Germany. For many West Germans, a possible consequence of adopting U.S. views on conventional deterrence could be, in the event deterrence failed, a full-scale conventional war limited to Europe. Hence many Germans continued to stress the importance of deterrence over defense, even if deterrence led to an overreliance on nuclear weapons.

These intra-Alliance debates over flexible response were taking place largely out of public view. At the same time, however, beginning in the mid-1970s there emerged a more open transatlantic debate over the fundamentals of East–West détente. The causes of these disputes were many and varied, and included the global economic crisis precipitated by the oil price shocks of the early 1970s. Yet the major threat to détente, especially as the United States saw it, was increased Soviet adventurism in the Third World, particularly in Africa.[8]

Increasingly in 1975–76, Soviet and Cuban intervention in Angola, Ethiopia, and elsewhere undermined support for détente in the United States and led to complaints that America's European partners were enjoying the benefits of détente while expecting Washington to shoulder the burden of Western interests elsewhere in the world. Conversely, many Europeans felt that the United States was unnecessarily introducing tensions into Europe by linking Soviet behavior elsewhere with détente in Europe.

In the context of U.S.–FRG relations, the weakening of American influence caused by Vietnam and Watergate was matched by an

8. An especially good overview of this period is provided in Raymond Garthoff, *Détente and Confrontation: American–Soviet Relations from Nixon to Reagan* (Washington, D.C.: Brookings Institution, 1985).

increasingly assertive West German foreign policy under Helmut Schmidt, who replaced Willy Brandt as chancellor in 1974. Whether the issue was détente, international economic policy, or East–West arms control, Schmidt was rarely hesitant in criticizing U.S. policy when he saw it as infringing unduly on West German interests. As Fritz Stern has noted, Schmidt personified a growing West German political influence; the chancellor "found his role of worldwide authority as natural to his temperament as Adenauer had found his role of reconciler with the West or Brandt his position of contrite authority vis-à-vis the East."[9] Schmidt's willingness and ability to promote West German national interests, even at the expense of intra-Alliance tensions, was to manifest itself in major policy disputes with the Carter administration on such issues as human rights, German economic policy, and the export of civilian nuclear power technology. Schmidt, with his experience as a member of parliament and as minister of defense, economics, and finance under Brandt, took exception to what he saw as the moralizing thrust of Carter's human rights policy and American heavy-handedness in pressuring West Germany to reflate its economy in order to provide a locomotive effect for the other Western democracies. Moreover, personality differences between the two often exacerbated policy differences between the two countries, especially when Schmidt was less than politic in letting slip unkind references to Carter's ability to handle the demands of the presidency.

Schmidt had spent more than fifteen years specializing in nuclear weapons and security issues before he entered the chancellery in 1974. With the exception of Franz Josef Strauss, no other West German politician was so well versed in the doctrinal and force planning elements of the NATO deterrent. Certainly no other chancellor before him was so capable of debating security and nuclear weapons issues on equal terms with U.S. officials. Schmidt's expertise in defense policy had its counterpart as well in the growing sophistication with such issues in the West German bureaucracy, political parties, and media. Hence the FRG was less dependent on American assumptions and analyses concerning NATO policy than it had been in the 1950s. What Catherine Kelleher has called the problem of "strategic grasp time"—the great gap between the United States' expertise on nuclear weapons and that of its European

9. Fritz Stern, "Germany in a Semi-Gaullist Europe," *Foreign Affairs*, 58 (Spring 1980): 875.

allies—had lessened considerably by the 1970s.[10] While growing nuclear expertise was most evident in the European nuclear powers, France and Britain, it was also increasingly evident in the FRG. Consistent with its status as the world's third largest repository of nuclear weapons, West Germany at last was coming of age in its familiarity with the arcane tenets of nuclear deterrence and strategy.

Of course, the West Germans' passage through nuclear adolescence had been anything but easy. The schizophrenic quality of depending for their security on U.S. nuclear weapons that could well destroy the FRG if the American deterrent failed had been ameloriated but not solved by the East–West détente and arms control efforts of the late 1960s and early 1970s. Indeed, by the mid-1970s, growing suspicions that U.S.–Soviet arms control talks were neglecting key elements of West German security reemphasized the essential dependence of the FRG, which was all the more glaring given West Germany's political and economic maturity in global affairs. The difficulty of the Schmidt government in particular and West German governments in general in seeking to limit this dependence while maintaining the viability of the U.S. and NATO nuclear deterrent for West German security was about to increase as NATO nuclear policy entered this third phase and NATO theater nuclear force issues emerged "from the wilderness" with a vengeance.

HELMUT SCHMIDT AND THE CONCEPT OF "GLEICHGEWICHT"

When Helmut Schmidt became chancellor in 1974, the eruption of a public debate over NATO nuclear weapons was still a few years away. The seeds of that debate were already present, though, in internal NATO disagreements over flexible response and in the divergence of interests between Washington and Bonn over East–West détente, superpower arms control, and Ostpolitik. Schmidt then injected into the equation his strong views on how best to protect FRG interests, both within the NATO Alliance and in the broader East–West relationship.

Ironically, although it was Schmidt who would ultimately be perceived as the architect of NATO's INF decision, the chancellor's views on the nature of conventional deterrence and the optimum

10. Catherine McArdle Kelleher, *Germany and the Politics of Nuclear Weapons* (New York: Columbia University Press, 1975), chap. 8 especially.

role of nuclear weapons in NATO strategy were not very different from those of McNamara and Schlesinger. This makes it all the more important to understand the underlying motivations that led Schmidt to go public, in his 1977 speech to the International Institute for Strategic Studies (IISS), with his concerns over the diverging interests of the United States and West Germany and the threat they posed to Bonn's foreign policy.

Central to this concern was Schmidt's concept of *Gleichgewicht* (equilibrium or balance of forces)—his belief that military parity in central Europe was an absolute precondition for the successful implementation of Bonn's Ostpolitik. A broad military parity between the superpowers at the strategic level, and between NATO and the Warsaw Pact in Central Europe, must not be threatened, he believed; otherwise Bonn would find itself increasingly susceptible to Soviet political pressure.[11] For Schmidt, the beginnings of superpower strategic parity in the 1960s and the continuing modernization of Soviet conventional and theater nuclear forces in the 1970s were increasing the political utility of Soviet military power. As Hans Speier and others had warned as early as the 1950s, "Soviet achievement of a respectable nuclear capability offers communist leaders novel opportunities to threaten or cajole the atomic have-nots in NATO."[12] Writing in the early 1960s, Schmidt himself said in his book *Defense or Retaliation* that the U.S. strategic deterrent "inevitably loses significance with the approach of a stable nuclear balance between the world powers."[13]

Yet if extended deterrence was being weakened by strategic parity, how could NATO best structure its own nuclear and conventional forces so as to maintain deterrence against the possibility of Soviet aggression? In a debate with Strauss in the early 1960s, Schmidt argued that theater nuclear forces could have only a deterrent value and that NATO must improve its conventional forces as a deterrent

11. The most complete exposition of Schmidt's concept of Gleichgewicht as a political necessity in East–West relations is found in his *Balance of Power* (London: William Kimber, 1971). As early as 1962, Schmidt had noted the advent of superpower strategic parity and the corresponding need to strengthen NATO's conventional forces to maintain military parity in Europe; see his "Die unvermeidbare Neue Strategie," *Die Zeit*, August 17 and August 24, 1962. Schmidt further expanded on the concept of Gleichgewicht in *Menschen und Mächte* (Berlin: Siedler, 1987).

12. Hans Speier, "Soviet Atomic Blackmail and the North Atlantic Alliance," Rand Research Memorandum RM-1837 (Santa Monica, Calif.: Rand Corp., 1956).

13. Helmut Schmidt, *Defense or Retaliation: A German View* (New York: Praeger, 1962), p. 100.

against Soviet conventional aggression.[14] Using arguments very much like those of McNamara and Schlesinger, Schmidt maintained that NATO would have to adopt a credible conventional deterrent, although some NATO theater nuclear forces (TNF) would still be needed as a deterrent against Soviet TNF. Where Schmidt differed with NATO policy was in his opposition to the use of theater nuclear weapons in case deterrence should fail. Using arguments similar to those advanced by advocates of a "no first use" policy twenty years later (one of whom, of course, was McNamara), Schmidt wrote, "The use of tactical nuclear weapons ... would ... lead to the most extensive devastation of Europe and to the most extensive loss of life amongst its peoples. Europe is the battlefield for these weapons. ... Those who think that Europe can be defended by the massed use of such weapons will not defend Europe, but destroy it."[15]

By comparison, Franz Josef Strauss argued that the U.S. nuclear guarantee to Europe must remain paramount and that any move by NATO to rely on conventional deterrence delinked from nuclear weapons would increase the possibility of Soviet conventional aggression, weaken deterrence, and undermine West German political support for the Alliance.[16] Not surprisingly, Strauss was one of the strongest German opponents of McNamara and Schlesinger's attempts to strengthen NATO conventional forces, asserting that at least sixty NATO divisions would be needed, not the thirty proposed by the Americans.

Despite their differences over how best to fashion the NATO deterrent, neither Schmidt nor Strauss tried to present a credible case for the military employment of NATO's theater nuclear forces. More than anything, it is this amorphous character of NATO's TNF that goes to the heart of the German nuclear dilemma, for to specify a military role for TNF would imply the possibility of a nuclear war limited to Europe, and with it the nuclear devastation of Germany.

Rather, Schmidt and Strauss concentrated on opposite extremes of the "continuum of deterrence" as most important for preventing a conflict in central Europe. For Schmidt, in an age of strategic parity

14. According to Schmidt, "the threat to use limited, or tactical, nuclear weapons against a nuclear-armed world power is no longer entirely credible in so far as it is meant to deter the latter from committing non-nuclear, or conventional aggression": Helmut Schmidt, "The Debate in Germany: The Opposition View," *Survival* 3 (July/August 1961): 179.

15. Schmidt, *Defense or Retaliation*, pp. 100–101.

16. Franz Josef Strauss, "The Debate in Germany: The Government's View," *Survival* 3 (July/August 1961): 176–178.

the primary need in Europe was for strong conventional forces, with theater nuclear weapons providing a link to the American strategic guarantee. Conversely, Strauss emphasized the threat of early employment of U.S. strategic nuclear forces to dissuade Soviet planners from even contemplating a conventional attack.

For both men, the importance of theater nuclear forces lay in their coupling of NATO's conventional forces to U.S. strategic forces, politically more than militarily. Where they differed was in the composition of NATO's theater nuclear forces: Schmidt argued for the equivalent of a "minimum deterrent" capability, while Strauss believed that a full range of theater nuclear force capability was required in order to expand NATO's range of options.

Not surprisingly, Schmidt and Strauss based their judgments on quite different readings of how a conflict in Europe was likely to start. Schmidt, for whom the operative experience was that of World War I, feared that misperceptions and miscalculations might draw East and West into a European conflict.[17] In this scenario, deterrence was a necessary but not sufficient condition for preventing war. Thus if war did come, NATO must have the conventional forces necessary to repel a Pact attack so as to reduce the likelihood that nuclear weapons would have to be used.

For Strauss, on the other hand, the blitzkrieg scenario of World War II, during which numerically inferior German forces attacked first in France and then in Russia, was more germane. Believing as he did that even a robust conventional deterrent would not dissuade the Soviets from attacking if they had made the decision to go to war, Strauss preferred to place his faith in the ultimate deterrent effect of nuclear weapons, even though their use once deterrence failed might lead, as Schmidt had remarked, to the destruction of what they were intended to defend.[18]

Given Schmidt's views in the 1960s on the role of theater nuclear

17. Ibid.

18. In this regard, it is Strauss rather than Schmidt who fits a general characterization of European attitudes toward deterrence provided by Ian Smart, who wrote that "West Europeans characteristically attach a peculiar importance to deterring the outbreak of a general war and have much less interest than North Americans in the eventual outcome of such a war. . . . Their perceptions of the threat are apt to generate pressure for or against military options, including nuclear options, in a way that reflects a sensitivity to the need to constrain Soviet intentions and to deter the outbreak of war, rather than to any argument for matching Soviet capabilities or for influencing a war's outcome." See his "European Nuclear Options," in Kenneth A. Myers, ed., *NATO: The Next Thirty Years* (Boulder, Colo.: Westview Press, 1980), pp. 116–117.

weapons in the Western deterrent strategy, it is surprising that he has come to be perceived as the architect of NATO's INF decision in 1979. By setting in motion the INF decision with his much-publicized London speech in October 1977, had Schmidt fundamentally changed his position? Did he, as the West German chancellor, feel the need for plugging the gaps in NATO's continuum of deterrence with INF systems? If deployed, such weapons would give the Alliance, for the first time ever, the capability to strike the USSR from bases in West Germany with missiles having flight times of ten minutes or less. Schmidt's support for qualitative improvements in NATO's nuclear posture, which could surely jeopardize his government's Ostpolitik, symbolized the fundamental security dilemma of playing a strong role in NATO while improving relations with the East.

In analyzing Schmidt's motivations for giving the IISS speech and the political circumstances in which it was given, however, I will argue that the chancellor had not greatly altered his views on the role of NATO nuclear weapons. Rather, his overriding concern with the political implications of a European military imbalance, combined with increased tensions between the FRG and the United States over other political and military issues, led Schmidt into an impolitic emphasis on INF, which in turn became subject to a great deal of misinterpretation.

SCHMIDT AND THE CARTER ADMINISTRATION

Before analyzing Schmidt's IISS speech in some detail, I should stress that what the chancellor said in London was less important than why he said it. In large part, Schmidt used the visible forum of the Alastair Buchan Memorial Lecture at IISS to draw attention to what he saw as the condominium aspects of U.S.–Soviet arms control, as well as the shortcomings he perceived in U.S. negotiating strategy in the SALT talks. Just as important was the strain in relations between Schmidt and the U.S. president by 1977, just nine months after Carter had taken office, over a wide range of issues, including economic policy, human rights, and Third World issues.

As noted above, sources of friction in U.S.–FRG relations included Schmidt's rejection of Carter's plea that West Germany reflate its economy to provide a locomotive effect for the economies of the industrial West; Bonn's irritation over Carter's nuclear nonproliferation policy, particularly U.S. attempts to block or modify West

Germany's sale of civilian nuclear energy technology to Brazil; and Schmidt's feeling that Carter's emphasis on the human rights issues was naive and would be counterproductive in East–West relations.[19]

Issues in the military sphere also complicated relations between Washington and Bonn. One was an internal Carter administration study that sought to lay out a global strategy for the new administration. Known as Presidential Review Memorandum 10 (PRM 10), this study suggested a possible change in NATO strategy from forward defense at the inter-German border to a mobile defense that would entail giving up large parts of West German territory to establish a more solid defense at the Weser River. Although PRM 10 was a conceptual document, intended to provide an overall framework for the foreign and security policies of the Carter administration, even the mention of possible abandonment of the forward defense strategy, which had long been a political sine qua non for the FRG, was bound to cause concern in Bonn.[20]

By the summer of 1977, the Schmidt government was also becoming concerned about the course of the SALT negotiations, especially in regard to the status of cruise missiles.[21] Following the Nixon administration's decision in 1972 to resume development of cruise missiles, some officials in both the British and West German governments had become interested in the possibilities of incorporating cruise missiles in the NATO deterrent.[22] At the Vladivostok summit in November 1974, however, the Soviets demanded that cruise

19. On the sale of technology, see Zbigniew Brzezinski, *Power and Principle: Memoirs of the National Security Advisor, 1977–1981* (New York: Farrar, Straus, Giroux, 1983), pp. 131–132. As Robert Jervis has noted, Carter failed to see the trade-offs inherent in emphasizing so strongly such issues as nonproliferation and human rights, with the result that an "overly ambitious initial policy jeopardized America's ability to achieve more limited goals." See his "Deterrence and Perception," *International Security* 7 (Winter 1982/83): 24.

20. Details of PRM 10 were leaked in the *Washington Post*, July 28, 1977. Although Secretary of Defense Harold Brown denied shortly afterward that the administration was contemplating any shift away from NATO's forward defense strategy, his repudiation of the options contained in PRM 10, among which the Weser-Lech line was only one, was compromised by the report in the original press leak that administration spokesmen should deny, for political reasons, that the administration was thinking of altering NATO strategy. See also *Washington Post*, August 2, 1977.

21. Early on in the Carter administration, SALT negotiator Paul Warnke "urged that the United States SALT position contain at least one provision that the Kremlin would welcome and some Pentagon planners would resist. This was to impose strict limits on the range of cruise missiles, particularly ground-launched cruise missiles": Strobe Talbott, *Endgame: The Inside Story of SALT* (New York: Harper & Row, 1979), p. 57.

22. Interviews with West German and U.S. government officials, summer 1980.

missiles be included in the ceiling of 2,400 "strategic launch vehicles" allowed each country.[23] Although the United States rejected this demand at the time, it offered not to "circumvent" the U.S.–Soviet equal aggregrate ceilings by increasing its forward-based systems (FBS). In addition to accepting this noncircumvention provision, the Soviets introduced an even more restrictive "nontransfer" provision, whereby each party would be required "not to transfer strategic offensive arms to other states, and not to assist in their development, in particular by transferring components, technical descriptions or blueprints for these arms."[24]

Although the Ford administration rejected the noncircumvention/nontransfer provision, it appeared to the Europeans in the summer of 1977 that the Carter administration might be on the verge of accepting a modified version of it.[25] Moreover, the administration seemed to be taking a wait-and-see attitude concerning cruise missiles. Policymakers within the administration realized that a wide range of issues, including various strategic missions, basing modes, and arms control ramifications, would have to be studied before the United States could consider the European theater applications for cruise missiles. A trip led by Leslie Gelb, director of politico-military affairs in the State Department, to the West European capitals in the summer of 1977 was designed to acquaint the NATO partners with official U.S. thinking. However, Gelb's "balanced presentation" served only to heighten European, and especially West German, concerns

23. The Soviet position was based on their definition of "strategic": i.e., any weapon that could strike the Soviet Union, no matter what its range. This definition included, of course, not only U.S. central systems but forward-based systems (FBS) in Europe and the Pacific, as well as British, French, and Chinese forces.

24. *SALT and the NATO Allies*, report prepared for the U.S. Senate Committee on Foreign Relations, Subcommittee on European Affairs, 1979, p. 30.

25. If the Soviets agreed to drop their insistence on the nontransfer provision, the Carter administration proposed to table a general clause reading: "In order to ensure the viability and effectiveness of this Treaty, each Party undertakes not to circumvent the provisions of this Treaty." As a fallback position, however, the administration was prepared to offer a modified version, but one that, to the Europeans, seemed more restrictive: "In order to ensure the viability and effectiveness of this Treaty, each Party undertakes not to circumvent the provisions of this Treaty, through any other state or states, or in any other manner." It was this second version that the Europeans feared might serve the purpose of a nontransfer provision, despite American assurances to the contrary. In the end, the Soviets did reject the first version, in January 1978; both countries agreed to the second version in April 1978, and it wasn't until SALT II was signed in June 1979 that the Europeans, especially the West Germans, were satisfied that this provision would not foreclose the option of deploying cruise missiles after the expiration of the protocol in December 1981. For more on this issue, see David Schwartz, *NATO's Nuclear Dilemma* (Washington, D.C.: Brookings Institution, 1983).

that the United States might be willing to bargain away the cruise missile at the SALT talks without receiving comparable restrictions on Soviet theater systems, especially the Backfire bomber.[26] As details about the SALT provisions became known—specifically, that sea-launched cruise missiles (SLCMs) and ground-launched cruise missiles (GLCMs) would be limited to ranges of 600 kilometers and some restrictions would be placed on the transfer of cruise missile technology from the United States to its allies—the Schmidt government became concerned not only that the United States would gain no concessions by limiting Soviet systems, but that it might find it politically expedient to extend the cruise missile limitations once the protocol expired in December 1981.[27] The feeling was shared by Gen. Alexander Haig, the current SACEUR, who was "very disturbed by the protocol" and by the fact that it had been brought up "at the initiative of the American negotiators, not the Soviets."[28]

At the same time that the West Germans felt they were losing a source of leverage over Soviet systems with the cruise missile provisions in SALT II, the neutron warhead issue appeared on the scene. A story in the *Washington Post* on June 5, 1977, reported that the Carter administration had given the go-ahead to the Department of Energy to begin producing enhanced radiation warheads (ERW) for short-range tactical nuclear delivery systems. Obviously applicable for use in the European theater against massed Soviet tank formations, the neutron warhead was seen by some Americans as providing a needed corrective to NATO's deficiencies in conventional forces.[29] During the summer of 1977, U.S. military officials touted

26. The United States' willingness to drop its insistence that SALT II cover the Backfire, as long as the Soviets gave assurances that the aircraft would not be given an intercontinental capability, further emphasized the Backfire's capability as a theater weapon for use against Europe. See Fred Kaplan, "Warring over New Missiles for NATO," *New York Times Sunday Magazine*, December 9, 1979.

27. Regarding West European fears that the United States might be bargaining away the cruise missile, see Flora Lewis, "U.S. Allies Afraid They May Be Denied Cruise Missiles," *New York Times*, November 7, 1977, and Herbert von Borch, "Mehrseitige europaische Atommacht am fernen Horizont," *Süddeutsche Zeitung*, November 28, 1977. See also Alex Vardamis, "German–American Military Fissures," *Foreign Policy*, no. 34 (Spring 1979).

28. See the interview with Alexander Haig in *Trialogue: The Trilateral Commission's Quarterly of North American, European, and Japanese Affairs*, no. 21 (Fall, 1979): 10.

29. For more on the technical and political issues involved in the ERW debate, see Fred Kaplan, "Enhanced Radiation Weapons," *Scientific American* 238 (May 1978); S. T. Cohen, "Enhanced Radiation Weapons: Setting the Record Straight," *Strategic Review*, Winter 1978; and Theo Sommer, "The Neutron Bomb: War without Tears," *Survival* 19 (November/December 1977).

ERW as providing a "usable" nuclear response to Soviet aggression, and just a few weeks before Schmidt's speech at IISS, Gen. George Brown, chairman of the Joint Chiefs of Staff, seemed to have ERW in mind when he said that "there is a recognition that we [NATO] do not have sufficient conventional forces to stop a Warsaw Pact penetration in Europe with non-nuclear forces."[30]

Although President Carter had made no firm decision to proceed with full-scale production of neutron warheads, preferring to gain NATO acceptance for their deployment first, the news that ERW components were being produced touched off a massive debate in Europe. Because ERW are designed to limit blast effects while increasing prompt radiation, many Europeans, as well as the Soviets, portrayed the neutron warhead as the ultimate capitalist weapon: one that would kill people while leaving property intact.[31] In West Germany, Egon Bahr of the SPD called the weapon a "perversion of human thought," and the magazine *Der Spiegel* ran a cover story on ERW titled "Neutron Bomb: America's Wonder Weapon for Europe."[32]

In the FRG and Holland especially, public demonstrations and opinion polls in the latter half of 1977 showed how difficult it would be for the Dutch and West German governments to approve of NATO deployment of ERW on their territory. For example, the Dutch defense minister, Roelof Kruisinga, resigned in early 1978 in protest over the refusal of Prime Minister Dries van Agt to reject the neutron bomb unilaterally.[33]

Given the sensitivity of the ERW issue in Western Europe, Schmidt and his counterparts in Holland and elsewhere did not want to be put in the position of supplicants, of having to come out in support of European deployment before Carter would agree to full ERW production. Politically, Schmidt preferred that Carter decide on production first; then the Alliance as a whole could decide on deployment. At the same time, Schmidt was interested in using the possibility of ERW deployment as a bargaining chip in the MBFR conventional force negotiations in Vienna, which were in their

30. *New York Times*, October 25, 1977.
31. Proponents of this view not only simplified the issue (they ignored the fact that the ERW blast and thermal radiation, especially in heavy concentrations, would indeed destroy buildings) but often conveniently passed over the converse of their claim: that standard battlefield warheads were somehow preferable in killing people as well as destroying property.
32. *Der Spiegel*, July 18, 1977.
33. *Neue Zürcher Zeitung*, March 7, 1978.

fourth year with little progress being made. In mid-September of 1977, representatives of the United States, United Kingdom, and West Germany agreed on a revision of the so-called Option III of 1975 to be offered in Vienna as a means of breaking the MBFR deadlock. As presented to all NATO members in October, this offer included U.S. withdrawal of 1,000 tactical nuclear warheads and 29,000 American troops in return for five Soviet divisions (65,000 to 70,000 troops) and 1,500 to 1,700 Soviet tanks. In addition, the possibility was left open that the United States might stop development of the ERW in return for the Soviets' acceptance of conventional parity in Europe.[34] However, given the stalemate at the MBFR talks, largely over the data base problem (i.e., differing NATO and Warsaw Pact figures on the number of Pact troops in Eastern Europe), it was apparent that no breakthrough was imminent. Thus Schmidt was still left in the position of having to declare his country's willingness to deploy the weapon before the Carter administration would begin production.

In addition to these major strains in U.S.–West German relations, there were also minor irritants, as well, mostly in the area of Alliance burden sharing. Issues such as West German support costs for the U.S. airborne command aircraft (AWACS), American reluctance to adopt the German 120-mm cannon for its new Abrams tank, and Bonn's insistence that Washington offset West German purchases of American weapons systems by purchasing more West German military goods (such as trucks and communications equipment) exacerbated an already strained relationship between the Schmidt and Carter governments.[35] However, it was the three main issues of PRM 10, SALT II and cruise missiles, and ERW that provided the context for the Schmidt speech at the IISS in October 1977.

THE SCHMIDT IISS SPEECH

Almost every analysis of the NATO INF affair of the late 1970s and early 1980s in some fashion refers to Schmidt's IISS speech of October 29, 1977, as the genesis of the NATO decision of December

---

34. The *New York Times* reported on October 25, 1977 (p. 12), that "a major impetus for revising the [1975 Option III] offer came this year when the West German Chancellor, Helmut Schmidt, made several public appeals for progress in the talks."

35. See Vardamis, "German–American Military Fissures," pp. 88–96.

1979. Excerpts from the speech are quoted at length by analysts to demonstrate that the chancellor was urging NATO to modernize its long-range theater nuclear forces as both a political and military response to improved Soviet INF capabilities, specifically the SS-20 and the Backfire bomber. Schmidt himself has at times contributed to the importance of this speech, claiming that he "created" the INF issue.[36] On the other hand, the chancellor has often tried to distance himself from the NATO decision, saying that his remarks in London were misconstrued, that he wasn't necessarily calling for a land-based NATO INF force, that an arms control agreement limiting INF was his main priority, and that if some deployment were necessary, he would have preferred a sea-based option.[37]

In certain parts of that speech, it does seem that Schmidt was urging the Alliance to modernize its theater nuclear forces. The passage most often quoted certainly leaves this impression: "SALT neutralizes [U.S. and USSR] capabilities. In Europe this magnifies the significance of the disparities between East and West in nuclear tactical and conventional weapons." Elsewhere, the chancellor implicitly criticized U.S. negotiating strategy at the SALT talks when he said that "we in Europe must be particularly careful to ensure that these [SALT] negotiations do not neglect the components of NATO's deterrence strategy."[38] Given that NATO's strategy of flexible response calls for an Alliance retaliatory capability at every rung of the escalation ladder, Schmidt seems to have been calling for improved NATO INF so as to tighten the link between NATO battlefield TNF and U.S. strategic forces.

A complete reading of Schmidt's speech, however, yields no reference to military deployment as the best means for reestablishing theater nuclear parity. If anything, Schmidt supported expanded East–West arms control efforts as a preferable solution for ensuring Gleichgewicht in central Europe: "Strategic arms limitations *confined* to the United States and the Soviet Union will inevitably impair the

36. The chancellor made these remarks at a conference I attended on German–American relations, sponsored by Friedrich Ebert Stiftung, in Bonn, June 13–14, 1980. See also Schmidt, *Menschen und Mächte*, pp. 230–235.

37. In a 1981 interview, Schmidt confirmed that he had originally favored sea-based INF, and that the High Level Group (HLG) had seriously reviewed such an option. According to Schmidt and other sources, there were two main arguments against SLCMs: they would have been too expensive, and the United States objected that sea-based INF would have "released the European allies from a nuclear risk which must be borne jointly." See *Die Zeit*, June 12, 1981.

38. Helmut Schmidt, "The 1977 Alastair Buchan Memorial Lecture," *Survival* 20 (January/February 1978): 4.

security of the West European members of the Alliance vis-à-vis Soviet military in Europe if we do not succeed in removing the disparities of military power in Europe parallel to the SALT negotiations."[39]

Moreover, Schmidt referred to both theater nuclear and conventional forces and emphasized the need to include theater nuclear systems in the SALT talks and to achieve progress at the MBFR conventional talks in Vienna. In addition, the chancellor's speech came just six months after NATO had launched an ambitious ten-year program to modernize its conventional forces. Initiated at the NATO Heads of Government meeting in London in May 1977, this Long-Term Defense Program (LTDP) called for substantial improvements in Alliance conventional forces. Of the ten areas included in the program, only one (point 10), specified a need for modernizing some of NATO's theater nuclear systems, but it made no reference to giving the Alliance a long-range INF capability, which NATO had not had since the mid-1960s, when the last of the Mace B cruise missiles were withdrawn from Europe. Indeed, Schmidt had given a forceful speech at the May meeting in which he emphasized the importance of parity in conventional forces, but made little mention of theater nuclear forces.

In his remarks to the closed NATO meeting in May (later made public by Schmidt), the chancellor reiterated his concern with the viability of extended deterrence. In a form reminiscent of his writings of fifteen years before, Schmidt stressed how the onset of strategic parity had called into question the deterrent value of U.S. strategic forces for the NATO Alliance. A full two years before Henry Kissinger's famous critique of extended deterrence, given in a speech in Brussels in September 1979, Schmidt emphasized that Soviet attainment of parity had ushered in a third phase in East–West military relations. No longer could the Alliance rely on the deterrent capabilities of superior U.S. strategic forces, as in the 1950s, or on the flexible response strategy of the 1960s and 1970s. Rather, the increase in Soviet strategic and theater forces had initiated a third phase, "making it necessary during the coming years, at least within the Atlantic and European framework, to reduce the political and military role of strategic nuclear weapons as a normal component of our defence and deterrence." Not one to leave anything to the imagination, Schmidt spelled out his concerns over the

39. Ibid.; emphasis added.

ability of the U.S. strategic umbrella to provide extended deterrence when he added: "The strategic nuclear component will become increasingly regarded as an instrument of last resort, *to serve the national interest and protect the survival of those who possess these weapons of last resort.*"[40]

Accordingly, Schmidt emphasized the importance of conventional forces in providing deterrence in Europe, given the diminished utility of U.S. strategic forces:

> This development must inevitably direct our attention even more towards strengthening our conventional defense potential, and towards the essential task of being capable of deterring and repelling military pressure or even military aggression by means of our conventional defense force, if pressure and aggression are mounted by non-nuclear, conventional forces. In other words, the more we stabilize strategic nuclear parity—an effort my government has supported from the beginning, and I have just stressed this again—the more it becomes necessary to achieve a balance of conventional forces as well.[41]

Indeed, it was Schmidt's preoccupation with continued Soviet modernization of its conventional forces in Eastern Europe, especially in the context of superpower strategic parity, and the political leverage such conventional forces might give the Soviets, that led the chancellor to stress this issue in his IISS speech, as he had been doing constantly since the NATO summit in May. As the chancellor noted in his talk at the IISS, "last May I said that the more we stabilize strategic nuclear parity between East and West, which my Government has always advocated, the greater will be the necessity to achieve a conventional equilibrium as well." Continuing, Schmidt made clear his preference for arms control:

> At the same meeting in May I said that there were, in theory, two possible ways of establishing a conventional balance with the Warsaw Pact states. One would be for the Western Alliance to undertake a massive build-up of forces and weapons systems; the other for both NATO and the Warsaw Pact to reduce their force strength and achieve an overall balance at a lower level. I prefer the latter.[42]

40. "The North Atlantic Summit Meeting, Remarks by Chancellor Helmut Schmidt, May 10, 1977," in *Survival* 19 (July/August 1977): 177–178; emphasis added.

41. Ibid., p. 178. Interestingly, some of Schmidt's aides convinced the chancellor that his concerns about the implications of strategic parity, which were expressed privately at the NATO meeting, were important enough for them to be published. Interviews with West German journalists and government officials, winter 1979–80.

42. Schmidt, "Buchan IISS Lecture," p. 4.

Schmidt then listed seven essential elements regarding the MBFR talks, insisting that "parity and collectivity must be recognized as the fundamental and determining principles," once again underlining the importance of military parity for the continuation of European détente.[43]

An additional aspect of Schmidt's IISS speech that is often overlooked is that the chancellor's comments on superpower arms control and the military balance of forces in Europe were a secondary component of his address. The main thrust of the speech dealt with international economic affairs and the need for greater Western coordination of economic planning to meet the challenge of rising energy prices and a global recession. As originally conceived, the chancellor's address was to have concentrated fully on economic problems and the dangers they posed for domestic stability in Western society. It is one of the ironies of the INF affair that Schmidt's remarks on arms control and European security were included in the speech at the last minute. Given that the forum was the Alastair Buchan Memorial Lecture, in honor of a former director of the IISS and a prominent British strategic thinker, one of Schmidt's aides thought the chancellor should pay homage to Buchan by including some remarks about the East–West military situation.[44]

In its report of the Schmidt speech the following day, the *Times* of London captured the essence of Schmidt's security remarks in a story headed, "Schmidt Calls for Mutual Cut in Conventional Forces."[45] The *Times* story noted Schmidt's concern that the Soviets had not yet accepted the principle of conventional parity in Europe and the chancellor's belief that neutron weapons might be effective in getting the Soviets to negotiate seriously at the MBFR talks.

> Until we see real progress on MBFR, we shall have to rely on the effectiveness of deterrence. It is in this context and no other that the public discussion in all member states of the Western Alliance about the "neutron weapon" has to be seen. We have to consider whether the

43. Ibid., p. 5.

44. Interviews with West German government officials, winter 1979–80. Among the strategic thinkers to whom Schmidt felt most indebted were Raymond Aron, Thomas Schelling, and, Alastair Buchan. See Schmidt's *Strategie des Gleichgewichts: Deutsche Friedenspolitik und die Weltmächte* (Stuttgart: Seewald, 1969), p. 17.

45. *Times* (London), October 29, 1977, p. 5. Actually, the *Financial Times* more accurately reported the overall thrust of Schmidt's speech by concentrating exclusively on what the chancellor had to say about global economic problems; see "Third World Warning Given by Schmidt," *Financial Times*, October 29, 1977, p. 1.

"neutron weapon" is of value to the Alliance as an additional element of the deterrent strategy, as a means of preventing war. But we should not limit ourselves to that examination. We should also examine what relevance and weight this weapon has in our efforts to achieve arms control.[46]

In accord with his ideas on incorporating a Western renunciation of ERW into a revised Option III proposal for MBFR, Schmidt was hoping to use neutron weapons as a bargaining chip, but a more effective bargaining chip than cruise missiles.

In sum, the essence of Schmidt's remarks on security made at the IISS come down to two essential points. One, strategic parity between the superpowers had magnified the imbalances in European theater and especially conventional forces and thus had weakened the political basis for détente generally and for West Germany's Ostpolitik in particular. And two, the best means for establishing parity at the European level was through arms control, not deployment of new weapons. For Schmidt, the significance of the new nuclear weapons being developed by the United States lay in the opportunities they provided for trade-offs with Soviet forces. By the fall of 1977, it was clear that SALT limitations on the cruise missile were not likely to lead to similar limitations on Soviet systems. Thus it was all the more important to Schmidt that ERW be used at MBFR talks to produce an agreement through which the Soviets accepted, both in principle and in practice, the concept of parity in conventional forces. For Schmidt, the issues of SALT, gray-area weapons, MBFR, conventional deterrence, and the role of nuclear weapons in NATO strategy were all related, and to deal successfully with only one or two of these issues made the lack of progress in the others all the more glaring.

INF AND NATO POLICYMAKING

The preceding discussion of Schmidt's speech at the IISS in October 1977, and the chancellor's concerns over the possible "decoupling" effects of superpower strategic parity makes clear that Schmidt was worried primarily about the growing disjuncture between successful superpower strategic arms control and the lack of progress in the MBFR talks. In addition, Schmidt was apprehensive

---

46. Schmidt, "Buchan IISS Lecture," p. 4.

over the apparent willingness of the Americans to submit to limitations on cruise missiles without receiving comparable restraints on Soviet long-range systems designed for use in the European theater.

Why, then, has the chancellor's speech been cited so often as providing the original impetus for the NATO theater nuclear force modernization program that was adopted by the Alliance in December 1979? As I have argued, a close reading of Schmidt's speech reveals that Schmidt was more concerned with imbalances in conventional forces than with inequalities in theater nuclear forces, and that he believed the best means for rectifying either imbalance was arms control, not new deployments.

Nonetheless, the chancellor seemed to be calling into question the entire notion of extended deterrence and the ability of U.S. strategic forces to deter conflict in Europe. In doing so, Schmidt was going against two decades of NATO strategy, when imbalances in certain weapons categories were tolerated as long as the Alliance maintained an overall military parity with the Soviet Union and Warsaw Pact. After all, NATO had tolerated an imbalance in long-range theater missiles since the mid-1960s, having no comparable systems to counter the 600 warheads on the Soviet SS-4 and SS-5 ballistic missiles. Was a West German chancellor now calling for "Eurostrategic parity," for an Alliance ability to match Soviet capabilities at every rung of the escalation ladder? Without explicity calling for INF parity, Schmidt did seem to be leaning in that direction when he spoke of the need for NATO to "maintain the balance of the full deterrence strategy."[47] Yet Schmidt's concern with an INF imbalance seemed at odds with his own thinking over two decades regarding NATO strategy. Consistently since the publication in 1961 of his *Vertidigung oder Vergeltung* (which appeared in English in 1962 as *Defense or Retaliation: A German View*), Schmidt had opposed an overreliance on theater nuclear forces and supported Alliance attempts to fashion a credible conventional deterrent.

There are two main reasons why Schmidt's speech at the IISS caused such a stir and why the chancellor's remarks have come to be seen as advocating INF modernization. First and foremost is that Schmidt chose to go public with his apprehensions that the SALT talks were neglecting European security concerns in a visible forum such as the Buchan lecture. In criticizing U.S. negotiating strategy at SALT, the chancellor was no doubt also venting his frustration with

47. Ibid.

what he saw as political insensitivity in the Carter White House to West German concerns over a broad range of issues. As we have seen, a combination of differences between the United States and the FRG over economic, human rights, and nuclear power issues had coalesced with tensions over arms control and security policies to make Schmidt uneasy about the competence of the Carter administration.[48] As was his wont at times, Schmidt did not hesitate to engage in public diplomacy by criticizing his main Alliance partner in an open forum.

The second reason Schmidt's remarks made such an impression in Washington was that the chancellor's speech did indeed reinforce the concerns being voiced to officials in the Carter administration by some of the chancellor's closest advisers. Walther Stützle, chief of the Defense Ministry's planning staff; Jürgen Brandt, inspector general of the Bundeswehr; and Gunther van Well, state secretary in the Foreign Ministry, had made known their displeasure at the cruise missile restrictions being contemplated in SALT II.[49] Arguing that Soviet deployment of the Backfire bomber and SS-20 was introducing a qualitatively new threat that the Alliance must counter, these officials and others were unhappy that Washington was bargaining away a NATO technological advantage. Stützle especially played a key role in this respect; having drafted the security portion of Schmidt's IISS speech, he apparently saw the Buchan lecture as an opportunity to reaffirm West German concerns about the negative effects of superpower arms control efforts on West European security.

Another important figure who stressed Bonn's unhappiness with the direction of Washington's SALT policies was Maj. Gen. Peter Tandecki, at the time the FRG representative to NATO's High Level Group, which consisted of eleven military experts from the NATO member states and was chaired by David McGiffert, assistant secretary of defense for international security affairs. Tandecki had played an important role in the deliberations of an unofficial body, the European–American Workshop, in 1975 and 1976. This group of influential, mostly academic experts, led by Albert Wohlstetter, sponsored a series of workshops and seminars on Alliance security problems and had developed into a major lobbying force for incor-

48. Doubts concerning Carter's handling of domestic affairs were also being raised in the United States at this time; see "Carter's First 9 Months: Charges of Ineptness Rise," *New York Times*, October 23, 1977, p. 1.

49. Interviews with U.S. government officials, summer 1980.

porating the cruise missile into the Alliance's force posture.[50] The recommendations of the members of the European–American Workshop, published in 1977 under the title, *Beyond Nuclear Deterrence*, were widely cited by supporters of the cruise missile on both sides of the Atlantic.[51] Just as important, the participants themselves, including Henry Rowen, Richard Burt and James Digby of the United States, Johan Holst of Norway,[52] and Uwe Nerlich of the FRG, acted as informal lobbyists in Western Europe, criticizing the Carter administration's cruise missile policy.[53]

While it would be overestimating the influence of the European–American Workshop to credit it with both stimulating European interest in the cruise missile and prompting European support for INF modernization once the cruise missile limitations in SALT had become known, its members did represent an important source of expertise outside the Carter administration. In providing further support for the views of Stützle, Tandecki, and others, the workshop did serve to heighten West German concern about the direction of NATO strategy.

As several members of the Carter administration noted in private interviews, Washington hoped in the summer of 1977 to assuage this concern and keep Allied differences within official NATO channels.[54] As already mentioned, Gelb's trip to Europe was intended less to downplay the significance of the cruise missile than to bring the Europeans up to date on American thinking concerning the pros and cons of this new weapon. Within NATO, American planners hoped to deal with the issue in the Alliance's Nuclear Planning

50. See Kaplan, "Warring over New Missiles."

51. Johan J. Holst and Uwe Nerlich, eds., *Beyond Nuclear Deterrence: New Aims, New Arms* (New York: Crane, Russak, 1977).

52. In 1976, Holst became under secretary of state for defense in Norway and the Norwegian representative to NATO's High Level Group, where he was able to support INF modernization in an official capacity. In the 1980s, Burt became the U.S. ambassador to West Germany for the Reagan administration and then the chief U.S. negotiator at the U.S.–Soviet Strategic Arms Reduction (START) talks for the Bush administration.

53. Richard Burt, for instance, was already writing early in 1977: "The most interesting military option available to the West for countering the expansion of Soviet Eurostrategic capabilities is already under discussion at SALT—the long-range, precision-guided cruise missile. In deciding whether to exploit cruise missile technology in this manner, the United States must therefore once again choose between placing priorities on strengthening the alliance ties and quickly obtaining a SALT agreement." See his "SS-20 and the Strategic Balance," *World Today*, January/February 1977.

54. Interviews with U.S. government officials, summer 1980.

Group. The Alliance itself had recognized the need for some TNF modernization at its London summit in May, when it included TNF as point 10 of its Long-Term Defense Program. At that time, however, the TNF issue took a back seat to the overall emphasis on the need for improvements in conventional forces, and the discussion on TNF modernization was limited to the possibility of improving the accuracy of the Pershing missile, not of extending its range.

Although the NPG was given responsibility for studying the TNF issue, under the rubric of Task Force 10, there was little movement on the issue in the summer of 1977. By the time of its mid-October meeting in Bari, Italy, however, European concerns about the need for a more serious study of the issue prompted the NPG to create the High Level Group (HLG).[55] The fact that the HLG was created even before Schmidt's speech at the IISS is one indication of how pressures within NATO were building for some type of Alliance response to Soviet TNF deployments.[56] The added visibility that the chancellor gave to the TNF issue served only to heighten the urgency of the task laid before the HLG. The HLG met three more times before the next scheduled NPG meeting, in April 1978, when the HLG recommended a "need for an evolutionary adjustment in NATO's TNF which would provide more in-theater long-range capability than at present."[57]

55. The NPG meeting of Oct. 11 and 12, 1977 was attended by the defense ministers of Belgium, Denmark, West Germany, Greece, Italy, the United Kingdom, and the United States, as well as Joseph Luns, secretary general of NATO, General Alexander Haig, Adm. Isaac Kidd (SACLANT), and Gen. Herman Zeiner Gundersen of Denmark, head of NATO's Military Committee. For the text of the communiqué issued following the meeting, which did not make any mention of the NPG's decision to set up the HLG, see *Europa Archiv*, April 10, 1978, pp. D195–196. Along with its consideration of INF, this meeting of the NPG also discussed the neutron bomb issue; indeed, one of Defense Secretary Harold Brown's main interests was to gauge European support for deploying neutron warheads. See *Times* (London), October 7, 1977.

56. In creating the HLG, the NPG asked this group to "examine the role of TNF in NATO strategy, the implications of recent Soviet TNF deployments, the need for NATO TNF modernization, and the technical, military and political implications of alternative NATO TNF postures." See *General Report on the Security of the Alliance—The Role of Nuclear Weapons,"* Report to the Military Committee of the North Atlantic Assembly (Brussels: NATO, November 1979). The report, written by Klaas de Vries (Holland), in his capacity as rapporteur, was accepted by NATO's Military Committee as representing the views only of the rapporteur and not of the study group that produced it. That the HLG was asked to do an in-depth study of TNF two weeks before the Schmidt speech at the IISS indicates the NATO bureaucracy's concern with the issue of TNF modernization.

57. The HLG met three times between October 1977 and the next scheduled meeting of the NPG in April 1978, and another four times before the NPG meeting

While the work of the HLG signified increased attention to the military aspects of the TNF issue, the Schmidt speech raised distinctly political questions regarding the Alliance's ability to maintain the "continuum of deterrence." As one member of the Carter administration noted, the Schmidt speech was troublesome in that the chancellor seemed to be suggesting that unless West European concerns were incorporated more strongly in the U.S. SALT negotiating strategy, European support for U.S. Senate ratification of a SALT II treaty might not be forthcoming.[58] While it is difficult to tell how serious a threat this was, officials in the Carter administration were concerned enough (given the difficulty the White House knew it would have in gaining Senate ratification) that a special interagency group was formed following the Schmidt speech to develop a specific position on INF that could be presented to NATO's High Level Group. The arguments developed by this group, known as the "mini-SCC" (Security Coordinating Committee), in favor of some type of INF modernization were detailed and complex; suffice it to say that they included a military rationale (the need to ensure the credibility of flexible response by strengthening NATO's theater nuclear posture) and a political rationale (the perceived need to demonstrate strong U.S. leadership in galvanizing the Alliance to respond to Soviet deployment of the SS-20 and Backfire bomber).

For many Americans, the additional capabilities provided by new INF systems would enhance both deterrence and defense in that deterrence would be strengthened by the deployment of weapons that, by countering Soviet INF, would make a defense of Europe more credible. As one analyst said, this "extension of deterrence into the conflict spectrum" was designed to avoid what many observers perceived as the shortcomings of an excessive reliance on U.S. strategic forces should deterrence fail.[59] Or, as a Congressional Budget Office report noted in 1977, "the basic idea is that a strategic nuclear response to Soviet aggression would be intuitively more plausible if theater nuclear weapons had already been used and had

---

at Homestead Air Force Base in Florida in April 1979. At Homestead the NPG requested that the HLG develop specific recommendations in time for the autumn 1979 meeting of the NPG. See Stephen Hanmer, "NATO's Long-Range Theater Nuclear Forces: Modernization in Parallel with Arms Control," *NATO Review* 28 (February 1980).

58. Interview with U.S. government official, autumn 1982.

59. J. J. Martin, "Nuclear Weapons in NATO's Deterrent Strategy," *Orbis* 22 (Winter 1979): 876.

failed to halt the Soviet attack."[60] By contrast, the offical German view, as contained in the 1976 West German Defense White Paper, was that "the initial use of nuclear weapons is not intended so much to bring about a military decision as to achieve political effect. The intent is to persuade the attacker to reconsider his intention, to desist in his aggression, and to withdraw. At the same time, it will be impressed upon him that he risks still further escalation if he continues to attack."[61]

The implicit notion of NATO's TNF providing a "triggering" response for U.S. strategic forces, in the event that the Soviets continued their aggression, was made more explicit as the INF issue evolved. In the 1979 Defense White Paper, the Schmidt government declared that it regarded INF as being "closely interlinked with the strategic long-range potential of the United States in terms of concept and structure."[62] Just two weeks before the Brussels decision on INF, a Schmidt government spokesman went even further, declaring that INF systems are designed to hold U.S. strategic forces "hostage" in the event of war: "The idea is certainly not to win a war. . . . Deploying a limited number of these [INF] systems . . . would not enable us to fight a nuclear war in Europe, but would enable us to escalate a conflict that we couldn't dominate otherwise."[63]

At the time of the IISS speech in 1977, however, it was not at all clear what function the West Germans perceived a new INF component as providing. While an improved INF capability might make an escalation to U.S. strategic systems more plausible, was there not also the risk that a future nuclear conflict would be limited to Europe? If any projected INF force was large enough to fill the gap in the "continuum of deterrence," might it not also be large enough to give NATO an "in-theater" capability that would in turn reduce the Alliance's need for U.S. central systems? Despite West Germany's continued emphasis on the political role of nuclear weapons in supporting deterrence, the Bonn government's concerns at this time were vague enough that the chancellor himself was accused of engaging in self-fulfilling prophecies concerning the decoupling of

60. Congressional Budget Office, *Theater Nuclear Forces* (Washington, D.C.: U.S. Government Printing Office, 1977), p. 6.

61. *White Paper 1976: The Security of the Federal Republic of Germany* (Bonn: Federal Minister of Defense, 1976).

62. *White Paper 1979: The Security of the Federal Republic of Germany* (Bonn: Federal Minister of Defense, 1979), p. 107.

63. Interview with Peter Corterier, SPD member of the Bundestag and party defense spokesman, *New York Times*, December 9, 1979.

Western Europe from the United States. When asked, following his IISS speech, whether the establishment of INF parity in Europe might not lead to the very decoupling that West German policy had always sought to avoid, Schmidt went to great lengths to explain that he did not favor "Euro-strategic" parity as such. Instead, he explained, he continued to support the U.S. strategic guarantee as the ultimate assurance of deterrence, while also supporting a stronger theater nuclear posture to solidify the continuum of deterrence.[64]

In effect, Schmidt was looking for a political response from the Carter administration that would take European security concerns into account and maintain the integrity of NATO's deterrent strategy. According to this view, the SALT process between the superpowers was an important component of détente, but must not be allowed to develop into a condominium at the expense of the European states. Similarly, the prospect of a successful SALT II treaty made progress at the MBFR talks all the more important. Given the steady growth of Soviet nuclear and conventional forces, it was imperative to Schmidt that parity in Europe, Gleichgewicht, be restored to reduce Soviet leverage over Bonn's Ostpolitik to manageable proportions. Finally, the growing problem of "gray-area weapons" not being covered in either arms control forum had to be addressed.

West German Leverage and NATO Policy

The central role played by Helmut Schmidt and members of his government in shaping NATO nuclear policy in the mid-1970s demonstrates the extent to which West German influence within the Alliance had grown since the Adenauer years. In the 1950s, and even during the debates over flexible response and MLF in the 1960s, Washington was the final arbiter on questions of nuclear policy. Although Adenauer initially opposed the U.S. preference for increased reliance on tactical nuclear weapons and concomitant cutbacks in conventional forces as proposed by Eisenhower's New Look policy, in the end he had little choice but to acquiesce. It is true, as Josef Joffe has noted, that the Adenauer government did

64. *SALT and the NATO Allies*, report prepared for the U.S. Senate Committee on Foreign Relations, Subcommittee on European Affairs (Washington, D.C.: U.S. Government Printing Office, 1979), p. 6.

intervene in the U.S. political process to modify the New Look and gained some measure of success when the Radford Plan was not implemented.[65] Moreover, as time went on, Adenauer sought to diversify the bases of West German security by strengthening relations with France, which culminated in the 1963 Franco-German treaty. Ultimately, however, the extant security environment—the anticommunist climate of the Cold War, continued European anxieties regarding West German power, and Adenauer's own preference for deepening West German integration within the Atlantic Alliance and Western Europe—relegated the FRG to secondary status in the shaping of NATO policy.

By the 1970s, the Federal Republic was well along in a political maturation process that included the important component of attenuating the legacy of its Nazi past (the so-called *Bewältigung der Vergangenheit,* or "overcoming of the past") through Willy Brandt's initiation of Ostpolitik.[66] It was this same Ostpolitik, however, that introduced new countervailing pressures into the conduct of West German security policy. In the early 1970s, possible tensions between Bonn's security role in NATO and its desire for an expanded Eastern policy were minimized by the confluence of superpower and European détente. Yet, as the United States has experienced in its own relations with the Soviets, where military competition and political cooperation coexist uneasily, the FRG was bound to be faced at times with conflicting priorities.

The summer of 1977, when the U.S.–Soviet SALT negotiations seemed headed toward an agreement that might neglect FRG security concerns, and when the continued failure of the MBFR talks was being accompanied by a steady growth in Soviet conventional and theater nuclear capabilities, was one such period. In the political sphere, West German relations with the Soviets were much improved. The achievements of Ostpolitik in the early 1970s were followed by the Helsinki Accords in 1975; West German economic and humanitarian contacts with the GDR were expanding; and relations with the other East European states were also improving. Yet the combination of Schmidt's dissatisfaction with Carter's political leadership and what the chancellor saw as the undermining of

65. Josef Joffe, "Society and Foreign Policy in the Federal Republic" (Ph.D. thesis, Harvard University, 1975), pp. 191–195.

66. For an especially good account, see Philip Windsor, *Germany and the Management of Détente* (New York: Praeger, 1971).

military Gleichgewicht in Europe threatened the security needs of the FRG and its continued pursuit of Ostpolitik.

To rectify the situation, what Schmidt was advocating in his NATO and IISS speeches was a greater political commitment to arms control, both to rectify the balance of conventional forces through MBFR and to include "Euro-strategic" nuclear forces in SALT II. While it is true that some of Schmidt's top aides were exploring the utility of the cruise missile to bolster NATO's deterrent, and while Schmidt would later come out more forcefully in favor of some form of INF deployment, in 1977 the chancellor seemed to hope that military parity in Europe could be reestablished primarily through arms control.

It was with these convictions in mind that Schmidt made the remarks he did at the IISS, taking the Carter administration to task for its conduct in the SALT negotiations. More than other West German chancellors before him, Schmidt took an activist role in seeking to shape Western policy, even when the issue was that of U.S.–Soviet arms control negotiations. While Schmidt's leverage over U.S. negotiating strategy was admittedly limited, he nonetheless was not reluctant to voice his criticisms when he felt West German interests were at stake.[67] From the NATO meeting in May 1977 to Schmidt's proposal in September that the West adopt a new negotiating proposal for MBFR (one that included the possible renunciation of ERW deployment) to the IISS speech in October, the chancellor was constantly, and forcefully, articulating West German security concerns.

Such forceful intervention by Schmidt can be attributed in part to temperament. Schmidt viewed himself as the elder statesman, especially in comparison with Jimmy Carter, and was impolitic enough to say so on a number of occasions.[68]

In a similar vein, West German officials by the 1970s had gained far more expertise and confidence in dealing with nuclear weapons

67. Gregory Treverton has noted, "Throughout the discussions of SALT II within the Alliance, West Germany was the ally most skeptical about American assurances on provisions, most concerned about cruise missile restrictions, and most eager that the United States commit itself, in the SALT III principles section of SALT II, to some negotiation of gray area weapons in SALT III"; see his "Nuclear Weapons and the 'Gray Area,'" *Foreign Affairs* 57 (Summer 1979): 1080.

68. See especially Jimmy Carter, *Keeping Faith: Memoirs of a President* (New York: Bantam, 1982), and Brzezinski, *Power and Principle*. For Schmidt's views on his relationship with the president, see *Menschen und Mächte*, pp. 222–229.

issues within the NATO decision-making process. The FRG had become a full partner in NATO's Nuclear Planning Group in 1967, and its nonnuclear status was no longer a major handicap in its dealings with American and British officials.

Most important, however, the "correlation of forces" within the Western Alliance (to borrow a Marxist-Leninist term) had greatly altered since Adenauer's time. In the 1950s, the Federal Republic had not yet become the primus inter pares of the European NATO states. Britain's postwar decline was still evolving, and France had not yet left the NATO military structure. By the 1970s, however, the NATO Alliance had to some extent become a Washington–Bonn coalition, with both partners perhaps expecting too much in the way of concurrence from the other. Partly as a result of frustration in Washington, evident in the Nixon and Ford administrations as well as Carter's, over the failure of the West Europeans to speak with one voice, the Federal Republic, as point man, "repeatedly found itself in a special role in its relations with the United States, alternating between being viewed as a 'scandalon' because of its lack of cooperation at one moment, and in the next being considered as a potential partner in a 'bi-gemony.' "[69] As Uwe Nerlich has noted, while the Federal Republic has "no choice but to be partner-in-stability" of the United States, the "continuity of this cooperation is, in the long run, a question of the art of political leadership."[70]

In the summer and fall of 1977, political leadership was lacking on both sides. The Carter administration had failed to satisfy Bonn that West German interests were being sufficiently protected in the SALT negotiations, while Schmidt can be faulted for having used the wrong channels to convey his displeasure. Unfortunately for both governments, and for the Alliance, the neutron bomb debacle in 1978 would further complicate not only intra-Alliance relations but the domestic politics of the FRG and Schmidt's bargaining position within NATO.

69. Uwe Nerlich, "Washington and Bonn: Evolutionary Patterns in the Relations between the United States and the Federal Republic of Germany," in Karl Kaiser and Hans-Peter Schwarz, eds., *America and Western Europe*, (Lexington, Mass.: Lexington Books, 1977), p. 366.
70. Ibid., p. 368.

[3]

The Social Democrats and
NATO Nuclear Policy: 1977–1980

When Helmut Schmidt became chancellor in May 1974, following Willy Brandt's resignation in the wake of a major spy scandal, the ruling SPD/FDP coalition was emerging from one difficult period of governing only to face another. The period from 1969 to 1972 had seen intense CDU/CSU opposition to the Ostpolitik of Brandt and Foreign Minister Walter Scheel of the FDP. During the bitter ratification debates over the Warsaw and Moscow treaties in 1972, Brandt had narrowly survived a vote of no confidence in the Bundestag, following which parliament was dissolved and new elections scheduled. Held in November 1972, this election was largely a referendum on the SPD/FDP Ostpolitik, and it resulted in the SPD's winning a plurality of Bundestag seats for the first time in the postwar period.[1]

Despite this victory, which was followed in December by the signing of the Basic Treaty with East Germany and a thawing of relations between the FRG and GDR, there continued to be major policy differences between the SPD and its junior coalition partner, especially in the domestic realm. These differences involved primarily economic issues (tax reform, social welfare benefits) but also included such civil liberties issues as the *Berufsverbot*, a law aimed at keeping political extremists (mainly German communists and other left-wing radicals) out of the West German civil service.

---

1. Public support for Brandt's Ostpolitik was widespread in the spring of 1972, with 66 percent of those polled in favor of the Moscow and Warsaw treaties, and 73 percent in favor of the Basic Treaty with East Germany. To a large extent, this support carried over into the November 1972 national election, in which the SPD won 46 percent of the vote to 45 percent for the CDU/CSU and 8 percent for the FDP. See David Conradt, *The German Polity* (New York: Longman, 1978), pp. 112–115.

Even in foreign affairs, the glow of the 1972 electoral victory proved short-lived as the October 1973 Yom Kippur War and resulting Arab oil embargo set in train the global recession of 1974–76. Adding to these difficulties when Schmidt took over in May 1974 were the beginnings of strains within the Alliance over Soviet conduct during détente.

Schmidt was also facing increased divisions within the SPD itself. Ever since the adoption in 1959 of the reformist Bad Godesberg program, some members of the party's left wing had been critical of the party for diluting its commitment to socialist principles. Such criticism was especially heated during the Grand Coalition between the SPD and CDU/CSU from 1966 to 1969. A combination of traditional blue-collar Marxists, Young Socialists (Jusos), and party intellectuals criticized the party leadership for forming a coalition government with the bourgeois CDU/CSU. During the Brandt years, from 1969 to 1974, a combination of Ostpolitik and social welfare legislation ameliorated left-wing restiveness. Also, the failure of the extraparliamentary opposition (APO) from 1966 to 1969 had led many of the younger left-wing socialists to adopt a strategy of working within the party to change SPD policies (the so-called long march through the institutions).

Brandt's replacement by the centrist Schmidt in 1974, however, and the scaling back of social welfare legislation because of the recession, soon led to renewed tensions between the "government" and "party" factions within the SPD. Matters weren't helped when, in the national election in October 1976, the SPD share of the vote declined for the first time since 1957, and the CDU/CSU again became the largest party in the Bundestag, with 243 seats to 214 for the SPD. It was only with the thirty-nine seats held by the FDP that the Schmidt government was able to stay in power (with a slim majority of ten seats), and in the formal Bundestag vote in December, Schmidt was reelected chancellor by only one vote.[2]

In many ways, the October 1976 election represented the nadir of Schmidt's tenure as chancellor (with the exception, of course, of his ultimate downfall in 1982). The government's slim majority provided increased leverage for the FDP in matters of policymaking, which in turn increased the dissatisfaction of the SPD left wing over what it saw as the compromise of SPD principles. Over a wide range of

2. In the 1976 election, the SPD slipped to 42.6 percent of the vote, while the CDU/CSU won 48.6 percent of the vote, and the FDP won 7.9 percent. See ibid., p. 113.

issues, from increased pensions to treatment of foreign workers (*Gastarbeiter*) to the building of civilian nuclear power plants, the Schmidt "government" wing and the leftist "party" wing of the SPD found themselves increasingly at odds.

Ironically, one issue that alienated many younger SPD members from the Schmidt government in the mid-1970s—that is, Bonn's curtailment of civil liberties to combat domestic terrorism—was also the issue that earned Schmidt a good deal of respect from the West German public at large. In seeking to deal with the rash of kidnappings and murders carried out by the Baader-Meinhof gang in 1976–77, the Schmidt government instituted such measures as the *Kontaktsperre* ("prohibition of contact"), which limited the ability of lawyers and those sympathetic to the terrorists to lend them aid. Younger radical socialists, as well as many civil libertarians in the FDP and other parties, criticized the Kontaktsperre and other measures as overreactions and threats to West German democracy, and added that such measures were being used only against leftist radicals, not against neo-Nazis and other right-wing extremists. At the same time, the doubling of the university student population from 1967 to 1977 had produced a chaotic situation in FRG higher education, and government attempts to impose stricter discipline in the governance of universities only added to the alienation of young people from the SPD/FDP coalition.

Such was the domestic political situation in West Germany as the SPD prepared for its party congress in Hamburg, November 15–19, 1977. Not surprisingly, despite the publicity generated by Schmidt's speech at the IISS only a few weeks before, the party's attention was focused primarily on domestic issues (civilian nuclear power and environmental issues in addition to economic and civil liberty concerns). The low salience of the INF issue for SPD and West German domestic politics in the fall of 1977 is evident from the party debates at the Hamburg congress. Attention to military issues was limited to the SALT and MBFR talks and, above all, to the neutron bomb. The various motions adopted by the party delegates stressed the need to break the MBFR logjam and ensure that no ERW deployment in West Germany would be necessary. Little attention was given to theater nuclear weapons, and then only in the context of the SALT negotiations. Two years later, at the December 1979 party congress in Berlin, the situation would be vastly different. Indeed, party opposition to Schmidt's INF policy was to be so great at the Berlin congress, which took place less than two weeks before the NATO meeting in Brussels, that the chancellor had to threaten to resign to enforce party discipline.

THE PARTY CONGRESS AND SPD POLICYMAKING

Before we examine the Hamburg and Berlin party congresses in greater detail, a word should be said about the function of party congresses in general in determining Social Democratic policy.

Beginning with the famous Gotha conference in 1875, when the German Social Democratic party was formed, party congresses have traditionally been the most important venues for debating, if not actually determining, SPD policy. From the initial congress at Gotha, when the followers of Karl Marx and Ferdinand Lassalle debated the advantages of revolutionary versus reformist strategies, party congresses have been the best barometer for gauging the balance of power between the party's socialist and social democratic factions. As Fritz Erler noted in the 1950s, the history of the SPD is one of generational shifts in power between the left socialists and moderate social democrats, as at the 1891 congress in Erfurt and the 1925 congress in Heidelberg.[3]

This was especially the case at the 1959 special party congress in Bad Godesberg, when the SPD shed many of its Marxist tenets and adopted moderate policies in an attempt to attract middle-of-the-road voters. Yet even a year earlier, the 1958 party congress in Stuttgart had been critically important in signaling possible changes in SPD policy, on both security and domestic issues. As we saw in Chapter 1, the efforts of a Gegenelite within the SPD (led by Erler, Carlo Schmid, Willy Brandt, Herbert Wehner, and Helmut Schmidt) to reorient party policy laid the foundation, first, for the adoption of those policies at Bad Godesberg in 1959, and ultimately, for the entry into power of the SPD as junior coalition partner in 1966 and as senior partner in 1969.

It is true that the adoption of more centrist security policies at the Stuttgart congress was the culmination of an internal debate that had been going on within the party since the party's defeat in the 1953 elections, when the reformers won Ollenhauer's agreement on the need to create a security committee (*Sicherheitsausschuss beim*

3. Fritz Erler, "Gedanken zur Politik und inneren Ordnung der Sozialdemokratie," *Neue Gesellschaft*, January/February 1958.

Vorstand) that could advise the party executive (*Vorstand*) on how to respond to Adenauer's plans for integrating West German forces into the ill-fated European Defense Community (EDC).[4] Although the creation of this committee was an early indication of the growing strength of the party's parliamentary group, its influence in determining party security was limited, as was demonstrated at the party congress in Berlin in July 1954. Despite Erler's arguments that continued SPD opposition to rearmament was tantamount to an abdication of party responsibility, the delegates at the Berlin congress overwhelmingly endorsed Ollenhauer's policy of continued resistance to West German rearmament. Just as significant, Erler and Willy Brandt were soundly defeated in their bid to be elected to the twenty-three-member executive committee. Finally, the strength of the opposition to rearmament at the time can be seen in a concession Ollenhauer was forced to make—not to the reformers, but to the more militant pacifists among the rank and file. As adopted by the Berlin congress in 1954, the resolution on security policy set down stringent conditions that would have to be met before the party could agree to support West German rearmament; in addition, the party leadership was forced to accept a clause stipulating that a special party congress, and not just the party executive, would be the final arbiter of whether those conditions had been met. As the *Times* of London noted, "the SPD leaders are left with their hands tied; before they can support any German military contribution to Western defense they are bound to face, and convince, a full party conference."[5]

This demonstration of rank-and-file strength at the 1954 SPD congress was indicative not only of the passions aroused by the rearmament debate but of the de jure importance of party congresses in general in determining SPD policy. As the party statutes state, the party congress (*Parteitag*) is the "highest organ" of the SPD, with responsibility for electing the executive committee and deciding on both policy and organizational issues. Meeting every two years, and composed of several hundred delegates elected by regional party organizations (*Bezirke*), the Parteitag in theory is the expression of the fundamentally democratic nature of the SPD. Given the hierarchical structure of the party, in which more than 9,000 local organi-

4. For more on the early stages of the reform movement in the SPD, see Gordon Drummond, *The German Social Democrats in Opposition, 1949–1960* (Norman: University of Oklahoma Press, 1982), pp. 120–128.

5. *Times* (London), July 26, 1954.

zations (*Ortsvereine*) are combined in twenty-two regional Bezirke, which in turn send their representatives to the Parteitag, the SPD has traditionally considered itself to be a model of participatory democracy. In practice, of course, party decision making in the SPD has been more oligarchic than representative, as the noted sociologist Robert Michels and others have pointed out.[6] As opposed to the bottom-up flow of decision making enumerated in the party statutes, organizational power in the SPD is wielded by the various factions that make up the party leadership. For all their importance in debating party strategy and policy, party congresses are expected to approve those policies decided upon well in advance of the biennial gatherings. The relative powerlessness of Parteitag delegates to shape party policies substantially, as Heino Kaack has made clear, makes them akin to customs officials who are permitted to open trunks for inspection but not to disturb the contents.[7] As Kaack observes, however, there is one plus for the party delegates in this customs official analogy, in that the party leadership, which has "packed" the trunk, is then not usually permitted to change the contents after inspection.

The style of SPD decision making in the Federal Republic, however, has veered noticeably from the oligarchic control described by Michels. Most important has been the evolution of the party itself from a class party to a *Volkspartei* and the concomitant rise in importance of the party's parliamentary group. Especially after Bad Godesberg, but even before, the perceived need to compromise on questions of ideology so as to broaden the party's electoral appeal necessarily increased the importance of the party's elected representatives in the Bundestag and in the regional governments. As we have seen, the locus of intraparty conflict in the 1950s was primarily between the doctrinaire party executive/bureaucracy and the reformist parliamentary group. As long as Ollenhauer and the traditionalists held sway, the reformers correctly saw it as being in their interest not to challenge the party leadership at the party congresses. As Douglas Chalmers notes, mounting such a challenge would have been "selecting as a battlefield the enemy's stronghold," given the

---

6. Robert Michels, *Zur Soziologie des Parteiwesens in der modernen Demokratie* (Leipzig: A. Kroener, 1925); for a more recent analysis, see Arthur B. Gunlicks, "Intraparty Democracy in West Germany," *Comparative Politics*, January 1970.

7. Heino Kaack, "Opposition und Aussenpolitik," *Politische Vierteljahresschrift*, no. 10, (1969), pp. 244–249.

activist, traditionalist composition of the Parteitag delegates.[8] Nonetheless, the existence of horizontal competition at the highest levels of the party diluted the concept of a rigid oligarchical structure of decision making. Moreover, as the reformers began to gain representation in the party executive, as they did at the 1958 Stuttgart conference, the party congress became increasingly attractive as a battleground on which to challenge the party bureaucrats. Thus, while the bulk of the reformers' efforts remained concentrated, from 1954 to 1958, within "the fragmented and specialized channels of committees and conferences leading to the party parliamentary delegations and the party executives,"[9] the party congress nonetheless retained a symbolic importance as the institution responsible for ratifying shifts in the evolution of the party's political strategy.

In the period following Bad Godesberg, as the SPD became more concerned with electoral politics than with ideology per se, the ability of the party congress to influence party policy directly weakened. Once the SPD gained power in Bonn, as Chalmers notes, the coordination of party policy was "undertaken with respect neither to ideology nor [to] the long-run impact of policies on each other, but rather with regard to the tactics of the party within the framework of elections and to the ever-present problem of the image of the party."[10] Once the SPD entered the government, this preoccupation with electoral success was joined by a concern with governmental stability, which reduced even further the ability of the SPD rank and file to effect the policies of the party qua governmental leadership. While the party congresses could and did continue to debate grand strategy and examine the long-term implications of SPD policy, the constraints imposed by holding governmental power meant that the Parteitag itself had become primarily an instrument for ratifying governmental policy. To be sure, the reformers' efforts to redirect party policy in the 1950s were mirrored in the 1970s by attempts of the left wing to hold the party leadership true to the party's ideological roots. In this respect, the party congresses in Hamburg in 1977 and Berlin in 1979 were as filled with dissension and debate as the congresses in the 1950s. Such debates, however, fulfilled more a safety-valve function than anything else, and the concern of the

8. Douglas A. Chalmers, *The Social Democratic Party of Germany* (New Haven: Yale University Press, 1964), p. 136.

9. Ibid., p. 137.

10. Ibid., pp. 137–138.

party leadership, along with ensuring ratification of party policy, was to impose party discipline to the extent necessary in supporting the government. It was only with the fall of the Schmidt government in 1982 that SPD party congresses regained some of their former influence in the actual shaping of party policy, as we shall note in Chapter 3.

SPD PARTY LEADERSHIP

The Hamburg and Berlin congresses in the late 1970s differed from the congresses of the 1950s in another important respect—the popularity of the party leader. In the 1950s, Erich Ollenhauer lacked the leadership abilities necessary to unify the SPD and compete with Konrad Adenauer. A product of the SPD bureaucratic *apparat*, Ollenhauer was consistently under attack both from the moderate reformers in the Bundestag Fraktion and from the militant left. Known as *der Mann des Ausgleichs* (the compromiser), Ollenhauer suffered greatly in comparison with his predecessor, the dynamic Kurt Schumacher, who died suddenly in August 1952. While Ollenhauer deserves some credit for having shepherded the SPD through its difficult adjustment from a class to a Volkspartei in the period preceding Bad Godesberg, it was obvious from the elections of 1953 and 1957 that the SPD needed a much more attractive candidate. The decision to drop Ollenhauer as the party's *Kanzler-kandidat* ("candidate for chancellor"), although not formally announced until 1959, was commonly accepted within the party even at the time of the Stuttgart congress in May 1958.[11]

Helmut Schmidt's popularity, by contrast, had begun to rebound after the 1976 election, and in the period between the Hamburg and Berlin congresses in the late 1970s, the chancellor was far and away the most popular politician in the Federal Republic.[12] Perceptions of

11. In a poll taken in July 1959, shortly after the announcement that Ollenhauer would not be the SPD candidate for chancellor in the next election, respondents were asked whether they welcomed that decision; 39 percent welcomed it, only 9 percent regretted it, while 52 percent were undecided or thought the decision immaterial. See Elisabeth Noelle and Erich Peter Neumann, eds., *The Germans: Public Opinion Polls, 1947–1966* (Allensbach: Institut für Demoskopie, 1967), p. 424.

12. In polls taken in February 1980, for example, respondents were asked to rate various politicians on a scale of −5 to +5. Helmut Schmidt was given a rating of +2.8, compared to Hans-Dietrich Genscher at +1.9, Helmut Kohl at +0.7, Franz Josef Strauss at +0.4, and Willy Brandt at −0.1. See *Die Welt*, March 4, 1980.

Schmidt as a forceful figure in international affairs (aided in part by the success of the hostage rescue operation at Mogadischu in 1978) made him more popular than the SPD. From October 1977 to December 1979, for example, an average of 58 percent of West Germans had a positive opinion of the Schmidt government, whereas the SPD was the preferred choice of only 40 percent of the electorate.[13]

These perceptions of the indispensability of Schmidt to continued SPD electoral success gave the chancellor significant bargaining power in the management of party affairs; this was true first at the Hamburg party congress in 1977, one year after Schmidt's victory in the 1976 election, and to even a greater extent at the 1979 Berlin congress, held nine months before the 1980 election. As we shall see, internal divisions over nuclear weapons issues were much more pronounced at Berlin than at Hamburg, and although Schmidt had to resort to the ultimate threat of resigning as the party's candidate for chancellor if the Berlin congress failed to support his policies, the lack of another viable SPD candidate helped ensure SPD endorsement of the Schmidt government's stand on the INF issue.

Yet Schmidt's popularity as a tool in the management of party affairs was offset somewhat by changes in the leadership structure of the SPD since the days of Ollenhauer. Up until 1959, the party had adhered to the Weimar tradition of naming one man as party chairman, chancellor candidate, and leader of the parliamentary *Fraktion*. When Willy Brandt replaced Ollenhauer as the SPD Kanzlerkandidat in 1959, however, he did not simultaneously become party chairman. Ollenhauer retained that title, albeit in name only, as his function of party leader was increasingly taken over by Deputy Chairman Herbert Wehner. Similarly, the three deputy chairmen of the Fraktion elected at the Stuttgart congress (Fritz Erler, Carlo Schmid, and Wehner), emerged in 1959 as de facto leaders of the Fraktion as Ollenhauer continued to recede into the background.[14]

By the 1970s, the divisions between party chairman, chancellor candidate, and Fraktion leader had become clearly delineated. Herbert Wehner became Fraktion leader, while Brandt, filling the role of elder statesman following his resignation as chancellor in 1974, became party chairman, leaving Schmidt as the party's nominee for

13. See *Frankfurter Allgemeine Zeitung*, March 1, 1980, and Elisabeth Noelle-Neumann, ed., *Allensbacher Jahrbuch der Demoskopie* (Allensbach: Institut für Demoskopie, 1977), p. 124.
14. See especially chap. 6, "The Leadership," in Chalmers, *Social Democratic Party*.

chancellor. Given the duties of running the government, Schmidt by necessity was more attuned to political maneuvering in the bureaucracy and the Fraktion than in the party at large. In addition, Schmidt's political philosophy was more in line with the moderate center of the West German electorate than with the sizable left-wing minority of the SPD. As Schmidt's popularity derived as much from the country at large as from the SPD rank and file, it is not surprising that the chancellor frequently had more trouble within his own party than with his coalition partner, the FDP, or even with the opposition CDU/CSU.

These difficulties were compounded by the division of party leadership among Schmidt, Brandt, and Wehner. Ideologically, Brandt and Wehner were to the left of Schmidt. In the case of Brandt, the former chancellor by the mid-1970s was giving increasing emphasis to many of the policy goals of the SPD left wing, such as calling for a halt to the arms race, criticizing civilian nuclear power, and championing the economic grievances of the Third World. While Brandt was not in full agreement with the party's left-wing faction, he increasingly came to be regarded as a counterweight to Schmidt's more centrist, realpolitik policies.

The situation with Wehner was a bit more complex. A former communist, Wehner was more to the left than Brandt on some issues. However, while ideologically sympathetic to many of the issues put forth by the left wing, Wehner was enough of a practical politician to realize that the sine qua non of SPD success in implementing Social Democratic policies was the retention of governmental power. In his position as Fraktion leader, Wehner was continuously managing the political differences within the SPD parliamentary group, which, as we have noted, were often more extreme than the differences between the Schmidt government and the CDU/CSU. Thus, while Wehner at times was even more outspoken than Brandt in his criticism of Schmidt's policies, he nonetheless put party unity above ideological considerations, especially when it came time for the party congresses to endorse Schmidt's government policy.

THE SPD HAMBURG PARTY CONGRESS

The two main security issues confronting the the SPD party congress in Hamburg in mid-November, 1977 were the interrelated issues of the neutron bomb and the lack of progress at the MBFR talks. As we've seen, Schmidt himself had linked the two issues in the hope of using the threat of ERW deployment in Europe to induce the Soviets to negotiate seriously on conventional forces in Vienna.[15] However, while the chancellor may have entertained hopes of using the neutron bomb as bargaining leverage, the prevailing sentiment at the Hamburg party congress was that ERW deployment by the Alliance could not be countenanced.

The party executive's motion (*Antrag*) number 1, adopted by the congress, called on the government to use its influence to ensure that "technological developments" in atomic weaponry would not lead "to a lowering of the nuclear threshold." Fearful that NATO planners might come to regard neutron warheads as a substitute for the Alliance's deficiencies in conventional forces, the Schmidt government was instructed to make sure that "the deployment of neutron weapons on the territory of the Federal Republic becomes unnecessary."[16] Recalling its commitment from the 1959 Bad Godesberg program to work for the complete elimination of all weapons of "mass destruction," the party congress emphasized that "there are in particular moral arguments, but also military/strategic as well as Alliance and political disarmament arguments, against the development, importation and stationing of neutron weapons."[17]

Other motions put forward by local and regional party organizations also expressed vehement opposition to neutron weapons. One such motion, tabled by the SPD local organization in the Poppelsdorf/Venusberg district of Bonn, summed up the arguments as follows:

1. Politically, the deployment of ERW would exacerbate (*verschärft*) the arms race and endanger the already problematic state of East–West détente.

2. Militarily, neutron weapons would blur (*verwischt*) the firebreak between conventional and nuclear weapons and lower the nuclear threshhold.

15. Alfons Pawelczyk, an SPD spokesman on security issues, wrote in "Neue Kraftprobe," *Der Spiegel*, December 5, 1977, p. 31: "We must attempt to induce the Warsaw Pact to settle the tank superiority in central Europe by the withdrawal of a significant quantity of tanks from this region. Against this we place our renunciation of the development of neutron weapons."

16. See *SPD Parteitag Hamburg, Dokumente: Frieden-Beschlusse zur Aussen-, Friedens-, und Sicherheitspolitik, Europapolitik, Nord-Sud-Politik* (Bonn: Vorstand der SPD, 1977), p. 7 (hereafter *SPD 1977 Congress*).

17. Ibid. p. 7.

3. Morally and juridically, neutron weapons could be compared to chemical weapons in their effects and thus should be subject to constraints such as those imposed on chemical weapons by the 1925 Geneva Protocol, to which, it was noted, the United States is a party.

Echoing Egon Bahr's comment that ERW represent "perverted thinking" (*Perversion des Denkens*), the motion called neutron weapons "a grotesque sadism of military planning."[18]

The general revulsion within the SPD over neutron weapons, as expressed at the Hamburg party congress, is instructive in two respects. First, it was indicative of the widespread negative publicity that the neutron bomb received in Europe following the June 5, 1977, story in the *Washington Post*, and it mirrored prevailing public opinion in the Federal Republic concerning the dangers of deploying such weapons.[19] Second, this revulsion pointed up the difficulties Schmidt would face in having to agree to the weapons' deployment in West Germany before President Carter would agree to full-scale production. Indeed, opposition at the Hamburg party congress to any compromises on the ERW issue was so strong that it took the combined powers of the party leadership, including Brandt, Wehner, and Defense Minister Georg Leber, to ensure that the wording of Antrag 1 was sufficiently flexible to leave the Schmidt government some leeway on the issue in the event that NATO agreed to production and deployment.[20] As we shall see, the chancellor would have to engage in some extensive political arm-twisting before he could be assured of party support in agreeing to ERW deployment. When, in the spring of 1978, he succeeded in getting that support, only to have Carter turn around and announce that Washington was deferring any decision on ERW production, Schmidt felt both aggrieved and betrayed.

The second major security issue addressed at the congress, the MBFR talks, was marked by an urgency similar to that of ERW. The

18. See Antrag 21, titled "No Neutron Warheads on the Territory of the Federal Republic," submitted by Ortsverein Bonn-Poppelsdorf/Venusberg, Bezirk Mittelrhein, in ibid., pp. 14–15. This motion, like others concerning ERW, was not adopted by the party congress as such, but was accepted by the party executive to the extent that it represented the sentiments contained in Antrag 1.

19. In a June 1978 poll, 49 percent of the respondents said they would feel "threatened" by deployment of neutron weapons, while 45 percent said they felt ERW were "protective measures."

20. As reported in *Die Zeit*, the party platform on ERW was essentially a "jein":

Vienna negotiations on conventional forces were stalled by an East–West dispute regarding Warsaw Pact force levels (known as the data-base issue). Within the SPD, there was growing sentiment on the need for a high-level political initiative to break the deadlock. Schmidt himself had sought to provide that initiative through NATO's revised Option III offer and by having the Alliance dangle the carrot of no ERW deployment in return for Soviet acceptance of strict parity of conventional force levels. In support of the chancellor's position, the party executive's security platform noted that the imminent conclusion of a SALT II agreement had given the MBFR talks a "new political quality" and that, in order to arrest the arms race and stabilize the security-political situation in Central Europe at the lowest level, a new political initiative was necessary.[21] A motion tabled by Ortsverein Waldkirch, in Baden-Württemberg, went further, calling on the government to help raise the MBFR talks from the level of experts to the status of "political summit talks" (*politischen spitzengesprächen*),[22] a recommendation that would later be actively pushed by Herbert Wehner.

While the party resolutions on ERW contained an implied criticism of the Carter administration for seeking to foist neutron weapons on the West Europeans, the SPD motions on MBFR were directed as much at Schmidt's coalition partner, the FDP, as at either of the two superpowers. While not explicitly mentioning either the FDP or its leader, Foreign Minister Hans-Dietrich Genscher, several leaders of the SPD, including Wehner and Brandt, felt that Genscher's preoccupation with the data-base problem was unnecessarily holding up the MBFR talks. While Genscher was only supporting a common NATO negotiating position, that reductions to a common ceiling of 700,000 ground troops could be achieved only when the Soviets were more forthcoming about the number of troops they actually had in Eastern Europe, the foreign minister nonetheless served as a lightning rod for left-wing SPD criticism of the two military blocs for failing to implement troop reductions. Perceptions of Genscher as too pro-American and too hard-line vis-à-vis the

---

the delegates could register their opposition to neutron warheads (*nein*), yet not totally foreclose government approval of any future NATO decision (*ja*); see "Neutronenbombe: Eine 'Ideale' Waffen," *Die Zeit*, November 11, 1977.

21. See Antrag 1, *SPD 1977 Congress*, pp. 7–8.

22. See Antrag 2, "Entschliessung," submitted by Ortsverein Waldkirch, Landesverband Baden-Württemburg, in *SPD 1977 Congress*, pp. 8–10.

Soviets made him the bête noire of the SPD left wing and the object of harsh criticism within the party.[23]

Finally, discussion of theater nuclear weapons at the Hamburg congress was, if anything, conspicuous by its absence. Of the various security motions introduced at the Hamburg gathering, only Antrag 1 made mention of the need to include gray-area weapons in the arms control process, and even then, no mention was made of long-range theater nuclear weapons.[24] Elsewhere, however, the arms control process was criticized as being the preserve of the United States, and suggestions were made that the Schmidt government establish an arms control bureau in the chancellery, where it could better monitor arms control talks so as to protect West German interests. One such motion contained an implied criticism of the SALT and MBFR processes when it suggested that the government consider "to what extent NATO can carry the process of military détente, or whether a European context, not parallel to NATO, should be created with the participation of the USA and Canada. Moreover, a national Disarmament Bureau should be created as a necessary instrument for the FRG."[25]

In the deliberations of the Hamburg Parteitag, not only was the issue of theater nuclear weapons very much secondary to those of ERW and MBFR, but also security issues generally took a back seat to the more contentious issues of civilian nuclear power and how the SPD should react to the growing environmental movement in the FRG. Increasingly in the late 1970s, the SPD found itself confronted by the problem of an extraparty environmental movement that threatened to cut into the party's electoral support. While the FDP and the CDU/CSU were similarly challenged, the SPD was most at risk, especially as the Greens evolved from a politically moderate to a left-wing organization and began to make common cause with leftist members of the SPD.[26]

23. For Wehner's especially harsh criticism of Genscher, see *Die Welt*, February 6, 1979.

24. The relevant paragraph in Antrag 1, read: "The SPD observes with growing concern the development of particular nuclear weapons systems that heretofore have not been included in either SALT or MBFR. It emphasizes its demand that arms control negotiations be broadened so as to include this category." See *SPD 1977 Congress*, p. 7.

25. See Antrag 3, "Friedenspolitik," submitted by Kreisverband Freiburg, Landesverband Baden-Württemberg, in *SPD 1977 Congress*," pp. 12–13. Proposals for an arms control office in the chancellery were also included in Antrag 27 and Antrag 29; see pp. 15–16.

26. Nicholas Ziegler, "Die Grünen" (unpublished paper, Harvard University, February 1983).

In a move designed to show its commitment to environmental issues, as well as to co-opt the growing strength of the environmentalists, the SPD in April 1977 issued a resolution, "Energy, Employment and the Quality of Life," which seemed to indicate that the party would come out in favor of a ban on the construction of new civilian nuclear power plants. At the Hamburg congress, however, the moderate wing of the party, backed by the trade union federation (DGB) leadership and the larger individual trade unions, fought back a challenge from the left wing that the party endorse such a moratorium.[27] Despite the outward show of unity forged at the congress, however, the leadership of the party realized that the SPD would continue to face competition from the Greens and a growing split within the party over environmental and security issues.[28] In the end, the SPD was able to paper over its differences and appear united. Forged largely by the combined efforts of Brandt, Wehner, and Schmidt,[29] the alliance was brittle at best, however, and it would be tested as the government was forced to take hard-and-fast decisions on such issues as nuclear power and the neutron bomb.

THE NEUTRON BOMB: DECIDING NOT TO DECIDE

In early 1978, with President Carter willing to announce production of neutron warheads only if the West Europeans committed themselves to deployment, the ERW issue had reached an impasse. In an attempt to end what had become an Alphonse-and-Gaston routine, Carter sent Deputy National Security Adviser David Aaron on a tour of the NATO capitals, but the report the president received in early February was anything but encouraging. Having been told that the Schmidt government would be willing to deploy ERW only if an arms control solution could not be found, and even then only if another European NATO member also agreed to deployment, Carter himself "began to question the advisability of our proceeding with the highly unpopular and very expensive project if it would never be implemented." Writing in his diary, the president complained

27. For more on the role of the trade unions, and especially DGB chief Hans Oskar Vetter, see "Gewerkschaften geben den Ton an," *Die Zeit*, November 18, 1977, p. 4.
28. See "SPD-Parteitag: Angst vor den Grünen," *Der Spiegel*, November 21, 1977.
29. For more on the leadership relationship of Brandt, Wehner, and Schmidt, see "Im Zeichen des Dreigestirns," *Die Zeit*, November 25, 1977, p. 4.

that "the Germans are playing footsie with us on the ER [enhanced radiation] weapons."[30]

Nonetheless, by early March a compromise was being worked out within NATO whereby the United States would announce that it was proceeding with ERW production, yet would defer deployment while trying to reach a successful arms control solution with the Soviets. Unlike the previous autumn, however, when the neutron warhead was seen as providing bargaining leverage at the MBFR talks, now there was talk of seeking a possible trade-off between ERW and Soviet SS-20s, 120 of which were then deployed.[31] This arms control option, supported by the West German foreign ministry and some members of the U.S. State Department, was one indication of the increasing attention Schmidt was beginning to pay to Soviet long-range TNF. The Alliance communiqué scheduled for release on March 20, at the conclusion of a meeting of the NATO Council in Brussels, was to have reflected such a compromise and the desire of the Alliance to pursue an arms control solution covering neutron weapons. Only a day earlier, however, while vacationing on St. Simon's Island off the coast of Georgia, President Carter decided unilaterally to cancel ERW production. Acting against the advice of his three principal national security advisers, Secretary of State Cyrus Vance, Defense Secretary Harold Brown, and National Security Adviser Zbigniew Brzezinski, Carter decided, seemingly for moralistic reasons, to cancel the neutron bomb and ignore the NATO compromise formula. Word was sent to Brussels to drop any reference to ERW in the statement to be issued on March 20; the excuse given was that the administration was too preoccupied by problems in the Mideast to give its approval to the ERW compromise. Schmidt learned of Carter's decision on March 31, when he met with Deputy Secretary of State Warren Christopher in Hamburg.[32]

When news of his decision became public in early April, Carter was immediately criticized not only by the allies, for having undermined a NATO position, but by his own advisers, the U.S. military, and Congress as well. Indeed, this criticism was so widespread that the

30. Jimmy Carter, *Keeping Faith: Memoirs of a President* (New York: Bantam, 1982), pp. 226–227.

31. As reported in the *New York Times*, April 4, 1978, p. 4, this compromise entailed a U.S. decision to begin ERW production, with a two-year deferral of deployment while "testing Moscow's reaction to limiting it in return for restrictions on the new SS-20 missile."

32. See especially the insightful article by Lothar Ruehl, "Ein Lehrstuck der Verworrenheit," *Die Zeit*, April 14, 1978, p. 3.

president was soon reported to be backing away from his position, at least to the extent of deciding to defer, not cancel, ERW production, in the hope of "inducing restraints" by the Soviets.[33] Yet the president's announcement on April 7 that he would only defer ERW production, leaving the door open to future production and deployment if the Soviets failed to come up with a suitable quid pro quo, did little to repair the damage already done. If anything, Carter compounded his reputation for unreliability, first by circumventing an Alliance position and then by reversing his own decision.[34] To make matters worse, there was widespread skepticism, both in Washington and throughout the Alliance, concerning the likelihood that the Soviets would see fit to offer anything in return for a U.S. decision merely to defer ERW production.[35]

Following Carter's announcement, the Schmidt government introduced a resolution in the Bundestag supporting the president's position. Foreign Minister Genscher called for a demonstration of bipartisanship in backing the president's attempts at arms control, while the opposition leaders, Helmut Kohl of the CDU and Strauss of the CSU, criticized the Schmidt government for not having agreed to ERW deployment so as to make Carter's production decision easier. In the end, the government's resolution passed 240 to 225, with the votes split along party lines.[36] Carter noted in his diary on April 13, the day of the Bundestag debate: "Chancellor Schmidt reported to me that he had gotten a 16-vote [sic] majority on the neutron bomb decision, approving both his and my position. Although this seems like a narrow margin to me, he was quite proud of it, and said the debate went well—there was no harsh criticism compared to what he had anticipated, and that the whole debate underlined the need for continued German–U.S. friendship."[37]

Although the Schmidt government resolution was not, strictly speaking, an endorsement for deploying ERW on West German

33. *New York Times*, April 5, 6, and 8, 1978.

34. In a satirical piece titled "Die Carterbombe" ("The Carter bomb") in *Die Zeit* on April 14, 1978, columnist Wolfgang Ebert answered his own rhetorical question, "What really makes this bomb so explosive?": "Its incalculability. It explodes one time here, and one time there . . . and makes absolutely no distinction between friend and foe."

35. A few weeks before, the Soviets themselves had ruled out any quid pro quo for a NATO decision to cancel ERW production; for a report on the Tass announcement, see *Times* (London), March 13, 1978.

36. *Süddeutsche Zeitung*, April 14, 1978.

37. Carter, *Keeping Faith*, p. 228.

soil,[38] the chancellor had nonetheless made known his government's willingness to agree to the NATO formula that Carter had blocked. Before the president's surprise announcement, the Federal Security Council in Bonn had endorsed a three-pronged approach concerning ERW and arms control, consisting of the alternatives of linking reductions of neutron warheads to reductions of Soviet troops in Eastern Europe; agreeing to only limited deployment of ERW in return for Soviet tank reductions; or trading a renunciation of ERW in return for a dismantling of the SS-20. As we have seen, officials in the West German foreign ministry favored the third approach, but met resistance from the White House, which opposed any trade-off of ERW for the SS-20 for fear of complicating the SALT talks, which President Carter was eager to conclude. Once again, Schmidt was made aware of the condominium aspects of superpower arms control and that Europe's concerns would have to take a back seat to U.S. and USSR interests, at least until SALT III.

The ERW episode was instructive as well for pointing up the misperceptions between Washington and Bonn, and for demonstrating Schmidt's growing concern with Soviet theater nuclear forces. In regard to the former, there were two main points the Carter administration failed to understand in its attempts to get the Schmidt government to agree to deployment before a production decision.

First, as Schmidt made clear in his address to the Bundestag on April 13, the 1954 prohibitions on West German control of nuclear weapons, plus Bonn's ratification of the 1969 Non-Proliferation Treaty, made it difficult for any West German government, over and above domestic political considerations, to be in the position of supplicant, of having to ask the United States to begin producing a particular nuclear weapon. Schmidt noted that

> The Federal Government has from the time of Chancellor Adenauer solemnly pledged itself to the renunciation of nuclear weapons. Any participation in the decision of a nuclear weapons state over the production of neutron weapons, for example, [or] over the production of nuclear weapons in general, would go against all previous practice in assigning to the Federal Republic, which is not a nuclear weapons state, a share of the decision over the production of nuclear weapons.

38. In a strict sense, President Carter was correct when he noted in his memoirs, "The fact is that to this day no European government has been willing to agree to their [ERW] deployment." See ibid., pp. 228–229.

Therefore any production decision must remain a sovereign decision of the United States of America.[39]

When Alois Mertes, foreign policy spokesman of the CDU, interrupted to say that Schmidt was engaging in semantics, the chancellor responded from the podium, "There are some, whom I know, who would like to have it otherwise. I have no desire to associate with them; I do not want to permit this impression [to enter] into relations with our Western friends and Alliance partners."[40]

While the argument of Mertes and the CDU/CSU that West Germany's agreement to deploy neutron weapons did not constitute a production decision was essentially correct, it ignored an important point. Given that neutron weapons were generally recognized as having few applications outside the European theater, and given that it made little military sense to station ERW anywhere but West Germany, a request by Bonn that Washington begin producing the weapons could certainly be viewed by the Soviets as constituting West German involvement in the production decision itself, and thus would constitute an abrogation of Bonn's obligations under the 1954 London and Paris Accords. Moreover, the very fact that NATO would have difficuly finding another country in which to station ERW pointed up the second issue the Carter administration failed to comprehend in pushing the FRG to ask for ERW production—that of nonsingularity.

Precisely because the Federal Republic is constrained by treaty from producing or controlling nuclear weapons, successive West German governments, whether SPD or CDU/CSU, have insisted that NATO deployment of U.S. nuclear weapons be an Alliance-wide affair. To avoid any impression of a U.S.–West German special relationship within the Alliance, especially on nuclear weapons matters, governments in Bonn have continually demanded that the FRG not be asked to deploy particular nuclear weapons that other NATO countries are not willing to deploy as well. As Schmidt noted in his Bundestag speech, his government had for months made it known not only that any decision to deploy ERW would have to be an Alliance-wide decision, but that West Germany could not be

39. For the complete text of the Bundestag debate, see *Deutscher Bundestag, Stenographischer Berichte*, 83 Sitzung, April 13, 1978 (hereafter *Bundestag ERW Debate*), p. 6502.

40. *Bundestag ERW Debate*, p. 6502.

[101]

placed in the position of being the only NATO country to deploy them. Yet Schmidt was aware as well that, with the possible exception of Italy, there were no other NATO countries where it made either military or political sense to deploy neutron weapons. The two "front-line" states on NATO's southern flank where ERW would be militarily available on a time-urgent basis were Greece and Turkey, and political tensions between the two ruled out any consideration of their receiving neutron weapons. As for Holland and Belgium, strong political opposition to ERW made them unlikely choices for deployment. Given that Denmark and Norway prohibit the stationing of nuclear weapons on their territory, while Britain was far removed from the central front, only Italy was left as a possible candidate, and even here, the deployment of neutron warheads was militarily questionable.[41] Schmidt realized that even if the Alliance as a whole decided to proceed with deployment, it would have difficulty finding other countries besides the FRG in which to deploy them. This was reason enough for Schmidt to be concerned about being put in the position of supplicant and for his stressing the point that any production decision must be a sovereign decision taken by Washington.

These issues, that Washington alone must decide to produce a particular nuclear weapon before NATO could consider deployment and that deployment itself must involve not only the FRG but at least one other non-nuclear state as well, were only two of the sticking points complicating NATO's handling of the ERW affair. In addition, the Schmidt government stressed the relationship of nuclear weapons modernization to arms control and the relationship of both to the military balance in Europe. All these issues that appeared in the ERW deliberations would surface again in NATO deliberations over INF.

In his address to the Bundestag on April 13, 1978, the chancellor made very clear his preference for the sequence of events to be followed concerning ERW: (1) a unilateral production decision by the United States; (2) the attempt at an arms control solution; and (3) if no arms control solution were forthcoming within two years, then the FRG would be willing to station neutron weapons, provided the Alliance decided such deployment was necessary and provided another NATO country also deployed ERW.[42] Not surprisingly, Schmidt

41. Surprisingly, Ruehl lists the difficulties of stationing ERW in countries other than West Germany, but doesn't mention Italy; see his "Ein Lehrstuck der Verworrenheit."
42. *Bundestag ERW Debate*, p. 6502.

was to demand a similar sequence of events for INF just a year later.

The other important point brought out by the ERW affair, aside from deepening suspicions within the Alliance over the steadiness of American leadership, was Schmidt's growing concern with Soviet theater nuclear forces. In his speeches in London in 1977 Schmidt had focused mainly on the modernization of Soviet conventional forces, but now he began to emphasize Soviet intermediate-range nuclear systems as a primary cause for concern. In his Bundestag speech the chancellor once again referred to his concern with "the shifting of the military balance of power in favor of the Warsaw Pact in Europe" and added that, if parity could not be restored through arms control, then the NATO Alliance would have to take steps in both the conventional and nuclear fields to protect its security.[43] Later in his speech Schmidt referred to both the SS-20 and the Backfire bomber when he noted: "We are concerned in several areas with the increase in the numerical superiority of the Warsaw Pact. This applies to the increased numbers of tanks as well as to the completion and the modernization of Soviet middle-range missiles and middle-range aircraft."[44]

After mentioning both MBFR and SALT as useful instruments for reestablishing a military Gleichgewicht through arms control, Schmidt reiterated his concern that such gray-area weapons as the SS-20 and Backfire be included in the arms control process: "We trust that European security interests will be protected in SALT, and built upon, and secured through close consultation with the United States of America. We consider it important, in this regard, that the existing disparity in the middle-range sphere will be considered in these negotiations."[45]

Finally, Schmidt caustically criticized the Soviet Union for having mounted a concerted campaign against the production of neutron weapons and their deployment in Europe while the Warsaw Pact was introducing new longer-range nuclear weapons systems.[46] When Leonid Brezhnev visited Bonn some three weeks later for summit talks with Schmidt, the chancellor used the occasion to criticize the Soviets again for continued increases in their nuclear and conventional military buildup. As expected, however, Brezhnev felt little obliged to offer anything in return for NATO's decision to defer

43. Ibid., p. 6501.
44. Ibid., p. 6503.
45. Ibid., p. 6503.
46. Ibid., p. 6502.

production of the neutron bomb. The most the Soviet leader was prepared to concede was that as long as the West refrained from injecting this "dangerous new element" into the arms race, then the Soviet Union would show similar restraint.[47] Coming just a month after Carter's hesitation on ERW, Brezhnev's remarks made it clear that the Alliance could expect to gain little leverage, either in the MBFR talks or over the SS-20, with the neutron warhead.

By and large, the Brezhnev-Schmidt summit was an uneventful affair, with little in the way of expectations or results.[48] Although the two leaders did sign a twenty-five-year economic agreement, this document was mainly a codification of existing trade relations, representing the desire of both parties to have the summit produce something concrete. However, Schmidt did succeed in having the joint communiqué endorse the concept of military parity, and the chancellor would later accuse the Soviets of having violated the spirit of the communiqué through their continued deployment of the SS-20. In linking the importance of military parity to the continuation of détente, the FRG and the USSR agreed that: "neither should seek military superiority. They proceed from the assumption that approximate equality and parity suffice for the maintenance of defense. In their opinion, suitable measures of disarmament and arms limitation in the nuclear and conventional spheres, which this principle expresses, are of great importance."[49]

In 1981, when the Alliance came under increasing Soviet criticism for proceeding with INF modernization and arms control, Schmidt would point to the Soviet "disregard" of the May 1978 communiqué as one justification for Alliance deployment of INF.

NATO and INF Modernization

The denouement of the neutron bomb affair in April 1978, unsatisfactory from almost every point of view, was a critical way station on the road to the Alliance's December 1979 decision to modernize INF. Within the Carter administration, it was recognized that the president had stumbled badly; in effect, Carter had pushed the West

47. *New York Times*, May 5, 1978.
48. See "Gespräche an Rhein und Elbe ohne Konkrete Ergebnisse," *Süddeutsche Zeitung*, May 8, 1978.
49. For the text of the communiqué, see ibid.

Europeans out onto a limb in getting them to agree to the NATO ERW compromise, only to saw the limb off behind them by his unilateral decision to cancel ERW production.[50] Although Carter reversed himself, announcing that he would defer ERW production instead of canceling the project outright, the damage had been done. The president had blocked an emerging NATO compromise, and the Alliance had lost whatever bargaining leverage it might have hoped for from ERW, as Brezhnev made clear during his visit to Bonn. For Schmidt, who had leaned on his party's left wing to keep them in line behind his government's position, Carter's action further diminished his own credibility and reinforced the chancellor's belief that the Carter administration little understood the constraints of West European domestic politics on NATO security policy. If there was any common denominator to come out of the ERW affair, it was that the Alliance would have to ensure that, when it came to future NATO nuclear weapons issues, the same mistake wasn't made twice. Above all, the feeling persisted that any decision on theater nuclear weapons would have to demonstrate a strong U.S. leadership, which had been sorely lacking during the neutron weapon affair.[51]

In June, as a first step in demonstrating U.S. resolve, the president created an interagency group to review NATO theater nuclear weapons and produce a study known as PRM-38, "Long-Range Theater Nuclear Capabilities and Arms Control." The group was charged with developing recommendations that the United States could take to NATO's High Level Group. The workings of this interagency group demonstrate how, given a strong presidential initiative, the

50. What made Carter's decision to cancel ERW production even worse, to some Europeans, was that the president had resisted the advice of his national security advisers, relying instead on Hamilton Jordan, his White House chief of staff, and U.N. Ambassador Andrew Young, two men with little experience in Alliance affairs; see *New York Times*, April 8, 1978.

51. As a U.S. House of Representatives report noted, "In the case of the United States, the INF decision became a test of American leadership within the alliance. Given perceptions of American vacillation and uncertainty in other fields and the legacy of the ERW episode, INF modernization was viewed as an opportunity for the United States to demonstrate its ability to lead the alliance, particularly in the crucial area of nuclear weaponry, and for the alliance to show its ability to respond to this leadership." See *The Modernization of NATO's Long-Range Theater Nuclear Forces*, report prepared for the U.S. House Committee on Foreign Affairs, Subcommittee on Europe and the Middle East (Washington, D.C.: U.S. Government Printing Office, 1980), p. 27.

White House can mobilize the disparate elements of the bureaucracy to reach a timely and comprehensive consensus.[52] By October, the PRM-38 working group had developed a series of recommendations, which the HLG then considered during its meetings of November 1978 and February 1979.

Before examining these HLG deliberations in greater detail, I must mention two other issues, both related to SALT, which affected West European considerations of theater nuclear forces. The first, that of the noncircumvention/nontransfer provisions, was in the process of being resolved by the summer of 1978. As we have noted, the United States and the Soviets had agreed in April 1978 to adopt the "fallback" version of the noncircumvention clause, which restricted the ability of the United States to provide its NATO allies with new weapons, such as cruise missiles. While accepting this provision, U.S. negotiators made it clear to the Soviets that Washington did not consider it to prohibit the ultimate deployment of cruise missiles in Europe once the protocol expired in December 1981. In consultation with West German officials, the Carter administration developed a unilateral interpretive statement to that effect and was ultimately able to assuage West European fears that SALT II would impair the Alliance's ability to modernize its theater nuclear forces.[53]

The second issue, the vulnerability of U.S. ICBMs, was also an outgrowth of the SALT negotiations, and was not so easily handled. Indeed, American critics attacked the SALT II treaty for allowing the Soviets to retain a heavy ICBM (the SS-18) that theoretically could threaten the ICBM leg of the U.S. triad (land- and sea-based missiles and long-range bombers), and this criticism continued long after SALT II was dead. In the summer of 1978, however, a growing debate in the United States over Minuteman vulnerability was reinforcing concern in Western Europe over the possibility that in any future conflict, the United States might find itself deterred from coming to Europe's defense by this growth in Soviet strategic forces. It was precisely this concern that Schmidt had articulated at the NATO summit in London in May 1977. While the issue of ICBM

52. In a story titled "A New Soviet Threat to Europe Spurs U.S. Decision on Missiles," Richard Burt reported that after Schmidt talked to Carter regarding a NATO response to the SS-20 at the NATO summit in May, the president ordered the interagency study to be completed within six months. See *New York Times*, July 29, 1978.

53. David Schwartz, "U.S. Policy and NATO's Strategic Dilemma" (Ph.D. thesis, Massachusetts Institute of Technology, 1980), pp. 391–392.

vulnerability is complex and contentious, and outside the scope of this study, the criticism by many American defense analysts of SALT II for supposedly allowing Soviet SS-18s to threaten an entire component of U.S. strategic forces was bound to have spillover effects in Europe. As one commentator put it, "the vulnerability of Minuteman feeds European concern over the implications of parity, psychologically if not analytically, by suggesting another reason for American caution if Europe alone is attacked by Soviet nuclear weapons."[54] Paradoxically, the Carter administration's solution to the vulnerability "problem,"—to develop the MX missile and deploy it in a mobile mode—made the problem worse, if anything, at least from the West European perspective. Given the difficulties the administration faced in 1979 and 1980 in first deciding upon a basing mode and then gaining domestic support for that plan, many Europeans rightly wondered why they should accept mobile basing of cruise missiles and the Pershing II when so many Americans were reluctant to accept a similar scheme for the new MX.

In the meantime, however, the Carter administration labored over the summer of 1978 to develop a consensus within the U.S. government on how NATO should deal with the theater nuclear force issue. By the end of the summer, agreement had been reached that, for political and military reasons, NATO should adopt a deployment and arms control option with which to counter the Soviet buildup of the SS-20. At the same time, however, any attempt to establish parity in Euro-strategic weapons was rejected, as such an effort might open the way for perceptions of decoupling, which had prompted concern over the INF issue in the first place.[55] In carrying the U.S. proposals to the HLG in the fall of 1978, McGiffert laid out the various choices open to the Alliance for modernizing its nuclear forces, including the following weapons systems: the ground-launched cruise missile, a modernized version of the Pershing IA (the Pershing II XR) with increased accuracy and extended range; a new medium-range ballistic missile (MRBM), called Longbow, which would utilize the existing Minuteman Mark 12A warhead; sea-launched cruise missiles (SLCMs); and the FB-111H, an improved version of the

54. Gregory Treverton, "Nuclear Weapons and the 'Gray Area,'" *Foreign Affairs* 57 (Summer 1979): 1077.

55. There were, however, some recommendations for deploying an INF force that would more than match the number of SS-20 warheads aimed at Western Europe. A report prepared by the Defense Science Board for Secretary Brown recommended the deployment of 2000 cruise missiles. See Lothar Ruehl, "Bummelraketen für Europa," *Die Zeit*, August 11, 1978.

FB-111A based in the United States. In considering these choices, the HLG was working by early 1979 under the following guidelines:[56]

1. Intermediate-range nuclear force modernization should not entail any increase in the role of nuclear weapons in Allied defense or any change in the strategy of flexible response.

2. There should be no change in the overall total of nuclear weapons in Western Europe.

3. There was no need for a direct matching capability to the SS-20; instead, the Alliance should create an offsetting capability that provided a "credible response."

4. The weapon systems themselves should have as much visibility as possible to enhance the force's deterrent value (thus a preference for land-based systems).

5. The weapons systems should strive for survivability (by mobility for example), penetrability, and accuracy.

6. There should be a mix of systems, for "synergistic" effect (e.g., to complicate Soviet defense planning and increase NATO targeting options).

Given these guidelines, it soon became apparent which systems were preferable. By a process of elimination, the lack of visibility (and thus tangible evidence of political commitment) of the sea-based systems militated against the SLCM.[57] As the FB-111H and the Longbow would not be operational until the mid-1980s, the need for a timely response argued against these systems. Thus by the spring of 1979 it was becoming apparent that the preferred systems were the GLCM and the Pershing II XR, and although a general range of 200 to 600 systems was being discussed, it would be several more months before an exact number could be agreed upon.

While the HLG was discussing various weapons systems and deployment schemes, less attention was being paid to the political and arms control implications of these weapons. Although the HLG was proceeding from the assumption that the Alliance would have to decide on deployments before the Soviets could be expected to

56. Klaas de Vries, *General Report on the Security of the Alliance—The Role of Nuclear Weapons*, report to the Military Committee of the North Atlantic Assembly (Brussels: NATO, November 1979), pp. 9–10.

57. Schwartz notes, "Interestingly enough, the option of an SLCM-based MLF force was once raised, in which a fleet of SLCM-carrying submarines would be multinationally manned, owned and operated; however, those who had lived through the MLF controversy were appalled at the suggestion, and even those who had not were aware of the unpleasant precedent, so the option was quickly dropped." See his "U.S. Policy," p. 409.

negotiate reductions in the SS-20, a gap was growing in late 1978 between the modernization and arms control components of the HLG deliberations. As Gregory Treverton has noted, "force planning in the HLG first lagged behind, then ran well ahead of arms control thinking. By 1979 there was the impression, most telling in the Federal Republic, that NATO was on the verge of deploying new weapons in Europe capable of striking the Soviet Union with little evidence of having analyzed arms control prospects or the impact of new Western weaponry on East–West relations."[58] Although preliminary discussions on arms control within the Alliance were being held by late 1978, many West European officials felt that NATO would have to examine its arms control options thoroughly and attempt to mobilize public support for its INF decision, especially given the recent neutron bomb experience. Accordingly, discussion within the Alliance in the autumn of 1978 focused on the desirability of setting up a new group, distinct from the HLG, to formulate arms control guidelines. During meetings of the NATO permanent representatives in October and November, preliminary plans were laid for the creation of the Special Group on Arms Control and Related Matters, which came into being in the spring of 1979.[59]

However, despite the progress being made in NATO and the various national bureaucracies in formulating a two-track decision on INF which would include both modernization and arms control, there was concern that not enough had been done to ensure that the ERW experience was not repeated. President Carter felt the West Europeans should first commit themselves to deploying INF before NATO made a formal decision, while Schmidt especially wanted reassurance that INF arms control would be seriously pursued. In

58. Gregory Treverton, "Long-Range Nuclear Weapons in Europe: The Choices," paper given at a conference, "New Approaches to Arms Control," sponsored by the International Institute for Strategic Studies, Great Windsor Park, England, May 16–18, 1979, p. 49. In 1977–78, Treverton was a staff member for Western European affairs on the National Security Council, and participated in the drafting of PRM 38.

59. According to an interview with one NATO official, the United States, contrary to press reports, did not drag its feet on arms control and fully supported the creation of the Special Group (SG). However, this official also noted that the United States did not want to be in the position of asking for the chairmanship of the SG, even though it would be the United States that negotiated INF limitations with the Soviets. In the end, political sensibilities were respected when the West German ambassador to NATO, Rolf Pauls, formally asked the United States to assume the chairmanship of the SG in early 1979. See also *Frankfurter Allgemeine Zeitung*, April 12, 1979, and Stephen Hanmer, "NATO's Long-Range Theater Nuclear Forces: Modernization in Parallel with Arms Control," *NATO Review* 28 (February 1980).

addition, the chancellor reiterated that, as with ERW, domestic political constraints meant that the FRG could not be the only non-nuclear NATO state asked to deploy INF. Following discussions with Schmidt, British Prime Minister James Callaghan, and French President Valéry Giscard d'Estaing in October 1978, National Security Adviser Brzezinski came away with the feeling that "what was striking in all three places was the degree to which gray areas issue [sic] is likely to become a major problem in alliance relationships in the 1980s... The more we can talk to them about it at the highest level, the better."[60]

Accordingly, Carter met with Schmidt, Callaghan, and Giscard d'Estaing on the island of Guadeloupe on January 5–6, 1979, for a wide-ranging discussion of Western security issues.[61] Although no concrete decisions were made regarding INF, this meeting did take up some of the slack left over from official NATO deliberations in giving the four leaders a chance to discuss INF modernization, the need to include INF in SALT III, and European concerns with SALT II. In the end, Carter was able to reassure his European counterparts that SALT II would not constrain NATO theater nuclear force modernization, while Schmidt and Callaghan for their part issued strong statements supporting SALT II ratification.[62] In addition, Schmidt seems to have convinced Carter of the need for NATO to create a formal body within the Alliance (the Special Group) that would prepare INF arms control options the way the High Level Group was considering modernization options.[63]

Nonetheless, Carter came away from the meeting with the same feeling he had had during the ERW affair: that no European member of NATO was willing to deploy new nuclear systems. According to the president, "Helmut was very contentious, insisting that he would permit the deployment of additional missiles on his soil only when other European nations agreed to similar arrangements. I

60. Zbigniew Brzezinski, *Power and Principle: Memoirs of the National Security Advisor, 1977–1981* (New York: Farrar, Straus, Giroux, 1983), p. 294.

61. Brzezinski notes that the initiative for the four-power meeting, the first such summit among the United States, United Kingdom, France, and West Germany to cover global affairs and not just issues pertaining to Germany and Berlin, came from Schmidt; see ibid., pp. 294–295. Schmidt, however, maintains the initiative came from President Carter; see his *Menschen und Mächte* (Berlin: Siedler, 1987), pp. 231–234. Whoever proposed the conference, one unfortunate by-product was that Italian Prime Minister Francesco Cossiga made known his displeasure at not being included.

62. *Christian Science Monitor*, January 6, 1979, p. 3.

63. Interviews with NATO officials, summer 1980.

replied that Helmut had initiated this entire discussion of a European nuclear imbalance, and that we must have German willingness to deploy these missiles in order to negotiate successfully with the Soviets . . . . [The] conversation was obviously inconclusive."[64] In his memoirs, Brzezinski is equally critical of Schmidt, noting that, where "Giscard was clear, to the point, and quite decisive," and Callaghan "displayed good political sense," Schmidt "was the one who was most concerned about the Soviet nuclear threat in Europe and the least inclined to agree to any firm response. He kept saying that he has a political problem and that he is not in a position to make any commitments."[65]

Just how severe a political problem Schmidt was facing would become clearer in a few weeks, when Herbert Wehner initiated a full Bundestag debate on the dangers of proceeding with INF modernization without paying sufficient attention to arms control. Even in late 1978, however, the chancellor was aware that the left wing of his party, under the direction of Willy Brandt, Egon Bahr, and Wehner, was seeking to develop a new, more political concept of arms control. As reported in *Der Spiegel*, Wehner continued to criticize current arms control efforts as being the "domain of specialists," while Brandt argued that arms control is "no more and no less a political partnership for the protection of peace."[66] In seeking a new strategy that would end the arms race and enhance the party's electoral appeal, especially among the young, both men stressed the need to divert funds from defense to development projects in the Third World and the opportunities that successful arms control might provide to create a new European security system that would not only supersede NATO and the Warsaw Pact, but even allow for consideration of the German question.

At the same time, the SPD left wing was restating its opposition to the Schmidt government's nuclear power policies. Although Schmidt had been able to deflect such opposition at the Hamburg party congress in 1977, the left wing was preparing to reopen the issue at the upcoming party congress in Berlin in December 1979. Indeed, given the growing electoral appeal of the Green movement and other environmental groups in the latter half of 1978, it was apparent that the Schmidt government would be facing more opposition to its civilian nuclear power policies than to its nuclear weapons

64. Carter, *Keeping Faith*, p. 235.
65. Brzezinski, *Power and Principle*, p. 295.
66. *Der Spiegel*, November 27, 1978.

policies. In state elections in Lower Saxony and Hamburg in June 1978, the environmentalists and their allies took enough votes away from the FDP, Schmidt's coalition partner in Bonn, to eliminate the liberals from both state parliaments.[67] This growing electoral pressure from the Greens, which not only threatened to cut into the SPD vote but could jeopardize the very existence of the SPD/FDP government in the 1980 election, ensured that the debate over how the SPD should react to the environmental movement would be repeated at the Berlin party congress.

What was not yet evident was the extent to which the civilian nuclear power opposition and any nuclear weapons opposition might coalesce. In early 1979, the Greens were concentrating primarily on nuclear power and other ecological issues, while the nuclear weapons debate remained primarily an internal SPD affair. This inattention on the part of the Greens to nuclear weapons issues can be explained in part by President Carter's decision to defer production of the neutron weapon and by the fact that the INF issue was still an internal NATO affair. Moreover, civilian nuclear power was primarily a domestic issue (although with some international ramifications—for example, the dependence of FRG nuclear energy companies on exports), in comparison with the Alliance issue of INF, and thus of more immediate relevance in West German domestic politics. Just two months after the Guadeloupe summit, however, the initiation of a full-scale Bundestag debate over INF heightened the visibility of the INF issue for the West German public. Although the INF debate throughout 1979 would remain primarily an issue of party, and parliamentary, politics, culminating in the December SPD party congress, the growing attention paid by the media to the INF issue indicated that the Alliance's nuclear weapons policies would not long remain a matter of purely internal concern.

The SPD Berlin Party Congress

Few SPD party congresses in the postwar period have been as politically significant as the one held in West Berlin December 3–7,

---

67. In Lower Saxony, the Green list won 3.9 percent of the vote, while the FDP dropped to 4.2 percent, below the 5 percent necessary to retain representation in the Landtag (Parliament); in Schmidt's native Hamburg, candidates from both the Greens and the communist-dominated Bunte Liste (Colored list) won a combined 4.5 percent of the vote, while the FDP won 4.8 percent; see *New York Times*, August 16, 1978.

1979. Although by the end of the congress Schmidt and the party leadership were able to win endorsement of the government's policies, especially on the contentious issues of nuclear weapons and nuclear power, much maneuvering and compromise were necessary to gain that endorsement. Indeed, Schmidt ultimately felt compelled to threaten to resign as the party's candidate for chancellor in the 1980 election in order to maintain party unity. Though he won party endorsement of his policies, however, Schmidt was faced with a growing opposition within the SPD which would ultimately contribute to the breakup of the SPD/FDP coalition in 1982.

The extraordinary contentiousness of the Berlin meeting can be traced to several factors. Far and away the most important was the way in which the growth of the Greens and other environmental organizations was exacerbating traditional divisions within the party between the moderate/social democratic and left/socialist wings. As we saw earlier, an appropriate response to the Greens had been much debated at the 1977 Hamburg party congress, when the left wing pushed the environmentalists' call for a moratorium on the construction of new nuclear power plants. The success of the Greens in the Hamburg and Lower Saxony state elections in June 1978 only added to the electoral pressure felt by the SPD.

Similarly, the upcoming 1980 national election and growing divisions within the Schmidt–Genscher government fueled the party debate at the Berlin congress. Domestically, a slowdown in West German economic growth was sharpening the policy debate within the government over possible cutbacks in social welfare spending. Economics Minister Otto Graf Lambsdorff of the FDP was especially criticized by the SPD left wing, advocating as he was the need for government retrenchment in the face of mounting public sector deficits and unemployment compensation. On foreign policy and defense issues, the pro-American stance of Foreign Minister Hans-Dietrich Genscher was seen by the SPD left as jeopardizing the country's Ostpolitik, especially as East–West relations were beginning to deteriorate.

Finally, there was the personality of Schmidt himself, who was seen as too moderate by the left wing, which continued to look to Willy Brandt for ideological guidance. For many party members, Schmidt's role in the NATO INF issue was at odds with an arms control strategy that the left wing had been developing since 1978. As formulated by Brandt, Bahr, and such younger SPD leaders as Alfons Pawelczyk, Karsten Voigt, and Horst Ehmke, a new political

[113]

emphasis on arms control, which the SPD left wing hoped would find support among younger voters in the 1980 election, was predicated in part on the view that previous U.S.-Soviet arms control efforts had not curtailed the arms race, but merely transformed a quantitative competition into a qualitative one.[68]

In regard to INF specifically, many in the SPD questioned the Schmidt government's description of the NATO modernization plan as only a response to Soviet deployment of the SS-20 (the standard government characterization was that of *Nachrüstung*, or "counter-armament"). Karsten Voigt argued that in fact the Pershing IIA and the cruise missiles represented an upward twist in the technological arms spiral and that deployment of such systems would undoubtedly force the Soviets to respond with a successor to the SS-20. Voigt was particularly concerned with the increased accuracies of the Pershing and cruise missiles, saying that the INF systems represented a "military response on a different, and indeed qualitatively higher technological level."[69]

In the weeks before the Berlin party congress, Brandt and others were urging that NATO defer an actual deployment decision until 1983 or 1984, when arms control efforts with the Soviets had been pursued and when the NATO systems themselves were capable of being deployed.[70] As Wehner had argued during the Bundestag debates the previous March, NATO should adopt a "negotiate first, deploy later" strategy. In part, the SPD left wing rejected the "bargaining chip" theory that the Soviets would not negotiate seriously unless the Alliance made a firm decision on production and deployment. In addition, many in the party warned of the dangers of "automaticity": the Alliance, they feared, having made a firm commitment to begin deployment by the end of 1983, would proceed with that deployment, regardless of the state of INF arms control negotiations. Finally, there was growing support within the party for committing the SPD to the ideal of the Zero Solution

68. In line with left-wing views that the North–South conflict represented a potentially explosive threat to global security, Alfons Pawelczyk described the need for diverting some of the $400 billion spent annually on armaments to Third World development aid. As he described it, "Security funds saved will remain security funds." See *Der Spiegel*, November 27, 1978.

69. See Voigt's "Schrittweiser Aussteig aus dem Rüstungswettlauf: Nach dem Berliner Parteitag der SPD," in *Neue Gesellschaft*, January 1980.

70. *Der Spiegel*, December 10, 1979.

(*Null-Lösung*): a successful outcome of arms control talks which would obviate the need for any INF deployment at all.[71]

As Alfons Pawelczyk noted, disagreement within the party on the INF issue centered on three key questions: (1) Was the NATO double-track decision, including a decision to deploy INF, a necessary precondition for successful INF negotiations, or would it in fact hinder or perhaps even block them? (2) Was the Zero Solution possible when the decision was taken not only to produce INF but also to deploy them? (3) Would such a decision to deploy INF lead to their automatic stationing, regardless of the state of negotiations in 1983?[72]

In addition to these three issues, there was the complicating factor of SALT II and the relationship of INF arms control negotiations with strategic arms talks between the superpowers. The Gaudeloupe summit had produced agreement between Schmidt and Carter that the chancellor would actively support SALT II in return for the president's commitment to INF arms control. By the fall of 1979, when the issue of the Soviet brigade in Cuba was delaying U.S. Senate consideration of the SALT treaty,[73] many in the Schmidt government and in the SPD were drawing an ever-tighter connection between the two, saying that Senate ratification of SALT II was a necessary precondition for NATO's adoption of the INF package. In October, FRG Defense Minister Hans Apel appeared before the Senate Foreign Relations Committee to reaffirm West German support for SALT II. In private conversations with Carter administration officials, however, Apel warned of the consequences for the NATO INF decision should the Senate fail to ratify SALT. When word

71. Unlike the Zero Option adopted by President Reagan in November 1981, the SPD Zero Solution did not explicitly specify that the Soviets would have to dismantle all of their intermediate-range missiles in return for no NATO deployment of Pershing and cruise missiles.

72. Alfons Pawelczyk, "Sicherheitspolitik im Rahmen der Friedenspolitik," *Neue Gesellschaft* (January 1980); Pawelczyk took the title of his article from the security platform of the West Berlin party congress.

73. Following the disclosure, in late August, of the presence of a Soviet "combat" brigade in Cuba, Senator Frank Church announced that the Senate Foreign Relations Committee was suspending hearings on SALT II so that the committee could hold closed-door hearings on the Soviet brigade issue. See *New York Times*, September 5, 1979. Church, who was facing a difficult reelection campaign in Idaho (he ultimately lost), had been fed the news about the Soviet brigade by the Carter administration, apparently so that Church could toughen his image. The issue ultimately turned out to be much ado about nothing, leading to the joke that "it was the first time a born-again Baptist made a mistake in going to Church."

leaked out that Apel was putting pressure on the Senate, Schmidt government spokesman Klaus Bölling tried to downplay the linkage between SALT and INF by saying that the West German government was not of the opinion that prior ratification of SALT was necessary for the Alliance INF decision, scheduled for December.[74]

For many in the party, however, such an "organic" link between SALT and INF did exist, precisely to avoid any codification of a separate Euro-strategic balance. Pawelczyk wrote: "We proceed from the assumption that the problem of nuclear middle-range systems must be handled in a real [*sachlichen*] association with the nuclear weapons of an intercontinental range, in order to avoid any decoupling of these two levels."[75]

On Monday, December 3, when more than five hundred party delegates convened in West Berlin for the opening of the party congress, SPD opponents of the NATO INF decision, scheduled to be affirmed one week later in Brussels, had been voicing various concerns about the double-track decision. Conversely, Schmidt, Defense Minister Apel, and other government leaders had been consulting for months with the party committee responsible for drafting the party platform (*Leitantrag*) that would be presented to the delegates and conferring with regional and local leaders in an attempt to construct a security issues plank that would gain the endorsement of a great majority of the party congress delegates. Given the importance of firm SPD support for Schmidt's INF position before the NATO Brussels meeting, and of demonstrating party unity before the 1980 election, the chancellor and the party hierarchy were wary of any major schism between the party at large and the Schmidt government.

THE BERLIN PARTY CONGRESS AND INF

For several months before the opening of the Berlin party congress, the party's *Antragskommission* (platform commission), comprised of some forty party officials and led by Herbert Wehner, had been drafting the SPD political platform to be voted on in Berlin.[76]

---

74. *Frankfurter Allgemeine Zeitung*, October 6, 1979.

75. Pawelczyk, "Sicherheitspolitik im Rahmen der Friedenspolitik," p. 43.

76. See "Materialen: Sicherheitspolitik im Rahmen der Friedenspolitik," *Leitantrag des Parteivorstands für den Parteitag in Berlin* (Bonn.: Vorstand der SPD, Abteilung Presse und Information, October 9, 1979) (hereafter *SPD Berlin Leitantrag*).

Within this commission a small working group had been created, chaired by Alfons Pawelczyk and including Karsten Voigt and Karl Kaiser (a Schmidt adviser), to draft the section on INF and nuclear weapons in Europe.

As published on October 9 for distribution throughout the party, the relevant section of the Leitantrag, headed "Im Bereich nuklearer Waffen" ("In the area of nuclear weapons"), was significant in that it consciously joined together defense and arms control issues so as to increase consensus building among the party delegates.[77] In particular, paragraph 28 presented as clear a statement as possible of the chancellor's view of the need for both arms control and defense efforts to rectify the existing imbalance in medium-range nuclear weapons: "The disparity in the nuclear medium-range potential must be met through a combination of defense and arms prevention political measures." For Schmidt, this meant "giving political priority to arms control arrangements in order to minimize instability in this area, at the same time adhering to the necessary defense options, in case these become necessary in the event of a miscarriage of arms control efforts."[78]

As we shall see, however, both paragraph 28 and the entire section on nuclear weapons would be subject to numerous challenges in the weeks preceding the Berlin congress and at the gathering itself.

As is customary in the preparation of a Leitantrag before a party conference, the text agreed upon by the Antragskommission also included amendments (*Änderungsinitiativen*), which were published alongside the commission report. Of particular importance was number 28, an amendment that incorporated some of the reservations being voiced by the SPD left wing. On the one hand, it referred to "no automaticity" ("an inevitable [*ausschliessliche*] stationing of nuclear medium-range weapons on German soil is not possible [*kommt nicht in Frage*] . . . . There may be no automaticity"). On the other hand, NATO was called on to determine, in light of arms control progress, whether the INF decision might not be changed ("to review decisions and, when necessary, to revise them").[79] This

77. According to one source, this fusing of arms control and defense policy issues was a conscious attempt to emphasize the complementarity of the modernization and arms control components of the NATO dual decision. Interviews with U.S. and West German government officials; *SPD Berlin Leitantrag*, pp. 15–16.

78. *SPD Berlin Leitantrag*, p. 15.

79. Ibid., p. 15.

latter point was to become extremely important following the Berlin congress, when many in the party argued that it allowed the SPD to review and possibly withdraw its support for the NATO INF decision. Finally, the amendment obliquely referred to the Zero Solution when it described the ultimate aim of the arms control efforts as making superfluous (*überflussig zu machen*) the introduction of medium-range systems in Western Europe.

In addition to those amendments included in the Leitantrag, the possibility remained open that additional changes, in the form of initiatives introduced by local party organizations, might further alter the platform on INF. For instance, INF opponents within the party tried to establish a clear linkage between SALT II ratification and the NATO INF decision, introducing an Initiativantrag that would allow the party to withdraw its support for INF should SALT II not be ratified.[80] If allowed to stand, such an amendment would have obviously tied the government's hands, and it was replaced with one that noted the dangers that the demise of SALT II would have for a Euro-strategic arms race, but that did not require SALT II ratification as a precondition for SPD support of INF.[81]

An indication of the care with which the INF section was constructed can be seen by additional changes that were incorporated in paragraph 26 of the section "Im Bereich nuklearen Waffen." A reference to the difficulties that a failure to ratify SALT II would cause for NATO (*"eine neue Lage im Bundnis schaffen"*: "create a new situation within the Alliance") was dropped to permit an open-ended interpretation.[82] Nonetheless, in his address to the congress, Karsten Voigt made clear his feeling that, although the reference to NATO had been dropped, the failure to ratify SALT II would most certainly cause difficulties for both the Alliance and the INF decision: "I proceed from the understanding that the Antragskommission has stricken the phrase 'within the Alliance' because it believes that, in the event SALT II is not ratified, a new situation will exist not only in the Alliance but far beyond the Alliance as well. I can support such an interpretation, because of course the effects of SALT II will extend far beyond the Alliance."[83]

80. The amendment called upon the government not to proceed with INF deployment in the event "that the SALT II Treaty does not come into force." See ibid., p. 4.
81. See Initiativantrag I/13, and "Empfehlung der Antragskommission I zu den Initiativeantrag aus Ihrem Bereich," in ibid., p. 12.
82. "Dokumente: Beschlüsse zur Aussen, Deutschland, Friedens und Sicherheitspolitik," in *SPD Parteitag Berlin, 1979* (Bonn: Vorstand der SPD, 1979), p. 20.
83. See "Unkorriegiertes Protokoll 5," in ibid., p. 38.

In effect, Voigt was telling the party delegates to read the passage as if the reference to NATO were still there. In doing so, Voigt was maintaining his credibility as a strong critic of INF, while allowing the party leadership to minimize any friction with the United States and other NATO allies which might arise from such a direct reference to the linkage between SALT II ratification and Alliance unity.[84]

Conversely, Defense Minister Apel sought to finesse the SALT II ratification issue, arguing in his speech to the party delegates that it should be the aim of the Alliance to begin INF talks immediately within a SALT III forum, but without necessarily waiting for the opening of formal SALT III negotiations. Without saying so explicitly, Apel was attempting to attenuate the damage that a U.S. failure to ratify SALT II would cause by asserting that bilateral U.S.–Soviet negotiations on INF could begin, and if all went well could be incorporated in the SALT process later.[85]

Numerous other examples could be given of amendments that expressed the dissatisfaction of factions within the party over the INF issue and that tried to qualify SPD support for the position of the Schmidt government. One such amendment, Initiativantrag I/17, referred to the destabilizing quality of the NATO systems and their potential use as first-strike weapons: "In general the SPD opposes the deployment of medium-range rockets in Western Europe, on the ground that the technical possibility exists of their being used from West European territory to conduct within a few minutes a surprise first strike against the USSR."[86]

While this and other such amendments were rejected, it was becoming increasingly apparent in the weeks preceding the Berlin congress that a number of tactical concessions would have to be made to party opponents of INF, estimated at 40 percent of the delegates, if the congress as a whole was going to endorse the Schmidt government's support for the NATO decision.[87] One such concession was the inclusion in the Antragskommission report of

---

84. Voigt had an especially narrow line to walk at the Berlin congress. Highly critical of the INF decision, as was his left-wing constituency in Frankfurt, Voigt nonetheless sought to build a consensus within the Antragskommission which would be acceptable to the Schmidt government and the party delegates at large. Interviews with SPD party officials, summer 1980.

85. "Arbeitsgruppe I, Unkorrigiertes Protokoll 4," in *SPD Parteitag Berlin, 1979*, p. 51.

86. See Initiativantrag I/17, in *SPD Berlin Leitantrag*.

87. For a discussion of the various amendments on INF that were being submitted by local party organizations before the congress, see "Die Gegner der Nachrüstung stellen etwa 40 Prozent der Delegierten," *Die Welt*, November 13, 1979, p. 2.

support for a moratorium on additional weapons deployments while INF arms control negotiations were in progress. As worded in the original report, this support was not wholehearted; the concept of a moratorium was merely to be explored as a means of contributing to the success of the INF negotiations themselves.[88]

As interpreted by the opponents of INF, however, such a moratorium could take the place of a ban on production of the INF systems during the negotiations, albeit a ban that would apply to the SS-20 as well. Here again, attempts at strengthening the party's commitment to such a moratorium were rejected by the party leadership.[89] However, the concept of a moratorium, which certainly was never part of the NATO double decision, was to reappear in the spring of 1980, when Schmidt himself broached the possibility of instituting a moratorium to facilitate the Geneva negotiations. This incident, which caused a great deal of trouble between Schmidt and the Carter administration, revealed the softness of the support for INF within the party and the chancellor's constant need to balance party constraints with his support for the Alliance position.

Far and away the greatest concession made before the Berlin congress was that over the Zero Solution.[90] Even those in the party who supported the need for a NATO counterbalance to the SS-20 were concerned that deployment schemes would run ahead of arms control and that the stationing of any new NATO INF systems would not only provoke Soviet military countermeasures but jeopardize West German Ostpolitik as well—hence the importance of committing the party, the Schmidt government, and the Alliance to the idea that the overriding aim of the INF arms control talks should be to render INF deployment unnecessary (*überflussig zu machen*). The difficulty with the Zero Solution, of course, was that it never made explicit what reductions in Soviet medium-range systems would be necessary to make the Zero Solution acceptable. As President Reagan interpreted it in 1981, the only acceptable Zero Solution (Zero Option) was a Zero-Zero Solution: the Soviets would destroy all their SS-4, SS-5, and SS-20 missiles in return for no NATO deployment of INF.[91]

For the left wing of the SPD, however, such a demand was

88. See *SPD Berlin Leitantrag*, p. 15.
89. An amendment that would have specifically tied the SPD to such a moratorium can be found in Initiativantrag I/2, para. 8, in ibid., p. 4.
90. Interviews with SPD officials and West German journalists, summer 1980.
91. See *New York Times*, November 19, 1981.

politically unrealistic, given that it would require the Soviets to dismantle a nuclear capability that had been in place for twenty years in return for a NATO pledge not to deploy systems that were not yet operational. Thus, while no precise figures were ever mentioned, the type of Zero Solution favored by the SPD left was a zero-plus arrangement, by which the Soviets would agree to keep their SS-20 deployment at a level low enough to allow the Alliance to forgo its INF deployment plans.

Not surprisingly, there was little interest in such a scheme either at NATO headquarters or in the Carter administration. The type of Zero Solution being discussed within the SPD was seen as tying the Alliance's hands even before INF negotiations had begun, and increasing the political difficulties NATO would face in deploying its INF systems should there be no progress in the arms control arena. Yet so strong was sentiment within the party that INF arms control be given priority over weapons deployment, expressed as well in the demand for "no automaticity," that the SPD leadership felt obliged to include a reference to the Zero Solution in the original Leitantrag.[92] Having done so, the party leadership then took the unusual step of privately informing the White House that such a change had been made, but that it had been done merely as a concession to the INF opponents within the party and did not represent the Schmidt government's position.[93]

Despite such concessions and continued negotiations within the party over the drafting of a security plank that would be acceptable to the Berlin delegates, endorsement of the INF provisions was by no means assured before the start of the Berlin congress. In talks with leaders of the party's regional organizations during the weekend of December 1–2, Schmidt became aware that criticism of the Leitantrag was growing.[94] While opponents of INF were partially mollified by the strengthening of the arms control component of the INF section, there remained strong sentiment for either delaying FRG support for a NATO decision to produce INF systems or at least postponing such a production decision until after SALT II had been

92. While para. 28 as originally drafted merely confirmed the equal weight to be given to both tracks of the NATO INF decision, changes decided upon by the Antragskommission did shift the emphasis toward arms control, especially with the reference to the Zero Solution (*Null-Lösung*). See *SPD Berlin Leitantrag*, p. 15.

93. Interviews with FRG government officials (summer 1980) emphasized the Schmidt government's desire to assuage American anxieties on this point.

94. *Süddeutsche Zeitung*, December 3, 1979.

ratified.[95] Given his commitment to both tracks of the NATO INF package, Schmidt reacted strongly, letting it be known that "he could not, as Chancellor, support any decision" to proceed with arms control but not modernization. Such a decision by the party, according to Schmidt, "would cause incredible harm to the solidarity of the Western Alliance."[96]

In retrospect, the chancellor was in a curious position vis-à-vis the party before the Berlin congress. Schmidt was aware of the widespread party opposition to the prospect of INF deployment. In addition to the reservations being voiced by Brandt, Bahr, Pawelczyk, and Voigt, leaders of regional party organizations were making known their displeasure with the Leitantrag. Erhard Eppler, a member of the party executive and leader of the Baden-Württemburg SPD, and Oskar Lafontaine of the Saarland SPD were especially critical of the government's INF policy. Most critical of all were the Young Socialists (Jusos), led by Gerd Schröder. As Schröder expressed it, the main concern of the INF opponents was that Schmidt's preoccupation with establishing a military balance of power in Europe would jeopardize the country's relations with Eastern Europe and call into question ten years of détente and Ostpolitik.[97] In order to allay such fears, Schmidt went to great lengths in the days preceding the congress to consult with party leaders in an attempt to reach accommodation on such points as "no automaticity" and the linkage between INF and SALT II.[98]

The chancellor even took the unusual step of publicly announcing, on the second day of the congress and before the SPD party plenum, that he would be meeting with East German leader Erich

95. One such amendment that was rejected read: "The approval of the party congress is given in the expectation that within six months SALT II will have been ratified and the appropriate negotiations will have begun." See Initiativantrag I/13.

96. *Süddeutsche Zeitung*, December 3, 1979.

97. *Frankfurter Allgemeine Zeitung*, December 6, 1979. Perhaps the best expression of this view comes from Karsten Voigt: "The credibility of our peace policy is even more important for our security than the credibility of the military deterrent. . . . Arms control for us has political priority over rearmament [*Nachrüstung*]": "Schrittweiser Ausstieg aus dem Rüstungswettlauf."

98. In drafting the address he would give at the conference, Schmidt sought the advice of numerous colleagues, including Carlo Schmid, who had played such an important role within the party during the nuclear weapons debates of 1957–58, as well as Richard Löwenthal, Research Minister Volker Hauff, and Hesse Minister-President Holger Borner. *Der Spiegel* reported on December 3, 1979, that although Schmidt had sought such advice before on important addresses, "never before had he considered it so important to prepare so intensively for a party congress as this one."

Honecker in the spring of 1980. Schmidt's surprise announcement, which was not made jointly with Honecker or even communicated to others in the SPD, was designed to convince opponents of INF that Bonn's Ostpolitik would continue and not be jeopardized by the upcoming NATO decision.[99]

Despite the scope of the opposition to his INF policy, however, the chancellor also realized that, with national elections less than ten months away, and with his own popularity in the country at large far outdistancing that of the party, he could exert strong leverage to fashion a consensus among the Berlin delegates. At the Hamburg party congress in 1977, *Die Zeit* recalled, the chancellor had "cautiously sought to make his peace and compromise with the party"; now he "was in line for conference acclaim for once, and he put the opportunity to good use." The complete lack of any alternatives to Schmidt—"other, that is, than to lose the next election"—provided the chancellor with what ultimately turned out to be a trump card.[100]

Yet so strong was the opposition to INF that Schmidt was forced to play that card. Votes taken during the congress on individual amendments, such as Initiativantrag I/13, which called for deferring any decision on production of INF, were supported by as many as 40 percent of the delegates.[101] Although the INF opponents could not muster a majority against the party platform, Schmidt was concerned with the ramifications of such a narrow majority in favor of the government's position. Not only was the SPD stand on INF important for the domestic political debates taking place in Holland, Belgium, and Italy, but the party's chances in the 1980 election could be compromised by an equivocal stand on what had become such an important issue of Alliance security. When votes on particular INF amendments continued to show a 60–40 split, Schmidt took the ultimate step of telling a session of the party executive, behind closed doors, that "he was no longer prepared to shoulder the burden of government without a clear mandate from the conference."[102]

This threat to refuse to run for reelection in 1980 soon made its way among the party delegates and had the intended effect.[103] The party leadership rallied behind the chancellor, and when it came time to vote on the INF section of the Leitantrag, with its dual

99. *Der Spiegel*, December 10, 1979.
100. *Die Zeit*, December 7, 1979.
101. *Der Spiegel*, December 10, 1979.
102. *Die Zeit*, December 7, 1979.
103. Interviews with SPD party officials, summer 1980.

commitment to arms control and modernization, 80 percent of the congress delegates supported Schmidt.

The final vote was an indication of Schmidt's importance to the party and the manner in which the top SPD leaders rallied around the chancellor. Herbert Wehner and Egon Bahr especially were instrumental in calling on the party delegates to unite behind Schmidt, referring to the dangers that a badly split SPD would pose both for the credibility of the Schmidt government and for the party's electoral fortunes in 1980. In contrast to the critical stand that Wehner had taken on INF early in 1979, the Fraktionschef urged unconditional support for Schmidt's position. As *Die Zeit* noted, Wehner subsumed his misgivings about INF under his overriding belief that "to achieve anything, you must have power and be in a position to govern," and thus this year "was . . . a far cry from last year, when he resorted to almost partisan measures in an attempt to further the cause of disarmament and foster understanding of Soviet interests."[104]

Egon Bahr, too, rallied to Schmidt's cause, emphasizing the importance of avoiding an open break in the party. Given his ideological stature within the party, as coarchitect with Willy Brandt of the FRG's Ostpolitik, Bahr's support was crucial, especially as so many of the INF opponents had pointed to the dangers that supporting INF would have for the country's relations with East Germany and Eastern Europe. Like Wehner, Pawelczyk, and Karsten Voigt, Bahr was a political realist and based his support for Schmidt on such political grounds. In his remarks to the party delegates, Bahr pointed to two overriding political considerations, prefacing them with a reference to his lifelong commitment to détente and West German Ostpolitik:

> As one who has spent a part of his life [working] for détente policies, I would reject the [INF] resolution, if I thought that détente would be destroyed by accepting such a resolution. . . . However, this is not the case . . . and for me there exists today a situation in which we have to recognize realities. . . .
>
> The first is: should there be an overwhelming majority against this resolution, it would, in my opinion, mean the beginning of the end of our ability to govern. And the second reality is, in my opinion: . . . I am convinced that only through this resolution can the United States be brought into [arms control] negotiations. In the event that the resolu-

104. *Die Zeit*, December 7, 1979.

tion is rejected, there will be no way to bring the United States into such negotiations, and we ourselves cannot negotiate arms control without the United States.

Therefore I come, not easily, to ask that the resolution, as endorsed by the Antragskommission, be supported.[105]

In the end, even Willy Brandt put aside his reservations about INF in the interests of party unity, although in his final speech to the party congress, according to Rolf Zundel, "Brandt resorted to wording so tortuous that there could be little doubt that he, for one, did not relish the prospect of NATO nuclear modernization. . . . Herr Brandt's choice of words testified to a contest between resignation and hope, between political skepticism and loyalty to Chancellor Schmidt."[106] While Brandt, in general terms, supported the INF resolution as passed by the party, he made clear that priority should be given to arms control and took the opportunity to call for ratification of SALT II and the beginning of INF negotiations within six months.[107] In the days following the party congress, several SPD leaders again emphasized the importance of U.S. ratification of SALT II so that INF systems could be brought into the context of SALT III negotiations. Both Brandt and Egon Bahr referred to the six-month time period, which was not an arbitrary figure, as the party would be meeting in six months for its electoral party congress (*Wahlparteitag*) in Essen. Although Schmidt had been able to avoid the drawing of a strict connection between SALT II ratification and the NATO INF decision, Brandt and Bahr hinted that the party might revoke its support for the INF decision at the Essen meeting in June 1980 in the event that SALT II had not been ratified and INF negotiations had not begun. In an interview in the *Süddeutsche Zeitung*, Bahr remarked that if SALT II "is not ratified and negotiations have not begun, then—and this is not great prophecy—it could happen that this subject will be taken up anew, and with a different result."[108]

A few weeks later, Brandt reiterated the priority of INF arms control and again referred to the Zero Solution as the ultimate aim of such negotiations: "I take the Berlin decision and the second component of the NATO decision very seriously. . . . For me, the offer of negotiations is not a sauce poured over the armament decision but

105. "Unkorrigiertes Protokoll 5," in *SPD Parteitag Berlin, 1979*, p. 106.
106. *Die Zeit*, December 7, 1979.
107. For the text of Brandt's closing speech to the congress, see "Unkorrigiertes Protokoll 7," in *SPD Parteitag Berlin, 1979*, pp. 74–91; the reference to SALT II is on p. 76.
108. *Süddeutsche Zeitung*, December 8, 1979.

an obligation to find out whether the stationing of missiles to the extent now envisaged is necessary. Helmut Schmidt himself said on this subject that, ideally, we could arrive at zero."[109]

And Karsten Voigt, criticizing those in the party who thought that the SPD was not committed enough to arms control, pointed to the changes that had been made by the Antragskommission in the INF resolution and the incorporation of party support for the Zero Solution and a possible INF moratorium. Moreover, Voigt called on party members to join fully in increasing the pressure on arms control efforts. In a prophetic call to action, Voigt urged SPD members to mobilize behind a political campaign that would take place "in the cities and communities, in the parties, unions, church groups, youth organizations and the groups of the peace movement," so as to give full substance to the SPD platform.[110]

In the immediate aftermath of the Berlin party congress, there was as yet no widespread peace movement in the FRG. Yet the depth of the opposition within the SPD to the stationing of INF systems in the FRG made it inevitable that, once such a peace movement coalesced, it would have widespread support among SPD members. For the moment, the party rank and file had acquiesced and given its support to the double-track INF package. As *Der Spiegel* noted, however, the support of the Berlin party congress was very conditional: "The affirmation of the Social Democrats for rearmament is limited and linked to the success of détente."[111] In addition, as Brandt, Bahr, Voigt, and others had stressed, the support of the SPD for the NATO double decision was predicated on continued success in the area of strategic arms control, beginning with U.S. Senate's ratification of the SALT II Treaty.

It was to be just a matter of days, however, before both SALT II and East–West détente were dealt a severe blow by the Soviet invasion of Afghanistan on December 27. In the ensuing months, Western governments quarreled among themselves on how to respond to the Soviet invasion, while the Western publics became anxious over deteriorating U.S.–Soviet relations. Schmidt came under increasing pressure from the Carter administration to respond more forcefully on Afghanistan, while the emergence of Ronald Reagan in the U.S. election campaign symbolized a growing hard-

---

109. Interview with *Kölner Stadt-Anzeiger*, January 4, 1980; reprinted in *German Tribune*, January 20, 1980, pp. 4–6.

110. Voigt, "Schrittweiser Ausstieg aus dem Rüstungswettlauf," p. 48.

111. *Der Spiegel*, December 10, 1979, p. 20.

line attitude in the United States. In such a situation, the NATO INF decision became a focal point for peace groups throughout Western Europe, especially in West Germany. Throughout 1980, an election year in the FRG, a coalition of Green supporters, peace activists, dissident SPD members, left-wing radicals, and members of trade union and church groups coalesced into the largest peace movement the country had seen since the late 1950s, one that would dominate West German politics for the next three years.

[4]

The Afghan Crisis and the Rise of the Peace Movement: 1980–1983

In the space of just a few months, separate strands in West German politics coalesced in 1980 into mass public opposition against the INF policies of NATO and the Schmidt government. Leaders of the West German peace movement (Friedensbewegung) exhorted their supporters to block deployment of the "Euromissiles" with such slogans as "No Euroshimas." Not since the late 1950s and the Kampf dem Atomtod (Fight Atomic Death) movement had hundreds of thousands of West Germans of all walks of life demonstrated in the streets against the security policies of a German government.

As important as the INF issue was, however, the Pershing II and cruise missiles (which were not scheduled for deployment until 1983 at the earliest) were only the most tangible symbol of growing German anxiety about developments in East–West and U.S.–FRG relations. In retrospect, the NATO INF decision of December 1979 provoked little reaction at the time from the West German media and public. It was only after East–West relations deteriorated with the Soviet invasion of Afghanistan, and the death of the SALT II Treaty signaled an end to U.S.–Soviet arms control, that many West Germans began to view INF deployment as but one pawn (albeit a nuclear one) in the match between Washington and Moscow, with the FRG as the chessboard.

THE INF DECISION AND EAST–WEST TENSIONS

In mid-December 1979, less than a week after the SPD party congress in West Berlin, NATO ministers met in Brussels to affirm

Alliance support for the INF double-track decision that had been evolving over the previous twenty-four months. Although Schmidt had been successful in winning his party's support for the SPD/FDP government position, it was by no means certain that the Alliance itself would reach a unanimous decision.

For one thing, the Dutch and Belgian governments continued to object to any firm Alliance commitment to deploy INF, arguing that a production decision was all that was necessary to get the Soviets to negotiate seriously. While generally supportive of the NATO dual decision, the Dutch government of Andreas van Agt found itself further constrained when, on December 6, the Dutch parliament voted against the upcoming Alliance decision.[1] Because the parliamentary vote came only a week before the NATO meeting in Brussels, van Agt was faced with the choice of ignoring it and thus risking a vote of no confidence (van Agt's majority in the Dutch lower house was a slim 77 out of 150 seats) or seeking a compromise at the NATO session which would mollify the Dutch parliament.

In Belgium the situation was a bit more complex, involving the inability of the government of Wilfrid Maartens to take a firm stand in the midst of a governmental crisis over the Walloon–Flemish reapportionment debate.[2] While the Belgian public did not exhibit the same degree of antinuclear sentiment as the Dutch, there was still enough apprehension at what the NATO INF decision might mean for détente and East–West relations that the Maartens government also sought to find a compromise formula by which it could support the Alliance decision.

In the end, the NATO ministers supported an INF resolution that called for both production and deployment should arms control fail, yet allowed the Dutch and Belgians to postpone a decision to deploy INF systems in their respective countries. In working out this compromise, the Alliance came under strong pressure from the Carter administration not to postpone an INF deployment decision. In a speech prepared for delivery by Secretary of State Vance (given by Under Secretary George Vest, as Vance was in Washington handling the Iranian hostage crisis), the Europeans were told that it

1. In November, van Agt had been able to win parliamentary approval for the Dutch position of agreeing to production but not deployment, but even this qualified support was overturned when nine members of the government coalition in Parliament voted against van Agt's policy; see *Neue Zürcher Zeitung*, November 11, 1979.
2. For more on the difficulties in Belgium of apportioning political power between the Flemish and Walloons and the attempt to set up regional assemblies for Flanders, Wallonia, and Brussels, see *Economist*, April 12, 1980.

would make "little sense" to delay any such decision "in the mere hope that talks might succeed . . . as the Soviets will have no visible incentive to negotiate reductions in forces."[3] Secretary of Defense Harold Brown had similarly objected in November to a Dutch proposal to defer deployment, saying that the U.S. Congress might not appropriate funds for weapons systems that might never be deployed.[4] In addition, the Schmidt government had been consulting closely with its counterparts in Holland and Belgium for several months to ensure Alliance unity for the INF decision. In part an effort to avoid another neutron weapon debacle, these consultations were necessary as well to ensure that the FRG would not be in the singular position of being the only non-nuclear West European country asked to deploy the INF systems. While Schmidt may have been confident that the Italians would satisfy the FRG's insistence on "no singularity," the chancellor wanted the NATO decision to be as broad-based as possible, and particularly wanted to prevent socialist opposition in Holland and Belgium from reinforcing SPD left-wing objections to INF.[5]

In a communiqué following the NATO meeting in Brussels, the Dutch and the Belgians voiced their support for the INF dual decision, with the proviso that the two countries would delay any decision on deploying INF systems for two years and six months respectively, so as better to gauge the progress of INF arms control negotiations.[6] As part of the compromise formula worked out to gain even this limited support from Holland and Belgium, the communiqué also emphasized the role to be played by arms control:

3. The Vest speech was given in West Berlin on December 10, just before the opening of the NATO meeting in Brussels; see *New York Times*, December 11, 1979.

4. See *Observer* (London), November 18, 1979. Of course, such arguments were precisely what the SPD left-wing objected to in its call for "no automaticity."

5. During the summer and autumn of 1979, consultations among the FRG, Holland, and Belgium included both governmental contacts and meetings between SPD party leaders and their counterparts in the Dutch Labor party and the Belgian socialist parties. For more on what was an intensive effort on the part of the Schmidt government to get the Dutch and Belgian governments to go along with the NATO INF decision, see *Süddeutsche Zeitung*, August 14, 1979; *Financial Times* (London), August 15, 1979; *New York Times*, October 18 and 19, 1979; and *Neue Zürcher Zeitung*, December 12, 1979.

6. In spelling out how the INF systems would be deployed, NATO Secretary General Joseph Luns explained that the 464 cruise missiles would be divided among the Federal Republic (96), Italy (112), Britain (160), and, if they accepted, Holland and Belgium (48 each). The Dutch in particular were so sensitive about even seeming to agree to any future deployment that they would not allow Luns's comments to be included in the final communiqué. See *New York Times*, December 13, 1979.

Ministers attach great importance to the role of arms control in contributing to a more stable military relationship between East and West and in advancing the process of détente. . . . Ministers regard arms control as an integrated part of the Alliance's efforts to assure the undiminished security of its member States and to make the strategic situation between East and West more stable, more predictable, and more manageable at lower levels of armaments on both sides. . . . Arms control efforts to achieve a more stable overall nuclear balance at lower levels of nuclear weapons on both sides should therefore now include certain U.S. and Soviet long-range theater nuclear systems.[7]

At the same time, however, the communiqué referred to the importance of the SALT II Treaty, still awaiting ratification by the U.S. Senate, both on its own merits and for providing a framework for INF arms control. In listing five principles to be followed in pursuit of an INF arms control agreement, the NATO communiqué called for "bilateral [U.S.–Soviet] negotiations in the SALT II framework."[8] This explicit reference to SALT was somewhat ironic, in view of the resistance of both the Carter administration and the Schmidt government to attempts, especially by the left wing of the SPD, to make ratification of SALT II a precondition of the NATO INF agreement. While the NATO INF communiqué did not refer to SALT II ratification per se, this connection between INF negotiations and SALT III obviously opened the door for misunderstanding in the event that SALT II was not ratified and SALT III died aborning.

Shortly after the Brussels meeting, on December 18, Secretary of State Vance presented the NATO INF arms control proposal to Vladillen Vasev, acting head of the Soviet embassy in Washington in the absence of Anatoly Dobrynin.[9] Based on the five guiding principles agreed upon by the Alliance in Brussels, the Vance proposal reflected a mixture of Alliance and specifically American concerns that the SALT II experience with gray-area weapons not be repeated in the INF negotiations. For instance, the first principle, that there

---

7. For the text of the communiqué, see *NATO Review* 28 (February 1980): 25–26.

8. The five principles were: (1) limitations on U.S. systems "principally designed for theater missions" should be "accompanied by appropriate limitations on Soviet theater systems"; (2) there should be bilateral INF negotiations in the SALT III framework; (3) the "immediate objective" should be mutual limitations, possibly leading to complete removal of INF (a concession to the Zero Solution); (4) agreements must be based on the principle of "equality, both in ceilings and in rights"; and (5) any agreement must be "adequately verifiable." See *New York Times*, December 13, 1979.

9. *New York Times*, December 19, 1979.

be no restrictions on American weapons designed primarily for the European theater without corresponding restrictions on Soviet systems also designed for the European theater, was meant to avoid the SALT II restrictions on cruise missiles and technology transfer without a reciprocal concession in regard to the SS-20 and Backfire bomber. Similarly, it was understood that the second principle, referring to bilateral U.S.–Soviet talks on INF within the framework of SALT, would in practice mean that the U.S. negotiating position would be determined as much in Brussels as in Washington.

Points 3 and 4 of the NATO position reflected the more specifically American concerns, and it was these points that were bound to be most troublesome to the Soviets. When Vance spoke of first limiting land-based missile systems, with submarine-based missiles and aircraft to be dealt with later, he was continuing ten years of U.S. policy of keeping American forward-based systems out of the arms control process. While there were convincing reasons for dealing with IRBMs and MRBMs first, given the special complexities of negotiating verifiable limits on aircraft, the Soviets would hardly be pleased with negotiations that focused on the SS-20. Point 4 was even more explicit on this point, as it called for equal limits, meaning that the Soviets would have to dismantle their existing missiles, as corresponding NATO systems did not yet exist.[10]

The formal Soviet rejection of Vance's proposal was given by Vasev on January 3: NATO must publicly renounce its Brussels dual-track decision before any INF talks could begin.[11] In the interim, however, the Soviets had invaded Afghanistan, thus calling into question not only East–West arms control efforts but what was left of détente as well. Yet even before the formal rejection or the move into Afghanistan, the Soviets had made known their position that the NATO decision to deploy new INF systems had removed any possibility of initiating INF negotiations. On December 13, at the conclusion of the NATO meeting in Brussels, TASS had issued a story that sharply criticized the Alliance decision on INF, saying that "the course chosen by the NATO leaders is fraught with the most dangerous consequences" and that "the dangerous decision by NATO is camouflaged by a call for talks with the Soviet Union, but talks that are conceived on an absolutely different basis from the ones proposed by the USSR" (i.e., the Brezhnev proposal of October

10. *Economist*, December 15, 1979, pp. 39–40.
11. *International Herald Tribune*, January 7, 1980.

1979). The prospect of moving quickly on INF arms control became bleaker when, following the Soviet move into Afghanistan, and on the same day that Vasev delivered the formal Soviet rejection in Washington, President Carter announced that he was deferring Senate consideration of the SALT II Treaty, knowing that he did not have the two-thirds majority necessary for ratification.[12]

In the midst of the Afghan crisis, with Schmidt attempting to devise a policy that would satisfy both his American ally and his own party, there occurred an event that, while somewhat lost in the midst of an international crisis, was to take on far greater proportions as the West German debate over INF intensified. In mid-January, Maj. Gen. Gert Bastian, commander of the Twelfth Panzer Division in Weitshochheim, was relieved of his post and denied early retirement after writing a personal letter to Defense Secretary Apel criticizing the NATO decision on INF.[13] In saying that, as a West German military officer, he could not support NATO deployment of long-range nuclear missiles, Bastian requested early retirement. In making the affair public, Apel said he would grant Bastian's request only if the general gave up his pension and retirement benefits. Bastian refused and forced Apel to fire him.[14]

Although the Bastian affair disappeared amidst all the attention being paid to Afghanistan, the general soon reappeared as a major figure in the growing West German peace movement. In November 1980, Bastian became one of the initiators of the Krefeld Appeal, which called upon Schmidt to renounce the INF decision and which by 1981 had collected over a million signatures. Bastian later joined the Green party and was elected to the Bundestag in March 1983.

In early 1980, however, Schmidt was more preoccupied with dampening the SPD's growing criticism of his INF policy and reconciling West German domestic and external interests in responding to the Afghan issue. The constraints the chancellor faced—from his American ally, from the CDU opposition, and from within the SPD—were a clear reminder that despite the increase in the FRG's

12. *New York Times*, January 4, 1980.

13. *Süddeutsche Zeitung*, January 18, 1980.

14. Bastian had first come to national attention when he attended a Young Socialists (Jusos) conference in Bad Mergentheim in March 1979. Although he took issue at that conference with Wehner's statement of the previous month that the USSR was a "defensive power," a Juso press release shortened Bastian's remarks and it appeared that the general was agreeing with Wehner. Bastian had to be defended by Apel from CDU/CSU calls for his dismissal. See *Süddeutsche Zeitung*, January 18, 1980.

political stature since the 1950s, West Germany continued to be circumscribed in the options available to square its three foreign policy circles.

THE AFGHAN CRISIS AND WEST GERMAN POLITICS

The ramifications for East–West relations of the Afghan affair, in which the Soviets for the first time in the postwar period used military force outside of the Soviet bloc, are well known and need not be discussed at length. What is germane to the INF issue, over and above the death blow that was dealt to a SALT II treaty that was already in trouble in the U.S. Senate, is how the crisis over Afghanistan affected the West German politics of the theater nuclear issue.

Many Western analysts have speculated that the timing of the Afghan invasion was predicated partly on the Soviet's belief that SALT II could not win Senate ratification anyway, and therefore they had little to lose in the arms control sphere by invading Afghanistan and posing a threat to Western interests in the Persian Gulf.[15] By the same token, it had been apparent by the fall of 1979, when Soviet preparations for the invasion were under way, that NATO would codify its INF decision in December. Not wanting to appear to have been pressured into INF negotiations by the NATO dual decision, the Soviets similarly would have little to lose from any hiatus in INF arms control resulting from the Afghan affair.

In one sense, the international condemnation of the Soviet invasion of Afghanistan allowed the Soviets to take the wraps off and counterattack vigorously on INF. Under attack from all quarters for its brutal use of force in Afghanistan, from Muslim and other Third World countries as well as the West, the Soviets sought to deflect some of this criticism by blaming NATO and the INF decision for having heightened East–West tensions. While any causal link between the INF decision and Soviet motives for invading Afghanistan was tenuous if not nonexistent, the Soviets could at least seek to make the best of a bad situation by shifting the blame for a break-down in détente onto the West.

Indeed, the severity with which Soviet criticism of the INF decision increased following its invasion of Afghanistan was consistent

15. interviews with U.S. government and NATO officials, summer 1980.

with traditional (i.e., pre-Gorbachev) Soviet negotiating behavior, in which "the relative weakness of their negotiating position [is] conversely proportionate to the intensity of their abuse and the outrageousness of their countercharges."[16] In the period preceding the Brussels conference, Soviet criticism avoided Helmut Schmidt, but now the chancellor himself was swept up in this stepped-up Soviet broadside. While Genscher was labeled a "demagogue" and references were again made to West Germany as the breeding ground of the horrors of World War II, Schmidt was pointedly warned of the "dangerous consequences" of a NATO decision that could reawaken "German militarism."[17]

Of course, there was method as well in the "madness" of this Soviet propaganda counterattack. At the same time that Soviet commentary excoriated the Schmidt government for its role in the INF decision, it pointedly referred to the dangers for Bonn's Ostpolitik of continuing to support INF deployment. An article in *Pravda* explicitly warned the Federal Republic that it risked becoming isolated from "the East" (i.e., East Germany) even in economic relationships.[18] In an editorial headed "A Cold Wind from Moscow," the *Süddeutsche Zeitung* noted that the Soviet references to a revival of German militarism seemed to be part of a campaign within the East bloc to impress the Schmidt government with this possible breakdown in his government's Eastern policy. Moreover, by concentrating on Schmidt's role in preparing the NATO INF decision, the Soviets were seeking as well to strengthen that part of the SPD which had only reluctantly supported the chancellor at the Berlin party congress.[19]

Not that opponents of INF within the SPD needed any prompting. In an atmosphere of increasing tension within the Alliance over how to respond to the invasion of Afghanistan, and with the Carter administration becoming more strident in its calls for Western punitive measures against the USSR, left-wing members of the SPD continued to warn of the dangers that a breakdown in détente would pose for the INF decision. Schmidt and his advisers were concerned that Carter's shelving of the SALT II Treaty would lead to

16. *Soviet Diplomacy and Negotiating Behavior*, report prepared for the Committee on Foreign Affairs, U.S. House of Representatives (Washington, D.C.: U.S. Government Printing Office, 1979), p. 137.

17. *Frankfurter Allgemeine Zeitung*, December 27, 1979, p. 3, and *Süddeutsche Zeitung*, December 31/January 1, 1979/80, p. 5.

18. As quoted in *Süddeutsche Zeitung*, December 31/January 1, 1979/80, p. 5.

19. Ibid., p. 4.

increasing calls from within the SPD for revising the NATO INF decision. To forestall any such attempts, the chancellor had the West German Foreign Ministry stress that "the arms control dialogue can proceed, independent of SALT III."[20]

Of more concern to Schmidt, however, were the dangers that the Afghan crisis posed for the entire fabric of East–West détente, especially in Europe. While the U.S. government was calling upon NATO to impose economic sanctions, boycott the 1980 Moscow Olympics, and prepare contingency military measures in the Persian Gulf, Schmidt government spokesmen stressed that the Afghan crisis was primarily a conflict between the USSR and the Third World, with only secondary importance for the East–West relationship.[21] At times the Schmidt government emphasized the necessity of dealing firmly with the Soviet invasion, as in communiqués following meetings of the Federal Cabinet and Federal Security Council on January 9 and 10,[22] yet the chancellor's overriding emphasis on salvaging East–West détente was prominent throughout the first few weeks of the new year. Kurt Becker, a close confidant of the chancellor's, wrote in *Die Zeit*: "The indivisibility of détente must not mean that tensions are introduced where none exist, especially in Europe. No West German politician can support a policy that calls into question the existence of the Eastern treaties."[23]

Schmidt himself voiced his displeasure with what he regarded as the overreaction of the Carter administration in a speech during a Bundestag debate on Afghanistan in the middle of January: "We must carefully consider our own German interests and those of the West. We must bring our land through this turbulence with a sure hand. We do not need nervousness, cries of alarm or strident speeches .... What we do need more than anything is careful 'crisis management.' "[24]

To reinforce his government's support for a measured response, Schmidt sent Alfons Pawelczyk (a poor choice, in view of Pawelczyk's lukewarm support for INF) to Washington in early January to convey Schmidt's feeling that European détente was still in the

20. *Der Spiegel*, January 7, 1980, p. 19.
21. *Süddeutsche Zeitung*, January 18, 1980.
22. Ibid., January 12/13, 1980, p. 1.
23. *Die Zeit*, February 8, 1980, p. 3.
24. In his commentary on the Schmidt speech, Martin Suskind noted that Schmidt made a point of saying "crisis management" in English, and that it took little imagination to understand that Schmidt was directing his remarks "in the direction of the Americans": *Süddeutsche Zeitung*, January 18, 1980, p. 3.

United States' interest, despite the crisis in East–West relations. The crux of Schmidt's argument that European détente must continue, that détente could after all be "divisible," was summed up by the argument that Pawelczyk pushed in his meetings in Washington: "After all, America is more sensitive to the Russian presence in Berlin than in Kabul."[25] Above all, Schmidt, as much as Egon Bahr and Willy Brandt, wanted to avoid what Brandt had called the danger of "Europeanizing a Near East and East–South problem."[26] For both Brandt and Bahr, the fundamental element of West German policy must be that while Western solidarity is important, European solidarity is "more important in this case."[27]

Not surprisingly, the Soviets played on such fears, especially in regard to Berlin. Valentin Falin, former Soviet ambassador to West Germany, warned in an interview with the West German news agency DDP in early February that a worsening of the international situation could directly affect Berlin.[28] A few days later, Pyotr Abrassimov, the Soviet ambassador to East Germany, linked the crisis in East–West relations with the INF affair when he not only reiterated that the NATO December decision had "destroyed the basis for arms control negotiations," but emphasized as well that Brezhnev's promise of a unilateral withdrawal of tanks and troops from East Germany, made in October 1979 to influence the NATO INF decision, might be in jeopardy because of the Western response to Afghanistan.[29]

Throughout the first six months of 1980, then, the Alliance was beset by the problem of devising a unified response to the Soviet incursion into Afghanistan. Ultimately, differences of opinion were subsumed to some degree within the concept of a "division of labor," whereby the United States and Britain took primary responsibility for strengthening military forces around the Persian Gulf while the FRG and other continental countries concentrated on increasing economic aid to such countries in the region as Pakistan and Turkey.[30] In the end, the Schmidt government did support Washington's boycott of the Moscow Olympics, the only major NATO partner to do so. Yet the entire affair dissipated the sense of

25. *Der Spiegel*, January 7, 1980, p. 19.
26. *Süddeutsche Zeitung*, January 18, 1980, p. 2.
27. *Die Zeit*, January 18, 1980, p. 2.
28. *Frankfurter Allgemeine Zeitung*, February 1, 1980, pp. 1–2.
29. *Foreign Broadcast Information Service: Soviet Union Daily Report*, February 8, 1980 (hereafter *FBIS*).
30. *Washington Post*, January 31, 1980, p. A16.

Alliance unity that had been present when NATO codified its INF position the previous December. As Stanley Hoffmann noted, the European response to Afghanistan may have been shortsighted, but the Carter administration's overreaction and its attempt to dictate a common Alliance policy served only to rekindle European anxieties regarding American steadiness.[31]

CRACKS IN THE WEST GERMAN SECURITY CONSENSUS

In the same way that the Afghan crisis split the Alliance, it also introduced new cracks in the foreign policy consensus that had existed between the Schmidt government and the moderate wing of the opposition Christian Democrats since the early 1970s. While criticism of the Schmidt government's pursuit of détente could always be expected from Franz Josef Strauss of the CSU, the chancellor was now attacked by CDU spokesmen for his lukewarm support for possible NATO sanctions against the USSR. Manfred Wörner, CDU defense spokesman, blasted the SPD/FDP government as "false apostles of détente," while Heiner Geissler, CDU general secretary, said Schmidt's reaction to the Afghan invasion was "naked opportunism."[32] In a special CDU/CSU security conference held in mid-January, the opposition parties, sensing an exploitable issue for the 1980 election, called the Schmidt government's security policies "halfhearted and insufficient," and warned that the Soviets were attempting, "with their defense and arms control policies, not to establish a military parity that would ensure peace, but to gain military superiority for political purposes."[33]

In early February, Helmut Kohl, CDU party chairman, took the Schmidt government and the SPD to task for their lack of cooperation in devising a common Alliance response to Afghanistan. Specifically, Kohl criticized the Social Democratic interpretation of NATO's "division of labor," saying that any such policy should not mean that the United States would bear the global burdens for Europe's security while Europe itself enjoyed a monopoly of détente.[34]

31. According to Hoffmann, in effect the Carter administration was running the risk of "sacrificing long-term coordination to short-term, artificially produced harmony." See his "Reflections on the Present Danger," *New York Review of Books*, March 6, 1980, p. 6.

32. *Süddeutsche Zeitung*, January 12/13, 1980, p. 2.

33. "Freiheit durch Sicherheit: Unserer Verantwortung für die Zukunft," in *CDU/CSU sicherheitspolitischer Kongress, January 11–12, 1980* (Bonn: CDU/CSU, 1980), p. 4.

34. *Frankfurter Allgemeine Zeitung*, February 7, 1979, p. 2.

Interestingly, Franz Josef Strauss, the CDU/CSU candidate for chancellor and usually the most outspoken critic of SPD détente policies, was relatively restrained in his criticism of the government. Although Strauss at one point did assert that if he were elected he would demand a renegotiation of the 1972 Moscow and Warsaw treaties, which had been the foundation of West Germany's Eastern policies for almost a decade,[35] Strauss was generally less acerbic in his comments than the more affable Kohl. In a reversal of roles since the 1976 federal election, when Kohl, as chancellor candidate, had had to restrain Strauss's outspokenness, in the 1980 campaign Strauss went to great lengths to moderate his extremist image to the West German public.[36]

Fundamental to Strauss's problem was his public image as a right-wing ideologue who, if elected, might increase those very tensions in Central Europe which the Ostpolitik of the 1970s had successfully diminished. Thus, far from presenting him with a ready-made campaign issue, the Afghan crisis demonstrated the need for Strauss to appear as a moderate, responsible statesman who could be entrusted with the country's security in times of crisis.[37] Although Strauss did take the high road during the campaign, the Afghan crisis ultimately redounded to the benefit of Helmut Schmidt, who continued to enjoy the confidence of the West German public as the most trustworthy and statesmanlike politician in the country. Polls taken in early 1980 showed voters preferring the CDU/CSU to the SPD by 47 percent to 41 percent, yet Schmidt was preferred over Strauss by 54 percent to 30 percent.[38] By the summer of 1980, the two parties were more evenly matched in public opinion polls (in July, 44.6 percent for CDU/CSU, 44.5 percent for the SPD), yet Strauss was never able to overcome his negative image among the West German voters, and Schmidt continued to be the preferred choice for chancellor by a margin of roughly 60 percent to 35 percent.[39]

On the level of German domestic politics, the issue of Afghanistan worked to Schmidt's advantage in the winter and spring of 1980, allowing the chancellor to capitalize on his international reputation and his political stature, in contrast to Strauss. Moreover, the preoc-

35. Ibid., February 25, 1979, p. 4.
36. Interviews with West German political analysts, fall 1981.
37. *Süddeutsche Zeitung*, January 25, 1980.
38. See *Die Zeit*, March 7, 1980; *Frankfurter Allgemeine Zeitung*, March 1, 1980.
39. *Die Zeit*, August 1, 1980.

cupation of West Germans with foreign policy issues effectively undercut the CDU/CSU campaign strategy of concentrating on domestic economic issues. Given the country's slide into the second recession induced by the oil price hike, with increasing unemployment and budget deficits threatening the government's social welfare programs, the CDU/CSU would have greatly preferred a campaign that revolved around domestic issues.[40] Whether the CDU/CSU could have won such a campaign even with Strauss is open to question. Still, it is doubtful whether Schmidt and the FDP would have enjoyed such a comfortable margin of victory—the government increased its majority in the Bundestag from ten to forty-five seats— had they been forced to contest the election on their domestic record.

From a longer-term perspective, however, the Afghan affair worked to Schmidt's disadvantage on three levels. First, it introduced new strains in the chancellor's relations with the Carter administration. Gone was the temporary pause in sniping between Bonn and Washington (largely between Schmidt and Brzezinski) which resulted from U.S.-FRG cooperation on the NATO INF decision.[41] Even more than the neutron bomb affair or the West German–Brazilian nuclear power agreement, the inability of the United States and West Germany to work out a common response to the Afghan crisis increased misunderstanding and apprehension of the other's foreign policy. In Washington, Brzezinski accused the Schmidt government of indulging in policies that would lead to the self-Finlandization of Europe.[42] For his part, Schmidt found naive Carter's pronouncement that the

40. For an analysis of how an election that focused on domestic issues would have been more to the advantage of the CDU/CSU, see *Rheinische Merkur/Christ und Welt,* February 22, 1980.

41. Schmidt and Brzezinski seem to have been at odds from the earliest days of the Carter presidency. During the Western economic summit in London in May 1977, Brzezinski noted he had "an unexpected clash with the German Chancellor. . . . Since I had known him for years, I greeted him warmly. To my surprise, he was rather haughty and distant. Moreover, he visibly recoiled when I responded to his 'Zbig' with 'Helmut.' Perhaps he felt that I should have used the more deferential 'Mr. Chancellor,' but in that case there was no reason for him to call me by my first name as if I were his employee": Zbigniew Brzezinski, *Power and Principle: Memoirs of the National Security Advisor, 1977–1981* (New York: Farrar, Straus, Giroux, 1983), p. 293.

42. In response, Marion Grafin Donhoff has written that "to pose such questions presumes a naiveté which simply cannot be attributed to a government that has had more experience with the communists than any of its allies in the West. No one has a clearer knowledge of communism than a people one part of whom has had to live under Marxist rule for over 30 years." See her "Bonn and Washington: The Strained Relationship," *Foreign Affairs* 57 (Summer 1979): 1054.

Soviet invasion of Afghanistan had opened the president's eyes overnight concerning the nature of the Soviet system, and the chancellor became even more worried over the incalculability of U.S. foreign policy.[43] In an attempt to reconcile their differences, Schmidt met with Carter in Washington in March. Although press reaction to the meeting was good, and the joint communiqué issued by the two leaders noted that they were "in almost total agreement in their evaluation of the world situation,"[44] both American and West German government officials noted that little progress had been made in settling differences over East–West trade, export credits, the Olympic boycott, and Western military measures in the Persian Gulf.[45] Moreover, Schmidt was impolitic enough to let slip to reporters on the plane back to West Germany that he thought the Carter administration's efforts to deal with inflation in the United States were, once again, "naive."[46] As before, the chancellor only made a bad situation worse with his habit of criticizing the Carter administration to third parties.

Schmidt's inability to get along with the Carter administration reinforced those strains that were beginning to appear in the West German security consensus. Admittedly, the fundamental issues raised by the Soviet move outside its own sphere of influence would have severely tested the conception of West German security that had been broadly adhered to by the three parties since the ratification of the *Ostverträge* (Eastern treaties) in 1972. Nonetheless, the CDU especially, but even Genscher and the FDP to some extent, had misgivings over Schmidt's inability to work constructively with the FRG's most important ally. The debate over the Afghan issue in 1980 brought into clear focus the difficulty that any West German government would face in seeking to reconcile conflicting foreign policy options in a period of crisis. For Helmut Kohl and the CDU, the clear priority Schmidt was giving to Bonn's Ostpolitik at the expense of relations with the United States seemed to signify a leftward drift on the part of the SPD. While Kohl, Strauss, and others in the opposition could not benefit politically by criticizing the need for a West German Ostpolitik, they could certainly criticize Schmidt for alienating the one country that made that Ostpolitik possible. Surveying the fundamental tensions that have always existed between Bonn's

43. See *New York Times*, January 3, 1980.
44. Ibid., March 10, 1980.
45. Ibid., March 7, 1980.
46. Ibid., March 10, 1980.

West- and Ostpolitik, Fritz Stern has summed up Schmidt's difficulty well: "It is once again a complicated hand that history has dealt the Germans: they must have Western support in order to carry out a policy [Ostpolitik] that at times will bring them into disagreement or even conflict with their Western protectors."[47]

These cracks in the security consensus would widen later with the rise of the West German peace movement and a further move to the left by the SPD. Yet the early months of 1980 were marked by increasing differences of opinion, both within the SPD/FDP government and between that government and the CDU/CSU opposition, on a range of foreign policy issues, including INF.

To some extent, the erosion of this security consensus was a product of deepening division within the SPD and Schmidt's difficulty in maintaining party support for his government's policies. An increased willingness of SPD party leaders to criticize the American response to Afghanistan and call into question SPD support for the INF decision was another difficulty Schmidt faced in seeking to reduce tensions between his West- and Ostpolitik. In the first few months of 1980, the chancellor sought vainly to maintain the viability of both. By and large, Schmidt continued to stress that though the Alliance should react firmly to events in Afghanistan, any Western response should not jeopardize European détente. As he noted in a speech in Stuttgart on February 21: "In no other country is the national interest in military parity and détente so vital as in the Federal Republic. We in Europe are in the most exposed position. We therefore have the greatest interest in seeing that the present international crisis is brought under control through deescalatory crisis management."[48]

By the same token, though, Schmidt labored for an equitable division of labor within the Alliance which would allow NATO to present a common front to Soviet aggression. In particular, Schmidt went to great lengths to persuade, though with not much success, Giscard d'Estaing of France to join in the Western effort.[49]

Despite his attempts to "make clear to the Americans that particular European concerns must influence" the decision-making process,[50]

---

47. Fritz Stern, "Germany in a Semi-Gaullist Europe," *Foreign Affairs* 58 (Spring 1980): 885.

48. *Stuttgarter Zeitung*, February 22, 1980.

49. For more on Franco-German deliberations over the appropriate Western response to Afghanistan, see *New York Times*, February 6 and 12, 1980.

50. *Frankfurter Allgemeine Zeitung*, March 10, 1980.

Schmidt continued to face mounting criticism within his own party. Brandt and Bahr became more forceful in their criticisms of U.S. policy, and especially of any talk of mounting an Allied military response in the Persian Gulf. Underlying their critiques of the Carter administration was the belief that West German national interests—that is, Ostpolitik—must remain paramount. As *Die Zeit* noted, they believed that "Germany can safeguard its own national destiny only by maintaining friendly relations with the East." For Bahr especially, the United States "is, in the end, but a power to be weighed on the scales of German national interest" ("nur ein Gewicht, das auf die richtiger Art und zur rechten Zeit zugunsten der Bundesrepublik auf die Waagschale geleft werden musste"). According to *Die Zeit*, Bahr was not "a convinced supporter of the Western community, but a German nationalist."[51]

A concern with German vulnerability to East–West tensions was also being voiced by Herbert Wehner, who echoed the calls of others in the SPD that the party reexamine its support for the INF decision. Inasmuch as the death of SALT II had made remote the possibility of an early start to INF arms talks, especially as it was an American election year, Wehner began to back away from the support he had given Schmidt at the West Berlin party congress. At a party meeting in the Saarland in mid-March, Wehner stressed the priority to be given to détente, warning that any stationing of INF systems would only "heat up the atmosphere." In particular, Wehner warned of the dangers of the central role the FRG would play in any such deployment, saying that "the arms race is a devil's circle, and we are not the Devil."[52]

By the spring of 1980, then, Schmidt was faced once again with mounting opposition to the NATO INF decision within the SPD. In particular, the chancellor was concerned that the SPD left wing would seek to reopen the issue at the party's electoral party congress (Wahlparteitag) in June in Essen, where the SPD would present its 1980 campaign platform. As had been noted often during the debate at the West Berlin party congress, INF opponents thought the party should review the INF situation within six months of the Brussels decision to see if changed circumstances demanded any revisions in the party's position. With the Afghan affair having all but killed East–West nuclear arms control efforts, there were indeed changes in the INF situation.

51. *Die Zeit*, January 18, 1980.
52. *Frankfurter Allgemeine Zeitung*, March 17, 1980.

To preempt any such challenges at the Essen party congress, and in response to Wehner's growing criticism, Schmidt took the unusual step of calling in April for a moratorium on any new INF deployments, by either the East or West, to improve the chances for an arms control agreement once negotiations had begun. In a speech to delegates at a regional party conference in Hamburg, Schmidt also criticized the two superpowers—the United States for failing to ratify SALT II and the Soviets for not being willing to begin INF negotiations.[53]

Although the chancellor may have hoped to keep his moratorium proposal within the confines of SPD party politics, press reports were soon carrying the chancellor's remarks across the Atlantic, with predictable results.[54] Reaction in Washington and at NATO headquarters in Brussels was immediate and critical. NATO officials claimed Schmidt was undercutting the December INF decision and that his moratorium proposal would legitimize those SS-20s already in place while making any eventual deployment of NATO INF more difficult. Moreover, these officials recalled that Schmidt had been a primary opponent of separating Alliance production and deployment decisions, and that his call for a moratorium now would make it more difficult to get the Dutch and Belgians to agree ultimately to INF deployment, should that be necessary. Finally, many officials wondered whether Schmidt's call for a "specific period" for such a moratorium was really intended to last only until December 1983, when NATO would be ready to deploy INF, or whether it might last longer.[55] In the Federal Republic, CDU/CSU spokesmen renewed their attacks on Schmidt, with Franz Josef Strauss denouncing the chancellor as "a security risk" to the Alliance.[56]

In an attempt to limit the damage, Schmidt responded by saying he had never explicitly advocated either a moratorium or a freeze on INF deployment. His main concern, the chancellor explained, was with the principle of negotiated arms settlements, and with the

53. The *Frankfurter Allgemeine Zeitung* reported on April 14, 1980, that Schmidt "proposed as a first step . . . a simultaneous renunciation by both sides of deploying new weapons, at the same time partaking of negotiations."

54. The original report in the *Frankfurter Allgemeine Zeitung* was buried in a longer story on p. 4 (April 14, 1980). The *New York Times* carried the story on April 17 and reported Schmidt as saying it would be a good idea "if both sides simultaneously renounced deployment of new or additional middle-range rockets for a certain number of years and used the time for negotiating."

55. *Frankfurter Allgemeine Zeitung,* April 17, 1980.

56. *New York Times,* April 17, 1980.

threat that an unrestrained arms race would pose for the arms control process.[57] Without saying so explicitly, Schmidt also implied that, for the time being at least, NATO had little to lose from any such delay in new deployments, as the Soviets were the only ones deploying new systems. As he expressed it to party delegates in Essen on June 9:

> My brief suggestion, that the upcoming period should be used for negotiations rather than a further exacerbation of the situation, has been rejected by the Soviets and painstakingly misunderstood by a few in the West. I stand by it, however: it would serve the cause of peace if neither side in the next three years further exacerbated the situation, but immediately began to negotiate bilateral limits.[58]

Even though Schmidt did not call for a moratorium in name, the concept of one clearly underlay the thrust of his "brief suggestion" and led to renewed tension with the Carter administration. The concept of a moratorium, while not explicity endorsed, had been contained in the SPD platform on INF adopted at the West Berlin party congress. To officials in the Carter administration, the fact that Schmidt seemed to be refloating the idea, especially when the Alliance was already divided over the Afghan affair, presaged a possible weakening of support by the Schmidt government for the NATO dual decision. Brzezinski noted in his memoirs:

> The problem of encouraging a stronger European response to Soviet expansionism was exacerbated that spring by a new proposal from the Chancellor. . . . Although the proposal actually did not entail a freeze, it was ambiguous enough to create the public impression that it was in fact a freeze. I feared that it would further undercut Western European support for the nuclear initiative. During lunch at the Pentagon the next day [June 11] Harold Brown, Ed Muskie [who had become secretary of state in May 1980] and I agreed that the President should send a toughly worded message to Schmidt on his new idea. The text that I proposed was approved, and I submitted it in the evening to the President.[59]

57. Remarks made by Schmidt at a conference on German–American relations sponsored by the Friedrich Ebert Stiftung, June 13–14, 1980, Bonn, attended by the author.

58. "Unkorrigiertes Protokoll 9," in *SPD Wahlparteitag Essen, 1980* (Bonn: Vorstand der SPD, 1980), p. 48.

59. Brzezinski, *Power and Principle*, p. 309.

As Brzezinski went on to note, Schmidt "was not pleased" when Carter subsequently admonished the chancellor, by letter, to steer clear of any commitments concerning NATO INF deployment during Schmidt's upcoming talks with Brezhnev in Moscow, scheduled for late June. In his journal entry for June 18, Brzezinski captured, at least from the viewpoint of the Carter administration, the essence of U.S.–FRG difficulties:

> Schmidt is furious over the President's message no doubt, and the President will have a confrontation of sorts with him when the two of them meet in Venice [for the Western Economic Summit in mid-June]. The problem is that Schmidt has undercut any sympathy for him by his derogatory statements about the President. Even though every meeting produces declarations of friendship, Schmidt then follows it up with back sniping.[60]

For his part, Schmidt claimed he had no intention of deviating from the NATO INF position during his talks with Brezhnev in Moscow. The chancellor went to great lengths to explain that he would in no way be "representing" the West during his talks with Soviet leaders. His main intention, at a time of East–West tension, was to represent and protect West German interests.[61]

Of course, a prime West German interest at the time was the lack of U.S.–Soviet arms control negotiations on INF, and the difficulties it caused Schmidt within the SPD. Thus, while Schmidt may have disclaimed the role of intermediary between the two superpowers, he nonetheless was vitally interested in having the Soviets drop their precondition that INF negotiations could not begin until NATO had renounced its INF dual decision. And in this task Schmidt was successful. In his meetings with Defense Minister Dmitri Ustinov and Marshal Nikolai Ogarkov, chief of the general staff, Schmidt was subjected to constant criticism concerning the INF decision. Yet the chancellor came away from the Moscow meeting impressed with the "depth and seriousness of the discussions."[62] Just a few days later, the Soviets did drop their objections to the NATO decision and agreed to begin INF talks with the United States.[63] Although those

---

60. Ibid. For Brzezinski's account of the Schmidt–Carter encounter in Venice, which "turned out to be quite a humdinger," see p. 310.

61. For Schmidt's recounting of the lively exchange with Carter during the Venice summit, see Helmut Schmidt, *Menschen und Mächte* (Berlin: Siedler, 1987), pp. 255–262.

62. *Frankfurter Allgemeine Zeitung*, July 2, 1980.

63. *New York Times*, July 3, 1980.

talks occupied only a few sessions in the fall of 1980, given Carter's defeat in the November election and the need to wait for the incoming Reagan administration, Schmidt could be somewhat satisfied that he had opened up at least one channel of communication between the superpowers.

Even more satisfying were the results of the November 1980 national election, when the SPD/FDP coalition took a combined 53.5 percent of the vote, compared to 44.5 percent for the CDU/CSU. The government's majority in the Bundestag increased from ten to forty-five seats, providing Schmidt with a bit more room for parliamentary maneuver.

Despite this victory, however, Schmidt's domestic political situation was anything but secure. Immediately after the election, long-simmering tensions within the SPD/FDP coalition flared anew over economic, social welfare, and defense budget policies, with the FDP economics minister, Otto Graf Lambsdorff, especially critical of SPD fiscal policies.[64] Moreover, the very fact that the SPD/FDP coalition had increased its parliamentary plurality meant that dissident SPD members of the Bundestag could be more vocal in their criticism of Schmidt and vote more freely against the government on important policy issues without risk of toppling the chancellor.[65]

The Green Party and the Rise of the Peace Movement

Tensions within the coalition were caused in part by the FDP's fear of the leftward drift of the SPD, which in turn was partly the result of the emergence of the Greens as a national political force. Hoping to build on their success in various Länder elections in the late 1970s, the regional Green parties and environmental groups decided, in January 1980, to form a national party to contest the upcoming Bundestag elections. Just two months later, in March, the Greens scored a major victory by winning seats in the Baden-Württemberg Landtag, with a total of 5.3 percent of the vote. While this was barely over the 5 percent minimum needed to win seats in the regional parliament, the Greens did demonstrate impressive

64. For more on SPD–FDP tensions, see *Die Zeit*, November 21, 1980.

65. For reports on increased SPD criticism of the INF decision following the 1980 election, see the article by Karsten Voigt, in *Frankfurter Rundschau*, May 20, 1981, and reports of opposition in the Baden-Württemberg SPD, *Frankfurter Rundschau*, May 15, 1981.

strength in cities with a large university population (11.6 percent in Freiburg and 10 percent in Tübingen), as well as a more than respectable 7 percent in Stuttgart.

Although the Greens won only 1.5 percent of the vote in the November national election and thus failed to win any Bundestag seats, their entry into national politics was significant both in terms of their appeal to many traditional SPD supporters and in the organizational framework they provided for the emerging German peace movement (Friedensbewegung).

As it gained momentum in 1980 in response to the NATO INF decision and deteriorating East–West relations, the peace movement in the FRG encompassed a diverse cross section of West German society.[66] Peace movement activists were drawn from across the political spectrum: from communists to clergy, ecologists to military figures, housewives to students. Although many of the movement's leaders came from the Green party, important organizational roles were also played by the Protestant church, the Young Socialists (Jusos), several trade unions and peace research institutes, and members of the media.[67]

It was from this organizational base that the Peace movement grew from what was initially an internal SPD split over the NATO INF decision into a broad-based campaign, symbolized by the Krefeld Appeal. This appeal to reject INF deployment, issued in November 1980 by, among others, General Bastian, Petra Kelly (then chairperson of the Greens), Pastor Martin Niemöller, and Christoph Strasser (a leader of the FDP), called on the Schmidt government to withdraw its support for the INF decision. By 1982 it had gathered 1.5 million signatures.

In the three-year period between the appearance of the Krefeld Appeal and the planned arrival of the first Pershing and cruise missiles on West German territory, the peace movement was able to mobilize hundreds of thousands of anti-INF demonstrators. Many of these demonstrations, such as one in April 1981 in Bonn to protest a meeting of NATO's Nuclear Planning Group, recalled the Easter peace marches of the early 1960s. Others were organized by the West German Evangelical (Protestant) church. In June 1981, for example, the Evangelical church adopted peace and disarmament as

66. See Jeffrey Boutwell, "Politics and the Peace Movement in West Germany," *International Security* 7 (Spring 1983).

67. For more on the involvement of the Protestant (and Catholic) churches in the peace movement, see *Der Stern*, June 4, 1981, pp. 20–31.

the theme for its national conference (*Kirchentag*) and drew more than 100,000 people to Hamburg.[68] In the fall of 1981 especially, peace movement demonstrations drew several hundred thousand people to massive rallies, not only in Bonn but elsewhere in the FRG and Western Europe. On October 10 in Bonn, more than 250,000 people demonstrated against the Pershings and cruise missiles, many carrying signs declaring "No Euroshima." Two weeks later, on October 24, a rally organized by the British Campaign for Nuclear Disarmament brought out 150,000 demonstrators in London, while more than 100,000 protestors gathered in Rome.[69]

To the extent that the heterogenous peace movement in the FRG had a coordinated strategy for blocking INF deployment, it consisted of following up the massive demonstrations of 1981 with widespread passive resistance measures in 1982, followed in 1983 by direct action against those military bases slated to receive the Pershings and cruise missiles.

The campaign of civil disobedience slated for 1982 was to consist of tax resistance, fasts and hunger strikes, and nonviolent encirclement of NATO and US military installations, such as the Pershing IA missile bases at Geilenkirchen and Schwabisch Gmund.[70] One group involved in the Friedensbewegung (the Federation of Citizens Action Groups to Protect the Environment) urged its members to withhold the symbolic figure of 572 DM from their taxes to protest the 572 INF systems due to arrive in Europe in the fall of 1983. Other groups planned nonviolent protests at U.S. and NATO military bases during the winter and began to organize fasts and hunger strikes thoughout the FRG.

Especially troubling to the Schmidt government in the fall of 1981 was a report prepared by the Federal Office for the Protection of the Constitution, which asserted that radical action groups within the peace movement had drawn up a three-year plan for militant "resistance actions" against U.S. and NATO military installations in the Federal

68. Despite widespread church involvement in the peace movement, the leadership of the Evangelical church at least became increasingly uncomfortable with the anti-American tone of many activists in the movement. See "The Preservation, Promotion and Renewal of Peace," *EKD* [Evangelische Kirche in Deutschland] *Bulletin* (Frankfurt, 1981).

69. *New York Times*, October 11 and 25, 1981.

70. In early 1981, the magazine *Der Stern* published a detailed map of the FRG showing the locations of Pershing IA and Lance missile launchers, nuclear-capable aircraft fields, and nuclear warhead depots. See "Die Versteckte Atommacht," *Der Stern*, February 19, 1981.

Republic.[71] With the cumbersome title of "Security-Endangering Left-Wing Extremist Trends in the Struggle for Peace," the report evoked painful memories of Baader-Meinhof terrorist acts in the late 1970s and violent confrontations between police and protestors at the Brokdorf and Gorleben nuclear energy facilities. When pressed, however, government spokesmen acknowledged that the report was both speculative and somewhat out of date, and that its main thrust was to evaluate "attempts by extremist groups to gain influence" on some of the organizations involved in the peace movement.[72]

In the end, violent protest against INF turned out to be minimal by the time the first Pershing II arrived in the FRG in November 1983. Some confrontations with police near military installations did take place, yet moderate elements in the peace movement were successful in isolating the more extremist factions. In part this success was due to the resumption of U.S.–Soviet negotiations over INF in Geneva in March 1983, and the prospect, however dim, that the superpowers might reach an agreement. Just as important, the CDU/CSU victory in the March 1983 election and the Kohl government's unswerving commitment to INF deployment produced a sense of resignation among many in the Friedensbewegung that INF deployment was inevitable.[73] Peace movement activists had been waging their campaign for three years, and a wearied frustration ultimately took the steam out of their efforts.

COMPOSITION OF THE PEACE MOVEMENT

Although outwardly similar in composition to the Kampf dem Atomtod movement of the 1950s, the 1980s peace movement in the FRG represented a marked change in West German domestic politics. Much of this change had its origins in the student protests of the late 1960s and in the rise of single-issue politics and the proliferation of citizens' initiative groups (*Bürgerinitiativen*) in the 1970s.[74] In the late 1970s, many of these organizations coalesced into various

71. *FBIS: Western Europe*, October 27, 1981, p. J3.

72. *Welt am Sonntag*, October 11, 1981.

73. For more on how members of the peace movement were alternating between resignation and anger on the eve of the arrival of the first Pershing IIs, see "Woche des Zorns," *Der Spiegel*, November 14, 1983, pp. 56–59.

74. See especially Werner Kaltefleiter, "A Legitimacy Crisis of the German Party System," and Jutta A. Helm, "Citizen Lobbies in West Germany," both in Peter H. Merkl, ed., *Western European Party Systems* (New York: Free Press, 1980).

regional Green parties, which began to contest state (Länder) elections. Although the Greens were initially unsuccessful in gaining representation at the state level, they posed an increasing electoral threat to both the SPD and FDP in such Länder as Hamburg, West Berlin, and Bremen, where they gained their first seats in a regional parliament in the fall of 1979. In addition, the public support they received for their environmental positions and their stance against civilian nuclear power put pressure on all three of the major parties to rethink many of their domestic policy positions.

Thus, by the time the peace movement began to emerge in 1980, there was already in place a well-established network of Green activists, environmentalists, opponents of nuclear energy, and citizen-initiative organizations that could give direction to and articulate the concerns of those West Germans, whether Green supporters or not, who were anxious about deteriorating East–West relations, symbolized above all by the INF issue. As the British historian E. P. Thompson, a leader of the peace movement in the United Kingdom, noted in the spring of 1981, "the anti–nuke energy people have moved very sharply in the last two or three months toward joining with the anti-missile people [and] traditional peace movements."[75]

Moreover, there was a synergistic relationship between the peace movement and the Greens, as the rising domestic debate over INF provided the Greens themselves with needed momentum. Following their disappointing showing in the 1980 national election, the Greens vowed to enter upcoming Länder elections in Hamburg and Hesse as "the sole legitimate representative of the peace movement."[76] Not only did the momentum of the peace movement help propel Green candidates into an increasing number of state legislatures in the early 1980s; it also was a factor in helping the Greens crack the 5 percent barrier at the national level when twenty-seven Green deputies were elected to the Bundestag in the March 1983 election.

Although the peace activists and the Greens were ultimately unsuccessful in their attempts to block the deployment of the first Pershing missiles in November 1983, they nonetheless had a substantial impact on the West German domestic debate over security issues in general and INF in particular. For one thing, the peace movement was aided by and helped give rise to a new generation of

75. See the interview with Thompson in *Boston Phoenix*, April 28, 1981, and also an article by Thompson in *Nation*, January 24, 1981.
76. Quoted in *Frankfurter Allgemeine Zeitung*, December 22, 1981.

defense policy analysts, the *Gegenexperten* (counterexperts). Centered in West German universities, peace research institutes, and the media, these analysts helped broaden the scope of the debate by criticizing the policies of the Schmidt government and publicizing alternative security concepts.[77] Unlike the situation in the 1950s during the Kampf dem Atomtod movement, in the early 1980s a growing network of West German elites outside the government and military were conversant with the more arcane tenets of nuclear weapons strategies and force postures. Together with a large number of "successor generation" journalists and editors who were highly critical of U.S. and NATO policies, these defense experts were able to provide the peace movement with a steady stream of alternatives to NATO policy.

Of course, the ability of the peace movement to mobilize tremendous demonstrations against INF was also a constant thorn in the side of the Schmidt government. In an attempt to deflect rising criticism of the chancellor's INF policy, SPD moderates and trade union leaders launched their own "peace initiative" (the *Frieden durch Abrüstung* [Peace through Disarmament] campaign) and sought to portray the SPD as the "biggest peace movement in the FRG."[78] At the same time, the SPD convened a "Peace Forum" with leaders of the peace movement on the topic of nuclear deterrence in a thinly veiled attempt to co-opt them.[79] Despite these and other efforts, however, the Krefeld Appeal continued to be the rallying point for the Friedensbewegung.

At times, Schmidt's irritation with the peace movement came out into the open, as in August 1981, when he castigated the Krefeld Appeal for failing to criticize Soviet policy, adding that the Appeal "is an instrument that will please the Soviet leadership."[80] Two months later, on October 9 (the day before one of the largest peace movement rallies in Bonn), Schmidt told the Bundestag that some

77. Among the better-known Gegenexperten were Dieter Lutz (Institut für Friedensforschung und Sicherheitspolitik, Hamburg); Horst Afheldt and Alfred Mechtersheimer (Max Planck Gesellschaft, Munich); and Gert Krell and Thomas Risse-Kappen (Hessische Stiftung Friedens- und Konfliktforschung, Frankfurt).

78. For more on the involvement of the German Trade Union Federation (DGB) in the INF debate and a DGB-sponsored rally in Düsseldorf on September 1, the forty-second anniversary of the start of World War II, see *Süddeutsche Zeitung*, September 2 and 3, 1981.

79. For a review of the SPD-sponsored Forum Frieden, see *Die Zeit*, September 4, 1981, pp. 9–11.

80. *Frankfurter Allgemeine Zeitung*, August 31, 1981.

members of the Friedensbewegung "want to persuade us that Soviet missiles serve peace, whereas American missiles serve war."[81]

Other Schmidt government spokesmen were even more strident in their attacks on the peace movement. Perhaps the strongest of these attacks came from Peter Corterier, minister of state in the Foreign Ministry, who shortly before the October 10 demonstration evoked painful memories of the Weimar period when he said that the upcoming demonstration was a "stab in back" for the Schmidt government. Corterier also hinted that the party leadership might seek to invoke the SPD "irreconcilability resolution" (prohibiting joint actions with known communists) against SPD members who joined the October 10 demonstration, adding that "anyone who continues to demonstrate with communists against the government must ask himself whether he can remain a member of this party."[82]

While it was true that communists and other left-wing extremist groups were involved in the peace movement, their influence was limited, a fact Schmidt himself acknowledged on numerous occasions. For example, the Deutsche Friedens Union, created in the 1950s to provide an organizational base for the outlawed German Communist party, was heavily involved in helping to organize anti-INF protests, and one of its leaders, Josef Weber, was an original signer of the Krefeld Appeal. In addition, it is more than likely that various peace groups in the FRG received substantial funding from Moscow and East Berlin.[83] Yet the relative weight of such groups in the overall Friedensbewegung was small and not very significant.

GOALS OF THE PEACE MOVEMENT

Given the many disparate strands that made up the peace movement, it was easier to tell what the eco-peace activists were against than what they were for. Beyond their opposition to the Euromissiles, many activists were in favor of the denuclearization of the two

81. For the text of the speech, see *FBIS: Western Europe*, October 13, 1981, pp. J1–J5.

82. Ibid., October 5, 1981, p. J2.

83. One assertion of Soviet covert funding of Western antinuclear groups comes from Stanislav Levchenko, a KGB officer who defected to the West in 1979, who claimed that Moscow provided $200 million to the campaign against the neutron bomb in 1977–78; see *New York Times*, July 26, 1983.

Germanies, if not Europe, as well as superpower military disengagement from the continent. Others called for the adoption of "nonoffensive" or "nonprovocative" force postures (that is, strict limitations on tanks, artillery, and ground-attack aircraft) to give NATO and the FRG a decidedly "defensive" orientation. There was much support for an end to military conscription and large cuts in the defense budget. The Greens advocated the dismantling of the Bundeswehr altogether and a strategy of massive civil disobedience (so-called social defense, or *Sozialvertidigung*) in order to deter a potential invader.[84]

Thus the opposition to NATO INF in the early 1980s was only one part of a broader security policy being advocated by leaders of the peace movement and the Greens. According to Peter Bender, one of the original theoreticians of the country's Ostpolitik in the 1960s, the INF issue was but a sympton of a dangerous dependency by which the FRG had become entangled in the U.S.–Soviet arms race. Bender argued that INF deployment would mean that Western Europe in the 1980s would be for the United States what Cuba had been for the USSR in the early 1960s: nothing more than a launching pad for nuclear missiles with flight times under ten minutes.[85] The fact that the Pershing II missiles would be able to strike deep in the Soviet Union, with almost no warning, was a major concern for many in the peace movement. In addressing the 250,000 demonstrators at the October 10 rally in Bonn, Erhard Eppler of the SPD voiced these fears when he spoke of "threatening the center of Russia from European soil with such a short warning time as to make political decisions impossible," thus putting "our own survival in the hands of a computer."[86]

Other speakers at the rally, such as Heinrich Albertz, a Protestant pastor and former SPD mayor of West Berlin, picked up on the Bender theme and argued that West Germany's situation was one of "complete dependency . . . without full sovereignty."[87] And for Eppler,

---

84. As contained in the Greens' party platform, the concept of social defense "means that West German society should be so organized and reoriented—in the direction of civil courage, resistance, alternative and decentralized structures—that it would be clear from the beginning to an aggressive foreign power that the attempt to occupy and dominate would bring such difficulties and burdens that the benefits in power and profits would not be worth the cost." See *Die Grünen: Das Bundesprogramm* (Bonn, 1980).

85. Peter Bender, *Das Ende des ideologischen Zeitalters* (West Berlin: Severin und Siedler, 1981), pp. 183–193.

86. Quoted in *New York Times*, October 11, 1981.

87. Quoted in ibid.

who held leadership positions in both the SPD and the Evangelical church, the Pershings and cruise missiles represented a striving for military superiority that not only endangered the Federal Republic's Ostpolitik but increased the risk that both West and East Germany would be subjected to nuclear devastation.[88]

Despite widespread opposition to NATO INF, however, most supporters of the peace movement were neither pro-Soviet nor united on how best to safeguard the security of the FRG. Although West German communists were heavily involved in the peace movement and the Greens, most activists in the eco-peace movement were just as critical of Soviet as of U.S. policy. For the most part, those who advocated a new security arrangement for West Germany proposed solutions that were either "European" or nationalist. Thus Eppler argued that the peace movement in the Federal Republic should link up with peace movements elsewhere in Europe so that the continent could become a "third force" in international politics. For others, such as Albertz and the Lutheran pastor Helmut Gollwitzer, the goal was more explicitly nationalist: to create a demilitarized, neutral, and reunited Germany.[89]

Admittedly, such sentiments represented only a small, albeit vocal, minority of West Germans. Despite the attention given to this minority, especially in the U.S. press, most West Germans continued to profess strong support for the FRG's role in NATO, even while expressing doubts about INF deployment. Thus, even at the height of the demonstrations in the fall of 1981, only 33 percent of West German respondents thought the country should adopt a neutralist foreign policy.[90] It is true that almost half (46 percent) of those aged sixteen to twenty-nine advocated such a policy, yet this was at the height of U.S.–Soviet tensions, and similar polls in later years showed diminished support for a neutralist foreign policy, even among the young.[91]

88. Erhard Eppler, *Wege aus der Gefahr* (Hamburg: Rowohlt, 1981), pp. 82–86.

89. See William E. Griffith, "Bonn and Washington: From Deterioration to Crisis?" *Orbis*, Spring 1982, pp. 117–133.

90. Respondents were asked, "What do you think would be the better foreign policy: Should we firmly link ourselves with the Americans militarily, or should we try to be completely neutral?" See *FBIS: Western Europe*, November 16, 1981, p. J5. A 1988 poll found 78 percent of the 16–24-year-old respondents saying that the FRG should remain in NATO; see *Das Parlament*, February 17, 1989.

91. In the mid-1980s, for example, 94 percent of CDU/CSU supporters and 85 percent of SPD supporters agreed with the proposition that NATO is essential to West German security; see Stephen F. Szabo, "West German Public Attitudes on Arms Control," in Barry M. Blechman and Cathleen Fisher, eds., *The Silent Partner: West Germany and Arms Control* (Cambridge, Mass.: Ballinger, 1988), p. 216.

Nonetheless, the activist core of the eco-peace movement did represent the political coming of age of a large segment of a postwar generation that was increasingly critical of West German society. In large part this dissatisfaction was the result of the economic recession of the late 1970s and the restricted opportunities for many of the "overeducated and underemployed" youth coming out of a liberalized and expanded West German university system, which had doubled in size from 1970 to 1980 (420,000 to 880,000 students). Highly critical of the centrist policies of the three main political parties and the materialist basis of West German society, these activists in the eco-peace movement stressed grass-roots political action and "quality of life" issues.[92]

By and large, supporters of the Greens in the early 1980s were highly educated, young, and of the urban middle and upper-middle class. Nourished by the breakdown of traditional societal units (whether based on family, religion, or socioeconomic class), support for the Greens was one manifestation of attempts by the postwar generation to develop alternative cultural lifestyles. As Gerd Langguth has noted, the Greens and other youth protest movements were also part of a "postadolescence" phenomenon that saw increasing numbers of young West Germans postponing entrance into the work force.[93] The university stipends and parental support that eased concern about individual economic security greatly reinforced the "postmaterialist" values and antiestablishment inclinations of many younger West Germans (in much the same way that they contributed to the counterculture of American youth in the 1960s).

In addition, the eco-peace movement in the early 1980s was spurred by the coming together of two strands in German–American relations which had not previously existed simultaneously. One strand was West German uneasiness with U.S. security policy, the other a rejection of American society as a model to be emulated. In the 1950s, for example, although many West Germans were critical of U.S. and NATO nuclear weapons policies, memories of Marshall

92. For more on the Green phenomenon, see Alfred Rothacher, "The Green Party in German Politics," *West European Politics* 7 (July 1984); and Gerd Langguth, *The Green Factor in German Politics*, trans. Richard Strauss (Boulder, Colo.: Westview Press, 1986).

93. Langguth notes that in 1970 about 44 percent of those aged 15–19 were working for a living, but by 1980 this figure had dropped to 28 percent; see Gerd Langguth, "The Green Movement in Germany," Konrad Adenauer Stiftung, Occasional Paper ser. no. 3–86 (Bonn, 1986), p. 3. See also Werner Hülsberg, *The German Greens: A Social and Political Profile* (London: Verso, 1988).

Plan aid and U.S. political support for the FRG were still dominant in a West Germany preoccupied with furthering its economic prosperity. In the late 1960s and early 1970s, the confluence of superpower détente and Ostpolitik muted differences over security policy, yet many younger West Germans especially were critical of what they saw as a bourgeois U.S. imperialism that led to race riots at home and the Vietnam conflict abroad.

In the early 1980s, however, there was a good deal of criticism across West German society of U.S. domestic and foreign policies. Many younger West Germans of the "successor generation," but others as well, were highly critical of the conservative swing in American politics and Reagan administration policies that cut social welfare spending while greatly increasing defense budgets. In October 1981, for example, the influential weekly *Der Spiegel* carried a long cover story, titled "Reagan's America—A Land for the Rich," which noted that "Ronald Reagan has undertaken the most far-reaching domestic political about-face in the U.S. since FDR."[94] In detailing the cuts in social programs being carried out by the Reagan administration, the *Spiegel* article mirrored the unease of many West Germans, both young and old, about this divergence in a commitment to basic social services in the FRG and the United States.

In addition, Germans across the political spectrum were upset by Reagan's description of the USSR as the "evil empire" and his calls for military superiority over the Soviets. Such feelings were exacerbated by loose talk in the administration of the possibility of a nuclear war limited to Europe. In short, for many activists in the Greens and the peace movement, as well as on the left wing of the SPD, criticism of Reagan security policies was reinforced by rejection of American society as a model, which in turn produced the anti-American tenor of the Friedensbewegung and increased calls for West Germany to find a "third way" between the superpowers.

In the end, the INF issue was only one of many factors that helped spark the peace movement and propel the Greens to national prominence. Yet these two developments in the early 1980s—a broad-based peace campaign against Schmidt's INF policy and the appearance of a viable political competitor to the left of the SPD—exacerbated existing tensions between Schmidt and his FDP coalition partner. By the middle of 1982, these tensions within the

94. *Der Spiegel*, October 26, 1981, pp. 158–169.

coalition had developed to the point where it seemed only a matter of time until Genscher and the FDP bolted to join the CDU/CSU. In September the inevitable finally happened, and thirteen years of Social Democratic governing came to an end.

[5]

The CDU/CSU and the
INF Treaty: 1982–1988

During the summer of 1982, tensions within the SPD/FDP coalition steadily increased as the Schmidt government sought to cope with stagnant economic growth, rising unemployment, and reduced government revenues. The chancellor was under pressure from his own party and the trade unions to increase public spending and create jobs, yet FDP leader Genscher and Economics Minister Lambsdorff openly rejected what they considered inflationary fiscal policies. Although the FDP supported Schmidt against a threatened vote of no confidence in February 1982, Lambsdorff in particular renewed his attacks on SPD budget policies in the spring of 1982. Following an SPD party congress in Munich in April 1982, at which the party again advocated tax increases to fund new jobs, Lambsdorff flatly rejected FDP support for what he called "torture instruments from the socialist chamber of horrors."[1]

In June, coalition unity suffered another blow when both the SPD and FDP suffered embarrassing losses in the Hamburg state elections. Schmidt had campaigned heavily in his native city on behalf of the SPD mayor, Klaus von Dohnanyi, to no avail. The Social Democrats suffered big losses in what had traditionally been an electoral stronghold, while the FDP failed to win 5 percent of the vote and was eliminated from the local parliament entirely. Adding insult to injury for both Schmidt and Genscher, the Greens replaced the FDP in the Hamburg parliament and began negotiating with the local SPD about a cooperative governing arrangement. Genscher

1. Quoted in Jonathan Carr, *Helmut Schmidt: Helmsman of Germany* (New York: St. Martin's Press, 1985), p. 179.

and the FDP were concerned by this renewed threat from the Greens to FDP electoral fortunes at the Länder level, while Schmidt was irritated by the tolerance shown by Brandt and other party leaders for the prospect of a "red-green" coalition.

By the summer of 1982, the chancellor needed a major policymaking success to arrest the growing fragmentation of the SPD/FDP coalition in Bonn. Ironically, such a success almost materialized, although Schmidt was probably unaware of it at the time. In mid-July, the U.S. and Soviet INF negotiators, Paul Nitze and Yuli Kvitsinski, came up with their famous "walk in the woods" accord for limiting medium-range missiles in Europe.[2] The outlines of the accord became public only after both Washington and Moscow had repudiated it, yet its implementation would have been a major coup for Schmidt.

The Nitze-Kvitsinski formula would have set equal ceilings of seventy-five launchers for NATO GLCMs and Soviet SS-20s in the European theater, while banning the Pershing II. Had the superpowers agreed to such an accord, left-wing SPD criticism of Schmidt's double track INF policy would have been blunted, and the peace movement and the Greens would have lost one of their major issues vis-à-vis Schmidt (especially as much of their criticism focused on the destabilizing aspects of the Pershing II, which many critics called a "first-strike" weapon because its flight time from the FRG to the Soviet Union was less than ten minutes). By securing his left flank from SPD radicals and the Greens on the INF issue, Schmidt might have been able to convince Genscher and the FDP that compromise was possible on economic and domestic issues.

In the absence of a major policy victory, Lambsdorff and others in the FDP continued to claim that Schmidt was being held hostage by left-wing elements in the SPD. In early September, Lambsdorff released an economic policy paper that called for large cuts in social-welfare spending which would allow for reductions in corporate taxes and increased public investment. The West German trade unions called the paper "a declaration of war," while Schmidt pointedly asked Lamsbdorff if the paper was meant to be a "writ of divorce" between the SPD and FDP.[3] Shortly thereafter, Schmidt decided to bring matters to a head by dismissing the four FDP cabinet ministers (they ended up resigning first) and calling for new

2. See especially Strobe Talbott, *The Master of the Game: Paul Nitze and the Nuclear Peace* (New York: Knopf, 1988), pp. 174–181.
3. Quoted in Carr, *Helmut Schmidt*, p. 184.

elections.[4] In a masterful speech to the Bundestag on September 17, the chancellor sought to convince wavering FDP deputies of the dangers to FDP electoral credibility of switching allegiance to the CDU/CSU, largely by spelling out for the public the culpability of FDP leaders in undermining the coalition.

In the period leading up to Schmidt's speech, Genscher had wavered in openly precipitating a break with the SPD. Content to let Lambsdorff orchestrate the FDP's criticism of its senior coalition partner, Genscher was concerned lest the FDP itself split over the fall of the Schmidt government. Genscher also feared that voter resentment at FDP tactics against a personally popular chancellor might cause the party to fall short of the 5 percent of the vote necessary to remain in the Bundestag when new elections were held.

Once Schmidt forced the issue, however, Genscher came to an agreement with the leader of the CDU/CSU opposition, Helmut Kohl, that their two parties would introduce a "constructive vote of no-confidence" in the Bundestag, which, if successful, would automatically replace Schmidt with Kohl. In addition, Genscher and Kohl agreed that the resulting Kohl-Genscher government would be interim only and that new general elections would be held on March 6, 1983.

In the days leading up to the Bundestag no-confidence vote on October 1, it appeared that Genscher's strategy might backfire. Regional elections in Hesse on September 26 (where the local FDP had recently deserted the SPD/FDP ruling coalition and switched to the CDU) produced a stunning SPD victory and eliminated the FDP from the Hesse parliament. In the last few days before October 1, SPD leaders hoped that enough FDP parliamentarians would stick with the Schmidt government to defeat the no-confidence vote.

In the end, however, Genscher and Lambsdorff were able to carry enough FDP Bundestag members with them, and the no-confidence vote carried, 256 to 235, with four abstentions. Helmut Kohl became the Federal Republic's sixth chancellor, and the CDU/CSU returned to power for the first time since 1969. It was only the second time in

4. In order to avoid an inherent weakness of the Weimar Republic, the Basic Law of the Federal Republic stipulates that a chancellor can be removed only if a majority of the Bundestag can agree on a successor (constructive vote of no confidence). A chancellor can ask the federal president to dissolve parliament if the chancellor fails to win a regular vote of confidence, but the ultimate power to call for new elections rests with the president. See Gerhard Loewenberg, *Parliament in the German Political System* (Ithaca: Cornell University Press, 1967), pp. 28, 219–221, 272–273.

the FRG's history that a constructive vote of no-confidence had been called, and it was the first to be successful.[5] Schmidt remained in the Bundestag as a member from Hamburg, and let it be known that he would not be the SPD candidate for chancellor when general elections were held on March 6 the following year.

In the 1983 election, Kohl was pitted against Hans-Jochen Vogel, a former minister of justice in the Schmidt government. A well-respected if somewhat colorless politician, Vogel had the unenviable task of campaigning against the now-incumbent Kohl while trying to heal those divisions in the SPD that had contributed to Schmidt's downfall in the first place.

The result was a disaster. Vogel and the SPD won only 38.2 percent of the vote, the party's worst showing in twenty years. The CDU/CSU, with 48.8 percent of the vote, fell just short of winning an absolute majority, while the FDP comfortably maintained its representation in the Bundestag with 6.9 percent of the vote. Certainly the biggest surprise, however, was the success of the Greens. Demonstrating nationwide strength for the first time, they won 5.6 percent of the vote, enough to send twenty-seven deputies to the Bundestag.[6]

The success of the Greens in establishing themselves as a fourth major party in the FRG was taken by some West Germans as evidence of the electoral salience of the INF issue—but only by a small minority. Indeed, Vogel and the SPD probably suffered by focusing much of their campaign on the Euromissiles. Polls taken shortly before the election showed that the CDU/CSU was the party deemed most competent to handle those issues of greatest importance to West German voters (unemployment, pension security, budget deficits). By comparison, the SPD was considered better able to strengthen the FRG's Ostpolitik and protect the environment, yet voters considered these issues of secondary importance.[7]

Like most FRG elections since 1949 (with the possible exception of the 1980 contest between Schmidt and Strauss), the 1983 contest

5. In April 1972, Rainer Barzel and the CDU/CSU initiated an unsuccessful "constructive vote of no confidence" against Willy Brandt and the SPD/FDP government. A few months later, Brandt himself called for and lost a regular vote of no confidence. He then asked President Gustav Heinemann to dissolve the Bundestag and hold a national election, which the SPD and FDP won in November.

6. *New York Times*, March 7, 1983.

7. David P. Conradt, "The 1983 Federal Election: A Preliminary Analysis," paper prepared for the 1983 American Political Science Association meeting, Chicago, September 1–4, 1983.

turned primarily on economic and social-welfare issues. In this regard, criticism of the SPD for concentrating on the wrong issues (such as INF and arms control) is misplaced. A combination of voter preference for having the CDU/CSU deal with the effects of the West German recession of the early 1980s, plus a natural desire for change after thirteen years of SPD rule and apprehension over the internal divisions within the SPD, made Vogel's task an almost impossible one.

The results of the March 6 election gave the Kohl-Genscher coalition a comfortable Bundestag majority of 58 seats (278 for the government, 220 for the SPD and Greens). With the CDU/CSU now firmly in power for the first time since the late 1960s, the Union had to begin the process of translating party security policies into governmental policy for the first time in a decade and a half. Conversely, Herbert Wehner and others in the SPD noted that divisions within the party were so deep that the SPD could well be facing an equally long stint in opposition.

THE SECURITY POLICIES OF THE CDU/CSU

In comparison with the pronounced divisions over security policy within the SPD, the image presented by the CDU/CSU has long been one of broad adherence to established NATO and U.S. doctrine, especially in regard to the centrality of nuclear deterrence (Table 2 shows the NATO nuclear arsenal in early 1984).[8] By the same token, during most of the postwar period the Union gave only grudging acceptance to arms control and Ostpolitik.

The traditional dividing line within the Union has been that between the "Atlanticist" orientation of CDU moderates and the "Gaullist" proclivities of CDU conservatives and most members of the CSU.[9] As during the Adenauer years, the Atlantic and West European orientations of the CDU/CSU have most often been complementary rather than divisive. The common denominator has been the perception that Soviet military and political power is the

8. See also Jeffrey Boutwell, "Party Politics and Security Policies in the FRG," in Stephen F. Szabo, ed., *The Bundeswehr and the Future of Western Defense* (London: Macmillan, 1990).

9. For a good analysis of CDU/CSU defense policy, see Clay Clemens, "The CDU/CSU and Arms Control," in Barry M. Blechman and Cathleen Fisher, eds., *The Silent Partner: West Germany and Arms Control* (Cambridge, Mass.: Ballinger, 1988).

Table 2. U.S. nuclear weapons and number of warheads in Europe, c. 1984

Nuclear weapon	Warhead	Number of warheads			Allied users
		U.S. use	Non-U.S. use	Total	
Bombs	B-61, B-57, B-43, B-28	1,416	324	1,740	Belgium, Greece, Italy, Netherlands, Turkey, West Germany
Depth bombs	B-57	129	63	192	Italy, Netherlands, United Kingdom
Long-range missiles					
Pershing II	W-85	54	—	54	
GLCM	W-84	100	—	100	
Short-range missiles					
Pershing 1a	W-50	120	100	220	West Germany
Lance	W-70	324	366	690	Belgium, Greece, Italy, Netherlands, West Germany, United Kingdom
Honest John	W-31	—	198	198	Greece, Turkey
Artillery					
8-inch	W-33	506	432	938	Belgium, Greece, Italy, Netherlands, Turkey, West Germany, United Kingdom
155-mm	W-48	594	138	732	Belgium, Greece, Italy, Netherlands, Turkey, West Germany, United Kingdom
Nike Hercules	W-31	296	390	686	Belgium, Greece, Italy, Netherlands, West Germany
ADMs	W-45, W-54	372	*	372	Belgium, Netherlands, West Germany, United Kingdom
All nuclear weapons		3,911	2,013	5,922	

*Unknown.

SOURCE: Adapted by permission from William M. Arkin and Richard W. Fieldhouse, *Nuclear Battlefields: Global Links in the Arms Race* (Cambridge, Mass.: Ballinger, 1985), p. 102.

overriding threat to West German security, necessitating tight FRG integration into the Western Alliance and dependence above all on the U.S. nuclear guarantee. Accordingly, it has been only during those periods when the U.S. commitment is called into question (as during Eisenhower's New Look policy and the Berlin crises of

1958–1961) that Atlanticist and Gaullist differences have been most pronounced and debate has been renewed on the extent to which the FRG should depend on the United States, as opposed to its West European allies.

Given this faith in the ultimate dissuasive power of nuclear weapons, the CDU/CSU has long considered the concept of conventional deterrence strictly secondary—hence the relative lack of Union interest in conventional arms control (until recently) and concepts of alternative defense, except as they would impinge negatively on West Germany's political status within the Alliance.[10]

Conversely, impending changes in NATO's nuclear deterrent and prospects for superpower arms control are of central concern to the CDU/CSU. The Union is never so united as when the Western deterrent is being modernized and strengthened (during the INF deployments) and never so at odds with itself as when arms control agreements presage major changes to that deterrent (the INF double-zero agreement and possible 35 percent reductions in U.S. and Soviet strategic systems under the START agreement).

At such times, and also during periods of U.S. political vacillation, the Gaullist proclivity for advocating a European nuclear force based on French and British forces comes to the fore. This happened following the Berlin crises of 1958–1961 and again during the Carter administration. For such Gaullists as the late Franz Josef Strauss of the CSU and Alfred Dregger of the CDU, a European deterrent would reduce overreliance on the vagaries of an uncertain superpower ally and concomitantly strengthen West Europe's political leverage. Such Atlanticists as Helmut Kohl and Manfred Wörner, on the other hand, consider any thought of replacing the U.S. guarantee with "a self-contained and independent defense of Europe [to be] illusory and dangerous."[11]

To be sure, as one analyst has noted, "even Union Gaullists have been frank in their skepticism about the possibility of real progress toward creation of a European deterrent; national rivalries and political inertia have come to be seen as intractable obstacles."[12] Given fundamental doubts about the willingness of France especially

10. See ibid., pp. 65–67.
11. Manfred Wörner, "West Germany and the New Dimensions of Security," in Wolfram Hanrieder, ed., *West German Foreign Policy, 1949–1979* (Boulder, Colo.: Westview Press, 1980), p. 41.
12. Clemens, "CDU/CSU and Arms Control," p. 66.

to entertain the notion of a true European deterrent, Strauss and other Gaullists recognized the need for the FRG ultimately to depend on the U.S. strategic guarantee.

Such dependence has been most palatable during periods of strong U.S. leadership and assertiveness, as during Reagan's first term from 1981 to 1985. When Washington's priority turns to improved U.S.–USSR relations and superpower arms control, however, as evidenced by the Reykjavik summit and the INF treaty, then CDU/CSU doubts reemerge in regard to the long-term viability of the U.S. nuclear guarantee. It is at such times that even CDU Atlanticists recognize the wisdom of hedging their bets by cultivating closer military ties with their West European allies, and especially France.

These attitudes emerge in response to both nuclear and conventional force issues. As David Yost has noted, Franco-German cooperation on military matters began to increase substantially in the mid-1980s, with the decision to implement the defense provisions of the 1963 Franco-German treaty signed by de Gaulle and Adenauer.[13] Regarding the *force de frappe*, France has acceded to West German desires for greater nuclear consultation, without, of course, granting much German influence in French targeting and employment plans.

Franco-German cooperation on conventional force issues has been a bit more substantive, as the two nations agree on the secondary importance of conventional deterrence. As the former French defense minister Charles Hernu said, "He who tells me that he prefers another division of soldiers to a missile-launching submarine has mistaken our epoch."[14]

Nonetheless, anxieties over the future U.S. role in NATO have helped push Paris and Bonn toward greater coordination of French conventional forces with the Bundeswehr. Such actions have included the establishment of the FAR (Force Action Rapide, comprising five divisions and 47,000 troops) for use in West Germany during a conflict; the creation of a joint Franco-German brigade (albeit outside the NATO command structure); and the 1987 "Bold Sparrow" exercises involving the largest number of French troops on FRG soil since the mid-1950s.[15]

13. David Yost, "Franco-German Defense Cooperation," in Szabo, ed., *Bundeswehr and Western Defense*.

14. Quoted in *Le Monde*, October 8, 1982.

15. See Klaus Naumann, "Forces and the Future," in Szabo, ed., *Bundeswehr and Western Defense*.

Ultimately, however, CDU/CSU security policies will be most shaped by the two major uncertainties facing the FRG in the 1990s: prospects for German reunification in a new European security framework and its effects on the evolution of German domestic politics. Also important will be impending economic and demographic constraints on West German military forces.

The growing pressure of fiscal and demographic constraints, coupled with uncertainties over the direction of U.S. policy, could well sharpen the Atlanticist–Gaullist split within the Union in the 1990s. Yet it is important to remember that debates within the CDU/CSU, unlike those in the SPD, tend to focus more on political strategy than on ideological issues. Differences between Atlanticists and Gaullists stem as much from struggles over Union leadership as from distinct policy options. Yet major challenges to the security status quo in Central Europe (such as dramatic reversals in the East European reform movements or the breakup of the Soviet empire) could provoke a major split within the CDU/CSU specifically and in West German domestic politics generally.[16]

It remains to be seen how CDU/CSU policies will evolve given the fluid situation produced by marked changes in East–West relations, as symbolized by the signing of the INF treaty. Franz Josef Strauss, for example, returned in early 1988 from a trip to Moscow (his first), declaring that the FRG should begin negotiating directly with Gorbachev over issues of common concern, given the unpredictable policies of the United States. And Alfred Dregger responded warmly to East German leader Erich Honecker's calls for moving quickly to the third "zero option," that is, banning short-range missiles with ranges of less than 500 kilometers.[17]

The irony of Union Gaullists endorsing follow-on arms control measures, to the consternation of officials in NATO and Kohl's defense ministry, is best explained by the traditional German Gaullist preference for insulating FRG security policy from the vagaries of American policy. Domestic political considerations are also relevant, given that the INF treaty will leave behind mainly short-range and battlefield nuclear weapons that can be used only on the territories of the two Germanies.

16. For a contrast of CDU/CSU security policies and those of the SPD, see Wolfgang Pordzik, "Aspects of the West German Security Debate," *German Studies Newsletter* (Harvard University Center for European Studies), November 1985.

17. See William Tuohy, "Bonn Resists NATO Policy on Short-Range Missiles," *Los Angeles Times*, January 11, 1988.

Most important, however, such attitudes represent a "reinsurance" policy on the part of the CDU/CSU for maintaining a strong West German role in European security negotiations. To the extent that current Union policies revive images of the Schaukelpolitik of Bismarck and an FRG playing off its Western and Eastern neighbors, they are causing no little concern within NATO. More to the point, however, the CDU/CSU is feeling its way in a rapidly changing landscape of East–West relations. The need to face difficult trade-offs in Bundeswehr budgeting, procurement, and manpower issues, as well as to cope with rapid developments in the arenas of NATO strategy and arms control, will continue to tax Union leadership and unity. In the 1990s, these issues could prove most difficult in the Union's relationship with its junior coalition partner, the Free Democratic Party.

THE FREE DEMOCRATIC PARTY

Out of all proportion to its electoral strength, which fluctuates between 5 and 10 percent, the Free Democratic Party has exercised a decisive influence on West German security policies throughout the postwar period. Capitalizing on the desire of West Germans for stability and continuity, the FDP has served in all postwar German governments save two (1957–1961 and 1966–1969) and has maintained control of the Foreign Ministry continually since 1969.[18]

The party sees itself as the defender of liberal, free-market policies, yet its success rests less on ideology than on the moderating influence it exerts on governmental policy. As the junior partner to the SPD from 1969 to 1982, and then in coalition with the CDU/CSU from 1982 to the present, the FDP has been seen by many West Germans as providing a necessary check on the excesses of both the SPD left wing and the CSU. The Federal Republic's electoral system of modified proportional representation is such that many moderate supporters of the SPD and CDU are able to cast their "second vote" for the FDP, thus ensuring that the FDP continues to function as a "coalition maker, safety valve, and corrective" vis-à-vis the policies of the major parties.[19] This strategy of "structural opportunism" (the

18. For a general analysis of the FDP, see Christian Soe, "The Free Democratic Party," in H. G. Peter Wallach and George K. Romoser, eds., *West German Politics in the Mid-Eighties: Crisis and Continuity* (New York: Praeger, 1985).

19. Barry M. Blechman and Cathleen Fisher, "Arms Control and the Free Democratic Party," in Blechman and Fisher, eds., *Silent Partner.*

term is Rudolf Wildenmann's) has ensured continued FDP participation in West German governments, even though the party itself remains divided between a commitment to social-liberal welfare policies and a deregulated, free-market economy.

In foreign affairs, the FDP, in the person of Hans-Dietrich Genscher, foreign minister since 1972, has been able to implement its concept of West German security predicated on continued strong integration in the Western Alliance, complemented by vigorous arms control efforts and political dialogue with the East. In doing so, Genscher and the FDP have embodied the desire of most West Germans for continuity and predictability in FRG security policies.

In addition, Genscher has been a forceful advocate of multilateral efforts at reducing East–West tensions, such as the Conference on Security and Cooperation in Europe (CSCE) and the Stockholm conferences on confidence-building measures. Indeed, the foreign minister talks often of a "European mission of peace" and of creating European and global "cooperative security measures."[20] Genscher sees this multilateral framework for FRG security policies— whether the NATO Alliance, the CSCE process, or U.N. efforts—as far preferable to either an overreliance on the United States or a too independent FRG Ostpolitik.

Accordingly, the FDP has been an important check on unilateralist tendencies in both the SPD and CDU/CSU. In the late 1970s, for example, Genscher was instrumental in affirming West German support for the NATO dual-track INF decision, despite calls from a large segment of the SPD for a unilateral moratorium on INF deployment. Similarly, after the FDP threw its support to the CDU/CSU in 1982, Genscher helped temper the hard-line preferences of Strauss and Defense Minister Manfred Wörner, and remained a constant advocate of arms control.

Although the party seems to have recovered from the internal crisis of confidence it suffered following its "betrayal" of the Schmidt government (when it lost thousands of party members and was voted out of all but five regional governments), the ability of the FDP to help maintain a West German security consensus in the face of increased party polarization is uncertain.

One major issue concerns Genscher, who since 1972 has embodied FDP security policies. Once Genscher retires, it is unlikely that his

20. For more on Genscher's foreign policies, see *Frankfurter Allgemeine Zeitung,* July 15, 1986, and *Die Zeit,* September 27, 1985.

successor as foreign minister will command the same respect from German voters and yield equal power within a coalition government with the CDU/CSU. In 1987, for example, Chancellor Kohl depended heavily on Genscher to counter pressure from Strauss and other Union conservatives who were critical of the impending INF agreement and who argued that the FRG should not give up its Pershing IA missiles to make an INF agreement more likely. Whether Genscher's successors will be able to play as pivotal a role remains to be seen.

A second point involves how the FDP positions itself between the SPD and CDU/CSU in the years ahead. Before the 1987 election, the new party chairman, Martin Bangemann, came down strongly for situating the FDP firmly on the conservative side of the German political spectrum. Bangemann maintained that the FDP must choose between two increasingly polarized camps of German politics, consisting of a solid moderate/conservative bloc (the FDP and CDU/CSU) and an unstable left-wing bloc (SPD and Greens).[21]

Genscher, in contrast, continued to advocate a swing role for the FDP and left open the possibility that in the future the FDP might entertain the notion of a governmental coalition with the SPD, provided that party returned to more moderate policies. On the other hand, the election of the conservative Graf Lambsdorff as FDP party leader in late 1988 indicates that the FDP will stay firmly wedded to its coalition with the CDU/CSU for the 1990 election.

Should the Union and FDP win that election, the FDP will continue to moderate CDU/CSU positions until well into the 1990s. However, should the FDP fall below the 5 percent threshold needed to gain representation in the Bundestag, the more conservative elements in the CDU/CSU would have a stronger hand in determining Union policy. This development could in turn exacerbate the left–right polarization on security issues in the Federal Republic. It is in this sense that the FDP is crucial to the maintenance of the West German security consensus as the Federal Republic faces difficult choices in the 1990s and beyond.[22]

THE CDU/CSU AND THE INF ISSUE

Beginning with the earliest reports of SS-20 deployments in 1975, CDU/CSU leaders were forceful advocates of NATO deployment of

21. *Frankfurter Allgemeine Zeitung*, July 1, 1986.

22. Christian Soe, "The Free Democratic Party: The Politics of Muddling Through," *German Politics and Society* (formerly *German Studies Newsletter*), June 1988.

new long-range nuclear systems. Union defense spokesmen during the Schmidt years, such as Manfred Wörner and Alois Mertes, constantly reiterated their party's support for land-based missile systems (whether cruise or ballistic) that could threaten Soviet territory and strengthen NATO's nuclear deterrent. As the INF issue moved through the NATO decision-making process, CDU/CSU leaders also cautioned against putting too much emphasis on INF arms control, arguing that NATO long-range systems were needed to couple European security to that of the U.S. nuclear guarantee.

As with the Multi-lateral Force (MLF) issue in the 1960s, CDU/CSU support for deploying INF epitomized the party's belief in the primacy of nuclear deterrence for NATO strategy. Specifically, the Union has long maintained that nuclear systems capable of striking the Soviet Union provide the most effective NATO deterrent against Soviet military action, whether conventional or nuclear, and the most important link to U.S. strategic systems.[23] Thus, while CDU/CSU spokesmen pay lip service to the strategy of flexible response, they are dubious about both the deterrent value and military utility of short-range battlefield systems. Many people in the CDU/CSU, especially Union Gaullists, are uncomfortable with the notion of controlled escalation (that the United States might pause rather than escalate), implying as it does the possibility of a nuclear war limited to Central Europe. For the same reasons, the CDU/CSU has never been totally convinced of the need to establish parity in conventional forces with the Warsaw Pact, given the primacy of nuclear deterrence.

For these reasons, the CDU/CSU was opposed to the NATO "Option III" proposal at the MBFR talks in 1975, which offered to reduce NATO nuclear forces in exchange for Soviet armored divisions. The Union was also disturbed (as was Schmidt) by the Carter administration's handling of the SALT II negotiations and the prospect of placing limits on NATO deployment of cruise missiles while leaving the SS-20 unconstrained. Accordingly, the CDU/CSU was not very upset when SALT II ratification was shelved following the Soviet invasion of Afghanistan.

Unlike Schmidt, the CDU/CSU did come out strongly in favor of deploying enhanced radiation weapons in 1977-78. Although the Union did not place great faith in battlefield nuclear weapons, the prospect of replacing outmoded nuclear artillery shells with more

23. See David S. Yost and Thomas S. Glad, "West German Party Politics and Theater Nuclear Modernization since 1977," *Armed Forces and Society*, November 16, 1982.

"usable" neutron warheads would, it was argued, strengthen nuclear deterrence at lower levels of the escalation spectrum. Such a case was easy to make while the party was in opposition, however, especially as West German public opinion was strongly against ERW deployment. When the CDU/CSU returned to power in 1982, it became lukewarm about neutron warheads, saying their deployment was no longer necessary, as the imminent deployment of INF systems would restore the nuclear balance in Europe.

During the INF episode itself, the CDU/CSU was largely supportive of the position of the Schmidt-Genscher government. Like Schmidt, the CDU/CSU considered land-based INF deployments as necessary to plug a gap in the continuum of deterrence, to solidify nuclear planning between West Germany and the United States, and to offset whatever political coercive leverage the Soviets might seek to gain from SS-20 deployments. Also, most members of the Union clearly favored a single American key for INF, giving the United States complete launch authority (the exception was Strauss, who favored a double-key arrangement).[24]

Yet Union leaders did differ from Schmidt on some key points. Wörner and others saw Schmidt's insistence on both the nonsingularity provision and the need to begin INF arms control negotiations before INF deployment as weakening the military rationale for INF systems.[25] For Union leaders, the SS-20 was only one component of a Warsaw Pact military edge that included increased numbers of shorter-range nuclear systems and superiority in conventional forces. Accordingly, NATO needed to deploy the Pershing II and cruise missiles to counter not only the SS-20 but an across-the-board Warsaw Pact threat.

This CDU/CSU preference for INF deployment over arms control did not, however, prevent the party from endorsing President Reagan's "Zero Option" proposal, announced in November 1981. Yet this support was largely tactical, in view of the apparent unlikelihood that the Soviets would ever agree to the complete elimination of INF systems. More to CDU/CSU liking was the 1982 Nitze-Kvitsinski "walk in the woods" formula, which would have permitted equal deployments of cruise missile and SS-20 launchers (seventy-five each). Although the U.S. and Soviet governments both repudiated the Nitze-Kvitsinski deal, such an arrangement would have allowed

24. *Frankfurter Allgemeine Zeitung*, February 1 and September 9, 1979.

25. For parliamentary debates over INF, see *Deutscher Bundestag, Stenographischer Bericht*, 8th Wahlperiode, 141 Sitzung, March 8, 1979.

for at least a minimum NATO INF capability. Some Union defense experts stressed, however, that the Pershing II, with its assured penetration capability and short flight times, was the more important system for NATO and should not be banned.

Up until the time the CDU/CSU returned to power, in October 1982, the party directed a constant stream of criticism at the Schmidt government for preferring an INF arms control solution over deployment. Despite strong West German antinuclear sentiment and large public demonstrations in West German cities in 1981 and 1982, the Union adhered to its position of giving primacy to INF deployment over arms control.[26] In this as in most other security matters, the CDU/CSU was far closer in spirit to the Reagan administration than was the Schmidt government.

Shortly after the election of March 6, 1983, however, the Kohl government received a shock when President Reagan unveiled his Strategic Defense Initiative in a nationally televised address. The prospect of a space-based defense that would protect the United States but leave Western Europe vulnerable to Soviet nuclear systems struck at the very foundations of CDU/CSU reliance on maintaining the coupling of European with American security. The president's rhetoric about making nuclear weapons "impotent and obsolete" undercut the CDU/CSU emphasis on the primacy of nuclear deterrence and provoked immediate criticism from Defense Minister Wörner and other Union leaders.[27] Government officials were also concerned that SDI budgetary demands might compromise the U.S. defense commitment to NATO, and the fact that the Reagan administration had not consulted with its European allies before the speech only added insult to injury.

Having articulated these concerns, however, CDU/CSU leaders soon began to recognize discretion as the better part of valor. By 1985, the Kohl government was moderating its criticism of SDI for various reasons, including a desire not to undercut the Reagan administration following the March 1985 resumption of U.S.–Soviet arms control talks in Geneva; a realization that the U.S. Congress was already slowing the pace of the SDI program through budget

26. The CDU/CSU position can be found in *Gemeinsam den Frieden sichern: Das Atlantische Bundnis—Garant unserer Frieden* (Bonn: CDU Bundesgeschaftsstelle, 1983).

27. Wörner raised this point especially forcefully at a meeting of NATO defense ministers in Turkey in April 1984; see *Süddeutsche Zeitung*, April 5, 1984; for a general review of West German sentiment regarding SDI, see Christoph Bertram, "Strategic Defense and the Western Alliance," in Franklin A. Long, Donald L. Hafner, and Jeffrey Boutwell, eds. *Weapons in Space* (New York: W. W. Norton, 1986).

reductions; and the dubious political wisdom of publicly challenging the president's vision of being able to protect the American people from nuclear weapons.[28]

Accordingly, the Kohl government took a lowest-common-denominator approach, expressing approval of SDI as a needed hedge against Soviet ballistic missile defense (BMD) efforts and as providing useful leverage in the Geneva negotations, while continuing to express skepticism over the military utility of space-based defenses, especially in providing protection for Europe. Moreover, there was growing interest in many Allied countries, including West Germany, in the potential technological and commercial benefits of participating directly in SDI research programs.[29] In part to help West German companies benefit from SDI development of advanced technologies, as well as to increase FRG influence in shaping the direction of the SDI program, the Kohl government in April 1986 signed a formal agreement with the United States regulating West German participation in the SDI program. To underscore the commercial rather than the military aspect of the agreement, however, the Kohl government sent Economics Minister Bangemann rather than Defense Minister Manfred Wörner, to Washington to meet with U.S. Defense Secretary Caspar Weinberger and sign the memorandum of understanding.[30]

In yet another twist to the SDI debate in 1986, Wörner came out strongly in favor of NATO programs aimed at providing a European defense against Soviet short-range missiles. Although antitactical ballistic missile (ATBM) defenses were not a high priority within the U.S. SDI program, the NATO Air Defense Committee had begun seriously to consider ATBM possibilities as part of an expanded air defense effort in 1984–85. It was only in February 1986, however, at the annual Wehrkünde conference near Munich, that Wörner generated heightened interest in ATBMs with his call for a NATO ATBM effort to counter what he perceived to be a growing threat from

28. For more on West German and West European reaction to SDI, see Jeffrey Boutwell, "SDI and the Allies," in Joseph S. Nye, Jr., and James A. Schear, eds., *The Future of SDI* (Lanham, Md.: University Press of America, 1988).

29. European participation in SDI technology projects evolved only slowly, however, and was predicted to amount to only 1 percent ($300 million) of total SDI spending of $30 billion in the period 1986–1990; see *Aviation Week & Space Technology*, January 20, 1986, p. 28.

30. Theo Sommer voiced the skepticism of many in the FRG regarding the economic benefits of West German participation in SDI contracts when he estimated the value of such contracts at DM 250 million over a five-year period, compared with annual expenditure of DM 35 billion on research and development by West German

conventionally armed Soviet theater ballistic missiles (SS-21, SS-23, SS-12/22), along with the pervasive threat posed by cruise missiles and aircraft.[31]

Wörner's interest in ATBM defenses, never fully shared by other CDU/CSU leaders, has moderated over time, given the difficult technical problems of defending against short-range missiles (with their low flight profiles, short flight times, and uncertainties over angles of attack) in densely populated Western Europe.[32] Just as important, the banning of missiles with ranges beyond 500 kilometers by the INF treaty in 1987 removed a large portion of the Soviet threat, leaving only the SS-21 to justify what would most likely be an expensive ATBM system.

In the fall of 1986, however, the Kohl government and other NATO partners found themselves contending with a far more momentous issue: the prospect of U.S.–Soviet agreement on the total elimination of nuclear missiles, as discussed by Reagan and Gorbachev at the Reykjavik summit in October.

The shock waves produced by the leaders of the two superpowers in their Reykjavik meeting on October 11–12, 1986, have been amply documented elsewhere and need only be summarized here.[33] In their series of free-wheeling discussions, Reagan and Gorbachev reached agreement on substantial cuts of about 30 to 40 percent in strategic nuclear weapons (that is, reducing delivery vehicles to 1,600 and strategic warheads to 6,000). The two leaders also agreed to ban long-range INF systems in Europe, while allowing the Soviets to keep INF systems with 100 warheads in Soviet Asia and the United States a similar number on its territory.[34] Having reached agreement on this general framework for deep reductions in nuclear weapons (while leaving unresolved such issues as SCLMs and sublimits on mobile and heavy missiles), Reagan and Gorbachev then discussed their ultimate goals for arms control.

---

industry (DM 6 billion by the Siemens company alone); see Theo Sommer, "Ein Schritt in die falsche Richtung," *Die Zeit*, April 4, 1986.

31. For a report of the Wehrkünde meeting, see *Die Zeit*, February 28, 1986; see also Manfred Wörner, "A Missile Defense for Europe," *Strategic Review*, Winter 1986.

32. A thorough analysis of the technical, military, and political components of the ATBM issue can be found in Donald L. Hafner and John Roper, eds., *ATBMs and Western Security: Missile Defenses for Europe* (Cambridge, Mass.: Ballinger, 1988).

33. See especially, U.S. House of Representatives, *Process and Implications of the Iceland Summit: Hearings before the Defense Policy Panel, Committee on Armed Services* (Washington, D.C.: U.S. Government Printing Office, 1987).

34. Spurgeon M. Keeny, Jr., "Reykjavik Revisited," *Arms Control Today* 16 (November 1986).

In the controversial aftermath of the Reykjavik summit, there were conflicting accounts of just what was agreed upon by the two leaders. Reagan administration officials claim the president offered to eliminate all strategic ballistic missiles (ICBMs and SLBMs) within a ten-year period, while Gorbachev maintained that the president agreed to the Soviet proposal to eliminate all strategic weapons (including long-range bombers and cruise missiles). Gorbachev also said that he and Reagan even agreed tentatively to consider banning all nuclear weapons within a specified period.[35]

In the end, U.S.–Soviet agreement on both initial reductions and possible elimination of nuclear systems broke down over superpower differences regarding strategic defenses. Whereas Gorbachev insisted on continued observance of the 1972 ABM Treaty, and the constraints it places on the testing and development of space-based defenses, Reagan staunchly maintained his "near metaphysical" attachment to the SDI (the term is François Mitterrand's) and sought to modify the ABM Treaty to permit SDI testing and deployment. According to former defense secretary Robert McNamara, the Reykjavik summit foundered when Reagan sought to convert the ABM Treaty "to a totally different agreement that would permit [SDI] activities and terminate the treaty in 10 to 12 years to allow for full-scale development of a nationwide strategic defense system."[36]

Confusion, irritation, and shock were the watchwords in the aftermath of the Reykjavik summit. Administration officials seemed confused over just what the president had said to Gorbachev about eliminating either strategic ballistic missiles, all strategic weapons, or all nuclear weapons of whatever range. Military and congressional leaders in the United States were irritated that the president had been on the verge of reaching sweeping agreements with the Soviets with no prior consultation within the U.S. government. Similarly, the NATO and European allies were shocked that a U.S. president had entertained in a single weekend the notion of dismantling the Western nuclear deterrent.

In a visit to Washington just a week after Reykjavik, Chancellor Kohl challenged the Reagan administration's attempt to reinterpret the ABM Treaty, stating that the West German government believed

35. The Gorbachev offer at Reykjavik was similar to his January 1986 proposal for completely eliminating all nuclear weapons by the year 2000; see Harrison Brown, "The Gorbachev Proposals," *Bulletin of the Atomic Scientists* 42 (March 1986).

36. Robert S. McNamara, "Reykjavik: Breakthrough or Blunder," *Arms Control Today* 17 (March 1987).

the traditional, restrictive reading of the treaty to be the "correct" one.[37] Kohl also criticized the outlines of the INF agreement discussed by Reagan and Gorbachev, saying that any prospective deal on European nuclear forces should also include those shorter-range systems that could be detonated only on German territory.[38] Kohl's sentiments were echoed by the other major NATO partners, whose officials were equally indignant that the Reagan administration was contemplating depriving NATO of the U.S. nuclear guarantee. To take but one example, the British defense minister, George Younger, called "unacceptable" any agreement "that involved the substantial reduction or complete elimination of nuclear weapons . . . if it left the conventional balance [in Europe] untouched" (Table 3 compares NATO and Warsaw Pact conventional force levels).[39]

In short, most NATO (and U.S. military) officials saw the Reykjavik summit as producing the worst of all possible worlds: a situation in which the U.S. nuclear deterrent was dismantled, leaving Western Europe to face Soviet superiority in conventional and short-range nuclear weapons. It was indeed ironic that, given general European wariness over SDI, even among Reagan supporters such as Kohl and Prime Minister Margaret Thatcher, it should have been SDI that blocked final agreement at Reykjavik.[40] What made the Reykjavik summit doubly troubling was that President Reagan seemed to be ready to bargain away U.S. nuclear weapons so soon after the NATO allies had invested much political capital to follow through with deployment of the Pershing II and cruise missiles in the face of

37. In October 1985, the Reagan administration claimed that a broader interpretation of the ABM Treaty would allow full-scale development and testing of advanced-technology ballistic missile defense (BMD) systems. While not officially adopted as U.S. policy, this reinterpretation of the ABM Treaty concerned both congressional and Allied leaders, who saw in it an attempt to justify the development and testing of SDI space-based defenses. The reinterpretation was contained in a letter from Abraham D. Sofaer, legal adviser to the U.S. State Department, to the Subcommittee on Arms Control, International Security, and Science of the Foreign Affairs Committee, U.S. House of Representatives, October 22, 1985. For a criticism of the administration's position, see Alan B. Sherr, "Sound Legal Reasoning or Policy Expedient? The New 'New Interpretation' of the ABM Treaty," *International Security* 11 (Winter 1986–87).

38. For an account of Kohl's visit to Washington, see *Washington Post*, October 22, 1986.

39. Quoted in *Wall Street Journal*, October 22, 1986, p. 37.

40. The relevance of strategic defenses for NATO is analyzed in Richard I. Brody, *Strategic Defenses in NATO Strategy*, Adelphi Papers no. 225 (London: International Institute for Strategic Studies, 1987), and Lawrence Freedman, *Strategic Defence in the Nuclear Age*, Adelphi Papers no 224 (London: International Institute for Strategic Studies, 1987).

Table 3. NATO and Warsaw Pact conventional forces, 1989

	NATO	Warsaw Pact
Population	647,000,000	396,000,000
GNP, billions of U.S. dollars	$7,975	$3,068
Military spending, billions of U.S. dollars	$410	$315
Military personnel worldwide		
Active	5,506,000	6,436,000
Reserve	8,242,000	8,276,000
Active-duty ground-forces personnel		
Worldwide	2,992,000	2,829,000
Europe: Atlantic to Urals	2,385,000	2,292,000
Central Europe with/without France	1,026,000/796,000	995,000
Divisions manned in peacetime		
Worldwide	125	128
Europe: Atlantic to Urals	105	101
Central Europe with/without Frace	41/32	49
Main battle tanks		
Worldwide	33,600	68,900
Europe: Atlantic to Urals	22,200	53,000
Central Europe with/without France	13,600/12,700	18,000
Artillery, rocket launchers, and antitank guns		
Worldwide	21,500	50,400
Europe: Atlantic to Urals	11,100	37,000
Central Europe with/without France	4,200/3,600	9,500
Land-based bomber and fighter/ground-attack airplanes		
Worldwide	5,873	4,200
Europe: Atlantic to Urals	3,215	3,218
Central Europe with/without France	1,238/973	1,024
Land-attack helicopters		
Worldwide	2,020	2,130
Europe: Atlantic to Urals	780	1,630
Surface warships and attack submarines		
Worldwide	775	616
European/Atlantic waters	578	561
Naval combat airplanes		
Worldwide	1,476	856
European/Atlantic waters	742	589

SOURCE: Updated from Jeffrey Boutwell et al., *Countdown on Conventional Forces in Europe: A Briefing Book* (Cambridge, Mass.: American Academy of Arts and Sciences and Ploughshares Fund, 1988).

serious domestic political opposition. Finally, there was the additional irony that the prospective Reykjavik agreement was supported most strongly by those European left-wing critics of the United States (such as the SPD in West Germany and Neil Kinnock of the British Labour party) who were advocating nuclear disarmament for Europe, either unilaterally or through negotiations.

In the months following the Reykjavik summit, events moved at a dizzying pace, especially in regard to the INF issue. The Soviets continued to take the initiative in offering new arms control proposals, all the while maintaining their adherence to a strict interpretation of the ABM Treaty. In February 1987, Gorbachev raised the possibility of linking limitations on short-range theater missiles with those being discussed for INF. The following month, the United States outlined a package of verification measures for an INF agreement which were far more intrusive than anything considered in more than four decades of superpower arms control.[41] This move was followed in July 1987 by Gorbachev's acceptance of an initial Western position for a global ban on all theater missiles with ranges greater than 500 kilometers (the so-called double-zero agreement), in part to ease the verification requirements for an INF treaty. In addition, the Soviets made known their willingess to accept on-site inspections to monitor compliance with an INF regime.

By mid-summer 1987, then, the broad outlines of an INF treaty were emerging. Emerging as well, however, was increased West German criticism of the prospective agreement. Given its long-standing position on the need for long-range theater missiles to strengthen the nuclear coupling of Europe to the United States, the Kohl government was critical of an agreement that would totally eliminate the Pershing II and cruise missiles, even though the SS-20s and shorter-range Soviet missiles (SS-12/22 and SS-23) would be banned as well. Defense Minister Wörner and the conservative CDU leader Alfred Dregger openly voiced their fears that implementation of the INF double-zero agreement would lead inexorably to the denuclearization of Europe.[42] Franz Josef Strauss of the CSU also castigated the double-zero proposal, saying it would "naturally mean a decoupling of America from Europe."[43]

For many members of the CDU/CSU, the double-zero agreement represented the worst of all possible worlds. First, there was the issue of decoupling. Union leaders feared that if all missiles of greater range than 500 kilometers were eliminated, and with them the ability to attack Soviet territory, the NATO nuclear deterrent would be decoupled from U.S. nuclear forces.

41. As contained in "U.S. State Department Press Statement," March 12, 1987. For more on the INF Treaty's verification provisions, see Jack Mendelsohn, "INF Verification: A Guide for the Perplexed," *Arms Control Today* 17 (September 1987).

42. Critics of the INF accord began referring to it as a "European Munich," recalling the fateful 1938 agreement between Hitler and Chamberlain; see Roger de Weck, "Angst vor einem europäischen München," *Die Zeit*, March 12, 1987.

43. Quoted in *Washington Post*, June 2, 1987, p. 1.

Second, Gorbachev's double-zero proposal posed a problem for the seventy-two Pershing IA missiles stationed in the FRG.[44] Gorbachev demanded that the Pershing IA, with a maximum range of 720 kilometers, be covered by the agreement. At first, U.S. and West German officials objected, claiming the Pershing IA was a West German system (the Pershing IAs were operated by the Luftwaffe, though the nuclear warheads remained in U.S. custody). Wörner, Dregger, and Strauss maintained the Pershings should fall in the same category as British and French systems; that is, "third party" weapons that Gorbachev had agreed would not be covered by the INF agreement. Yet Genscher and CDU General Secretary Heiner Geissler were wary of the political consequences, both domestic and international, if the Pershing IA issue blocked an INF accord. These political considerations became all the more important (especially in U.S.–FRG relations) in July 1987, when Gorbachev agreed to the U.S. demand for the complete global elimination of missiles with ranges greater than 500 kilometers. With the Soviets having compromised on several U.S. demands, Kohl felt he could not permit the INF treaty to abort over the single issue of seventy-two aging missiles (the Pershing IAs were first deployed in 1971). Accordingly, the chancellor agreed that the FRG would unilaterally dismantle the Pershing IAs once the implementation of the INF treaty had begun, thus removing the final obstacle to the December 1987 signing of the treaty.[45]

When it became apparent in the summer of 1987 that the United States and the Soviet Union would reach agreement on the double-zero arrangement, conservatives in the CDU/CSU began to call for a "third zero" to be added to the impending treaty. Although it seemed ironic for the Union leaders to advocate the abolition of all theater ballistic missiles (TBMs), their position stemmed not only from their concern with Soviet superiority in short-range TBMs, but from the fact that such missiles could not reach much beyond the territory of the two German states (a common aphorism in the FRG at the time was "the shorter the range, the deader the Germans").

44. Clemens, "CDU/CSU and Arms Control," pp. 112–114.

45. On August 26, 1987, Kohl announced that the 72 West German Pershing IA launchers and missiles would be dismantled following "the final elimination of all Soviet and American INF systems." In order to maintain the point that these were "third-party" systems, the West German Pershing IAs were not formally included in the INF Treaty (the 178 Pershing IA missiles referred to on p. 294 of the INF memorandum of understanding are American systems based in the United States). See "Germany, U.S. Remove Last Obstacles to INF Agreement," *Arms Control Today* 17 (September 1987): 30.

In effect, the INF treaty would decouple NATO from the United States, yet allow the Soviets to retain hundreds of short-range missiles (the SS-21) that could threaten only West German territory.

On the other hand, CDU/CSU opponents of the agreement had a difficult time denying the Soviets' obligation under the treaty to destroy far more theater missiles and warheads than the United States (and the FRG). As Table 4 shows, the Soviets would have to destroy 910 INF missiles (compared with 689 for the United States) and 926 shorter-range missiles (178 for the United States and FRG). The number of warheads to be removed was even more asymmetrical (2,572 for the Soviets, 931 for the United States), given that the 405 deployed SS-20 missiles carried three warheads each.[46]

Table 4. Number of U.S. and Soviet launchers and missiles covered by INF treaty

	Launchers			Missiles		
	Deployed	Non-deployed	Total	Deployed	Non-deployed	Total
USA						
LRINF						
Pershing II	115	51	166	120	127	247
GLCM	99	17	116	309	133	442
All LRINF	214	68	282	429	260	689
SRINF						
Pershing IA	—	1	1	—	178	178
All INF	214	69	283	429	438	867
USSR						
LRINF						
SS-20	405	118	523	405	245	650
SS-4	79	6	85	65	105	170
SS-5	—	—	—	—	6	6
SSC-X-4	—	6	6	—	84	84
All LRINF	484	130	614	470	440	910
SRINF						
SS-12	115	20	135	220	506	726
SS-23	82	20	102	167	33	200
All SRINF	197	40	237	387	539	926
All INF	681	170	851	857	979	1,836

SOURCE: Adapted from *Survival*, March/April 1988 (London: International Institute of Strategic Studies), p. 180.

46. The text of the INF Treaty can be found in *Survival* 30 (March/April 1988): 163–180. The Soviets began the destruction of the SS-20 missiles on August 28, 1988 at the Kapustin Yar military range, 56 miles southeast of Volgograd, while the United States began destroying its INF missiles in September 1988 at a base near Marshall, Texas; see *Boston Globe*, August 29, 1988, p. 42.

Politically, Chancellor Kohl could not afford infighting within the CDU/CSU over a treaty of such obvious importance to both a U.S. president and the West German public. Increasingly during 1987, there was widespread public support in the FRG for the INF treaty, which some observers believed contributed to the poor showing of the CDU/CSU in two state elections in May 1987, and the concomitant strong showing of Genscher's FDP. In addition, both France and the United Kingdom opposed CDU/CSU attempts to obstruct the INF negotiations by demanding reductions to equal ceilings on shorter-range TBMs, instead of the "second zero." Finally, Kohl was wary of jeopardizing the planned visit of East German leader Erich Honecker to the FRG in September 1987, the first such visit by a GDR head of state in the postwar period.

Accordingly, once Kohl had agreed that the FRG would unilaterally give up the Pershing IA, one of the last major stumbling blocks to an INF double-zero agreement was removed. During the autumn of 1987, U.S. and Soviet negotiators reached agreement on the complex verification details, and the treaty was formally signed by Reagan and Gorbachev during the Washington summit on December 7, 1987.

CDU/CSU Policy in the Wake of the INF Treaty

In the period following the Washington summit, confusion and conflicting positions proliferated within the CDU/CSU. On the one hand, Dregger, Strauss, and other Union conservatives continued to voice their fears over the decoupling effects of the INF treaty and that the implementation of the double-zero agreement would only highlight Soviet superiority in short-range TBMs and conventional forces. Dregger, for example, warned that Western Europe was running the risk of falling "beneath the military domination of the Soviet Union."[47] In an article that appeared in the December 1987 issue of *Europäische Wehrkünde*, Dregger echoed the Gaullist theme of forging a stronger European defense partnership founded on Franco-German cooperation.[48] For Dregger, such a partnership would not supplant the U.S. contribution to Western Europe's defense, but it

47. *Frankfurter Allgemeine Zeitung*, February 8, 1988.
48. Alfred Dregger, "Entwurf einer Sicherheitspolitik zur Selbstbehauptung Europas," *Europäische Wehrkünde*, no. 12 (December 1987).

would strengthen a deterrent capability that had been weakened by an INF treaty that removed the link between NATO's tactical nuclear capability and U.S. strategic systems. Dregger especially called for greater coordination between France and the FRG in regard to the French nuclear deterrent, in terms of both strategic systems and those "prestrategic" systems (Pluton and Hades short-range missiles) whose range limited their use to German territory.[49]

Certainly the biggest split within the CDU/CSU in the months following the signing of the INF Treaty revolved around the twin issues of attemping to negotiate a "third-zero" agreement on nuclear systems of under-500-kilometers range and proceeding with extant NATO plans to modernize those short-range systems. In the Alliance as a whole, the U.S., British, and French governments were uniformly opposed to beginning negotiations on a third zero and uniformly in favor of implementing NATO's 1983 Montebello decision to modernize short-range nuclear artillery, missile, and aircraft capabilities.[50] In the opinion of the former NATO SACEUR Gen. Bernard Rogers, the Montebello decision, which had included the unilateral withdrawal of 1,400 nuclear warheads from Europe, was made doubly important by the imminent withdrawal of the Pershing and cruise missiles under the INF agreement.

In the FRG, however, the political difficulties encountered in deploying INF systems in the first place made it unlikely that the West German public would find much enthusiasm for deploying new short-range systems that, after all, would be used only on German territory in the event of war. In part to reassure West Germans on this score, such Union leaders as Dregger were receptive to notions of eliminating all land-based nuclear systems with ranges of less than 500 kilometers. In January 1988, for example, in response to an initiative from Erich Honecker that NATO and the Warsaw Pact agree not to modernize short-range systems and then to eliminate them entirely, Dregger responded: "We welcome East Germany's support for an inclusion of land-based atomic weapons with a range of under 500 kilometers in the arms control process. These systems threaten Germany almost exclusively on both sides of

49. Dregger referred to a February 28, 1986, letter from Mitterrand to Kohl which signaled progress in Franco-German consultations on nuclear weapons; see Dregger, "Entwurf einer Sicherheitspolitik," p. 705.
50. See James M. Markham, "Arms and Allies: NATO A-Arsenal Cuts Disputed," *New York Times*, January 21, 1988.

the partition border. Therefore, it is in our interest for disarmament to be applied in this area."[51]

If the sight of Dregger warmly responding to an East German arms control proposal was surprising to many in NATO, even more shocking was the attitude of Franz Josef Strauss on his return from a series of meetings with Gorbachev in Moscow (Strauss's first visit to the Soviet Union in his forty-year political career). In commenting that West Germany should be prepared to deal independently with the Soviets on security issues, given the unpredictability of the Reagan administration, Strauss was perhaps playing to West German public opinion, which regarded Gorbachev more favorably than it did Reagan.[52] Nonetheless, Strauss's comments were upsetting to other NATO officials, who saw in them "a resurgence of German national interests" at the expense of allied unity.[53]

Not surprisingly, the aspects of the nuclear issue emphasized in CDU/CSU policy statements varied with the intended audience, domestic or external. Thus Dregger was also on record as saying that reductions in short-range nuclear systems could be implemented only in conjunction with progess in conventional and chemical arms control.[54] Chancellor Kohl went even further, flatly opposing a third zero option and adding that any agreement establishing equal ceilings on short-range TBMs must be worked out "in conjunction" with East–West agreements on both reductions in conventional forces and the elimination of chemical weapons.[55] This was the official NATO position, as agreed on at the meeting of NATO heads of government in Brussels in March 1988. In return, however, Kohl exacted a concession for the FRG. Instead of endorsing the U.S.– British–French preference for the deployment of modernized short-range nuclear systems, the NATO communiqúe deferred to West German political considerations by stating that nuclear systems "will

51. Quoted in William Tuohy, "Bonn Resists NATO Policy on Short-Range Missiles," *Los Angeles Times*, January 11, 1988.

52. Although this was the first time a Soviet leader was regarded more favorably than a U.S. president, West Germans continued to feel far more positively about the United States than about the Soviet Union; see *Economist*, February 27, 1988, p. 38. In the United States as well, favorable attitudes toward Gorbachev were on the rise, from 44 percent of those polled in November 1985 to 66 percent in October 1987; see *Americans Talk Security* (Boston: Marttila & Kiley, November 17, 1987), p. 3.

53. Quoted in *Los Angeles Times*, January 11, 1988.

54. Dregger, "Entwurf einer Sicherheitspolitik," p. 706.

55. *Frankfurter Allgemeine Zeitung*, February 8, 1988.

continue to be kept up to date where necessary."[56] This vague reference to modernization reflected Kohl's ambivalence about taking a hard-and-fast decision on a successor to the Lance short-range missile, which he feared could lead to West German protests similar to those engendered by INF deployment.

Of all the CDU/CSU leaders, the most supportive of NATO nuclear modernization programs was Manfred Wörner (who in July 1988 replaced Lord Carrington as NATO secretary general, the first German ever to hold the post). Yet even Wörner soft-pedaled the modernization program when he addressed domestic audiences, focusing mainly on the modernization of NATO sea-based and air-based systems, rather than land-based (i.e., FRG-based) weapons.

As for the FDP, Foreign Minister Genscher was vocal in his opposition to the Montebello modernization program, yet did not go so far as to embrace the third zero option. As with the Pershing IA issue, Genscher did not want the modernization of the Lance missile or other weapons systems to block progress on further cuts in European nuclear forces. On the other hand, the foreign minister did link such cuts to progress in reducing the asymmetries in NATO–Pact conventional forces and progress in banning chemical weapons.

CDU/CSU Nuclear Policy and Domestic Reassurance

By the end of 1988, then, the Kohl government's policy was in a state of flux regarding the complementarity of NATO nuclear modernization with further reductions in the NATO arsenal of 4,600 nuclear warheads. The FRG had bought a little time with the compromise wording of the March 1988 NATO declaration, yet decisions would have to made soon regarding the modernization of various NATO nuclear systems (especially the Lance missile).

If nothing else, the support of many in the CDU/CSU for further nuclear reductions in Europe signaled a remarkable turnaround from the policies the Union brought into the government when Kohl became chancellor in 1982. Wörner, Dregger, Strauss, and other leaders of the CDU/CSU had forcefully advocated the deployment of ERW weapons in the late 1970s and were strong critics of Helmut

56. For the text of the NATO communiqué, see *NATO Review* 36 (April 1988), 30–31.

Schmidt's INF arms control policies right up to the chancellor's fall in October 1982.

In a seeming paradox, CDU/CSU receptivity to arms control increased considerably only *after* Kohl's convincing electoral victory in March 1983, when the Union might have felt less bound by domestic opinion. After all, Konrad Adenauer, having won a resounding election victory in 1957, responded to massive domestic opposition to additional nuclear deployments in 1958 (as high as 80 percent against) by chastising one of his aides with the dry retort: "Those are interesting statistics: how do you intend to change them?"[57] In the 1980s, however, Kohl and the CDU/CSU, faced with marked changes in West German domestic politics, greater fluidity in East–West relations (especially with the appearance of Gorbachev), and the institutionalization of inter-German relations, could not afford Adenauer's studied imperviousness to public opinion.

In regard to West German domestic politics, Kohl did not have Adenauer's good fortune of having an SPD opposition that lacked credibility with the voters. While the SPD in the 1980s was indeed suffering through internal crises of conscience and seeking to find a post-Schmidt identity, the party in the 1950s labored even more under its doctrinaire quasi-Marxist policies and Adenauer's ability to equate SPD goals with those of East Berlin and Moscow.

Nonetheless, the appearence of the Greens in the 1980s was a complicating factor not only for the SPD but for the CDU/CSU as well—not so much electorally as in the way the Greens (and the peace movement generally) symbolized changing West German attitudes toward nuclear weapons and the FRG's role in NATO.

In the 1950s, antinuclear attitudes focused almost exclusively on the nuclear weapons themselves. In the 1980s, nuclear angst in West Germany was equally bound up with apprehension over the confrontational policies of the Reagan administration and growing distrust of U.S. policies, even among staunch CDU/CSU supporters. In one poll taken in 1982, 61 percent of respondents who identified themselves as CDU/CSU supporters (and 70 percent overall) agreed with the premise that Bonn must safeguard its own national interests, even if friction with Washington increased as a result.[58] In a

57. See Hans-Peter Schwarz, "Das Aussenpolitische Konzept Konrad Adenauers," in Rudolf Morsey and Konrad Repgen, eds., *Adenauer-Studien* (Mainz: Matthias Grünewald, 1971), 1:97–102.

58. The poll, conducted by the television organization Zweites Deutschen Fernsehen in the spring of 1982, is cited in Clemens, "CDU/CSU and Arms Control," pp. 85–86.

period when Reagan administration officials were letting slip loose comments about nuclear wars limited to Europe (Secretary of State Haig), and when Soviet policy had ossified during the transition from Brezhnev to Andropov to Chernenko, West Germans across the political spectrum were feeling increasingly uneasy about the stalemate in East–West relations.

As Michael Howard has noted, European public opinion during this period was characterized by a widespread lack of "reassurance" concerning Western security and nuclear weapons policies.[59] In Howard's view, deterrence should serve as much to reassure Western publics regarding the rationality of NATO defense policies as it should deter the Soviets and Warsaw Pact from aggression. The problem, of course, was that by the 1980s NATO nuclear policy was characterized neither by the West's strategic superiority of the 1950s nor by the quiescence of the 1960s and 1970s (Lawrence Freedman's "years in the wilderness," when NATO nuclear weapons issues were overshadowed by East–West détente and strategic arms control).[60]

Certainly the steady growth of Soviet military power in the 1960s and 1970s in strategic, theater nuclear, and conventional forces contributed to a growing sense of unease among some portions of the Western public. On the other hand, Soviet belligerence toward Western Europe had eased considerably since the high-water mark of the 1958–59 Berlin crisis and the 1961 building of the Berlin Wall. Accordingly, West German and European public opinion (save in France) was increasingly divided as to whether the USSR was intent on using its military might for political coercion or was a "defensive, status-quo power driven to compete in a perilously accelerating arms race."[61] Public opinion polls in the early 1980s, for example, showed deep cleavages between FRG party supporters on the causes of East–West tensions. A majority of CDU/CSU supporters blamed the Soviet military buildup (63 percent); Green party supporters thought the U.S. military buildup more important (69 percent); SPD supporters were evenly divided.[62]

59. Michael Howard, "Reassurance and Deterrence: Western Defense in the 1980s," *Foreign Affairs* 61 (Winter 1982–83).

60. Lawrence Freedman, "The Wilderness Years," in Jeffrey Boutwell, Paul Doty, and Gregory F. Treverton, eds., *The Nuclear Confrontation in Europe* (London: Croom Helm, 1985).

61. Philip A. G. Sabin, "Reassurance, Consensus, and Controversy: The Domestic Dilemmas of European Defense," in Stephen J. Flanagan and Fen Osler Hampson, eds., *Securing Europe's Future* (London: Croom Helm, 1986), p. 139.

62. Cited in Stephen F. Szabo, "West German Public Attitudes on Arms Control," in Blechman and Fisher, *Silent Partner*, p. 215.

Public indecision regarding the threat posed by the Soviet Union (and the concomitant need for such measures as INF deployment) became even more pronounced with the coming to power of Mikhail Gorbachev in March 1985. Under Gorbachev, Soviet policy was no longer so rigid, doctrinaire, and overtly propagandistic as it had been during Brezhnev's last years and then under Andropov and Chernenko. In arms control especially, Gorbachev and Foreign Minister Eduard Shevardnadze (who replaced Andrei Gromyko in 1985) adroitly captured the initiative by first agreeing to and then going beyond various Western proposals (for example, on intrusive verification measures, on the double zero for INF, and on chemical weapons and confidence-building measures).[63] As we know, by 1987 West Germans had a higher regard for Gorbachev's commitment to arms control and East–West political accommodation than they did for Reagan's.

The third major factor influencing CDU/CSU attitudes on arms control and security issues, the institutionalization of inter-German relations, was arguably the most important. As we shall see in Chapter 6, the CDU/CSU chose to continue the Deutschlandpolitik of Brandt, Schmidt, and the SPD practically unchanged when it came to power in 1982. The consensus in the FRG on the need for expanding inter-German relations had become so broad (and impervious to ups and downs in East–West relations) that even such staunch critics of SPD Ostpolitik as Strauss were accommodating themselves to the reality of normalized relations with East Germany.

The significance of this CDU/CSU desire for stable relations with the GDR is important for understanding how fissures within the West German security consensus shifted, from Ostpolitik in the 1970s to military policy in the 1980s. Just as significant, this CDU/CSU acceptance of Ostpolitik has influenced the Union's position on arms control and could perhaps lead to a recasting of the West German security consensus.

Generally, West German security policy can be described as comprising three overlapping spheres—military policy (NATO nuclear policy, defense budget, and procurement issues), the management of East–West relations (arms control, the U.S.–FRG relationship), and Ostpolitik (inter-German and FRG–USSR relations).[64] While the

63. For a thorough analysis of Soviet arms control negotiating strategy in this period, see Jonathan Dean, *Watershed in Europe* (Lexington, Mass.: Lexington Books, 1987).
64. See Boutwell, "Party Politics and Security Policies."

SPD was in power, Ostpolitik was the major divisive issue between the CDU/CSU and SPD, from the bitter ratification debates over Brandt's Eastern treaties in the early 1970s to CDU/CSU criticism of Schmidt's response to the Polish crisis in the early 1980s. Party differences over military policy were less severe, given Schmidt's ability to keep the SPD left wing in line and maintain steady SPD/FDP support for NATO INF policy and Bundeswehr budget increases.

Upon regaining power in 1982, the CDU/CSU muted its criticism of Ostpolitik and largely absorbed the policies of the SPD. On the other hand, the Kohl government ardently supported INF deployment (which the SPD rejected at its Cologne party congress in 1983) and only tacitly supported East–West arms control efforts. Yet the public appeal of Genscher's support for arms control, followed by Soviet and U.S. flexibility in arms control negotiations, put the CDU/CSU in an awkward position. The public "reassurance" engendered by stable inter-German relations had now become a central factor in discussions of INF arms control and the possibility of a third zero option, given that the weapons being discussed involved the two Germanies most directly. As Kohl discovered to his electoral dismay in the spring of 1987, when his government equivocated about its support for an INF Treaty, public concern about reducing the nuclear threat to West Germany had become so intertwined with public support for the continuation of Ostpolitik that many West Germans viewed the issue as reducing the nuclear threat to *both* Germanies.[65]

At a minimum, such attitudes made it necessary for Kohl to give up the Pershing IA and support the INF Treaty. Beyond that, however, a growing sense of the "community of responsibility" between the two Germanies (the term is Honecker's) has meant that the CDU/CSU is rethinking its attitudes on further reductions of nuclear weapons in Europe, the need to foster intra-European defense cooperation in light of shifting U.S. global commitments, and the concomitant necessity of the FRG to establish closer relations with the Soviet Union to ensure a strong West German influence in evolving European security arrangements.

If the concept of "reassurance" has influenced evolving CDU/CSU security policies, no less important has been the concept of

65. For more on how Kohl's policy on INF contributed to CDU setbacks in the Land elections in Rhineland-Palatinate and Hamburg in May 1987, see *Economist*, May 23, 1987, pp. 9–10, 43–44.

"reinsurance," in the Gaullist sense of providing the FRG with multiple security options.[66] Hence the importance of strengthening West German ties with Paris, Moscow, and East Berlin to protect against the vagaries of the U.S.–FRG relationship. Yet current CDU/CSU policy has gone beyond pure Gaullism to include, at least in part, an acceptance of the SPD and Genscherite notions of a European security partnership. Whether the Union continues to move in this direction will depend on many factors, including changes in the U.S. commitment to Europe, the success of the Gorbachev experiment, the attitudes of younger CDU/CSU leaders, and developments in the process of German reunification. Yet it is not farfetched to imagine that, in tandem with a return by the SPD to more moderate policies, a new security consensus could develop among the major political parties in the FRG in the 1990s. The outcome of such a consensus could well be a more independent German security policy, founded more on German national interests, which could alter the parameters of the German nuclear dilemma.

66. The historical reference here is to the 1887 Reinsurance Treaty, which Bismarck signed with Russia to forestall Franco-Russian collaboration at Germany's expense; see Gordon A. Craig, *Germany, 1866–1945* (New York: Oxford University Press, 1978), pp. 130–131.

[6]

Nuclear Weapons and Inter-German Relations: 1980–1989

One of the more intriguing aspects of the INF controversy in the 1980s was the way in which nuclear weapons issues accelerated an ongoing process, in both West and East Germany, toward a greater articulation of German interests and a heightened sense of German identity. In part this development was due to the natural vulnerability of being front-line states in the confrontation between NATO and the Warsaw Pact. Even before the onset of the INF issue, however, both German states had been articulating more distinctly "German" national interests, in part because of the expanded Ostpolitik of the 1970s and the benefits of increased contacts between the FRG and the GDR. Yet the two Germanies were also coming increasingly to appreciate the bonds of history and culture they shared, despite the ideological chasm between them.

The signing of the INF Treaty in December 1987 only partially mitigated the sense of urgency in this ongoing process. In some ways, in fact, the INF accord transformed and exacerbated the German nuclear dilemma. With the abolition of medium- and long-range INF systems, the majority of remaining NATO and Pact nuclear weapons could be used only on German territory. Hence the interest shown in both the FRG and the GDR for a "third zero option" that would ban missiles with ranges of less than 500 kilometers. Moreover, during the evolution of the INF controversy, the East German public became aware for the first time of just how many Soviet nuclear weapons were stationed in the GDR (see figure 2).

By the late 1980s, then, the two Germanies found themselves with a shared "German nuclear dilemma," albeit with quite different political implications. When massive public demonstrations in East-

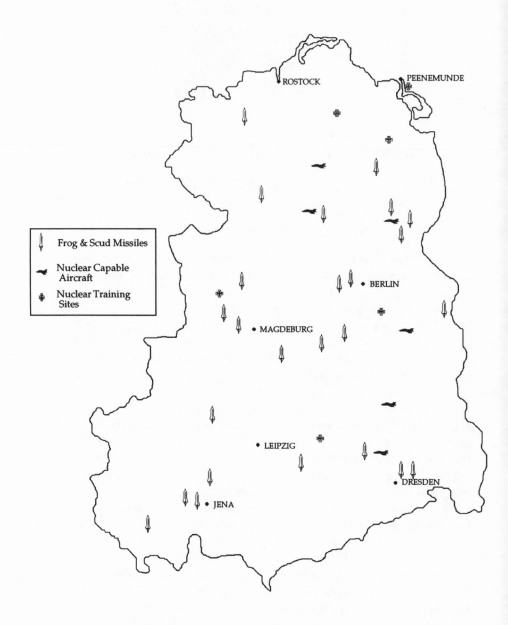

Figure 2. Deployment of Soviet nuclear weapons in East Germany, 1982. Adapted from a map, reportedly from a U.S. Defense Intelligence Agency report, that appeared in the West German weekly *Stern*, December 16, 1982, p. 20.

ern Europe in late 1989 led to the downfall of the Honecker regime and other old-guard communist leaders, the German nuclear dilemma took on quite a different hue. Suddenly German reunification had elbowed its way onto the East–West political agenda. Political events in Eastern Europe rushed far ahead of the ability of governments to respond, forcing leaders in both West and East to grope for formulas by which an eventually united Germany could be tightly integrated in a stable European security framework.

Whatever the ultimate pace of East bloc reforms, the German nuclear dilemma was fundamentally transformed by the opening of the Berlin Wall on November 9, 1989, and the subsequent flood of contacts, both private and governmental, between the two Germanies. Though one can't discount the possibility that economic and political chaos in Eastern Europe will result in a reimposition of Soviet control, such an outcome seems unlikely. What seems more probable is that the pace of East bloc reforms will be uneven, with great political uncertainty and confusion well into the 1990s. At least initially, the German nuclear dilemma has taken a back seat to all that is going on in Eastern Europe. Yet at some point, the presence of thousands of nuclear weapons on German soil will become a major factor in the way the United States and the Soviet Union, the two Germanies, and the rest of Europe come to grips with these new challenges to European security.

THE EVOLUTION OF INTER-GERMAN RELATIONS

It was a paradox of East–West relations from 1961 to 1989 that the region where the armed forces of the two blocs most directly confronted each other, along the border between East and West Germany, was regarded as one of the least likely flash points of a future conflict. In listing possible scenarios for the outbreak of a major conventional or nuclear war between the United States and the Soviet Union, most analysts believed that such a conflict, though it might spread to Central Europe, would not begin there.[1] Unlike the situation from the late 1940s to the early 1960s, when the status of the two German states and the city of Berlin were major sources

---

1. A range of scenarios that might lead to nuclear war is discussed in Graham T. Allison, Albert Carnesale, and Joseph Nye, eds., *Hawks, Doves, and Owls: An Agenda for Avoiding Nuclear War* (New York: W. W. Norton, 1985).

of East–West tension, the "German problem" in the 1970s and 1980s had become one of quiescent normality, greatly overshadowed by the clash of superpower interests in the Third World, from Latin America to the Middle East and Southeast Asia.

This lessening of tensions in Central Europe was facilitated (tragically) by the building of the Berlin Wall in 1961, and accelerated in the late 1960s with détente between the superpowers and between their European allies. By the early 1970s, the signing of the Berlin Quadripartite Agreement, the FRG's Eastern treaties with Poland and the USSR, the SALT I accords, the FRG-GDR Basic Treaty, and the Helsinki agreements had all paved the way for expanding contacts between the two Germanies. Afterward the inter-German relationship (Deutschlandpolitik) managed not only to survive but to expand, despite severe fluctations in relations between the United States and the Soviet Union in the 1980s.

As Fritz Stern noted in 1980, the West German Ostpolitik initiated by Willy Brandt in the late 1960s had "built up its own momentum. To most Germans it has ceased to be an option and has become a national necessity."[2] The reasons go well beyond the increased stability that inter-German relations helped create in Central Europe. For Germans living on both sides of the Elbe, improved relations between the FRG and the GDR produced tangible benefits.

For the Federal Republic, the gains were primarily humanitarian (increased resettlement of East Germans in the FRG and improved access by West Germans to friends and family in the GDR) and legal (a normalizing of the status of West Berlin). In addition, West Germany gained economically from the increase in inter-German trade that followed the improvement in relations in the early 1970s. As the mayor of Hamburg had foreseen as early as 1958, when he criticized the Adenauer government's Westpolitik as an "outmodedly rigid foreign policy" that robbed the port city "of half its hinterland,"[3] ultimately trading patterns in Central Europe would have to return to normal if West Germany was to realize its economic potential. Once these trading patterns were reestablished, inter-German trade expanded steadily, reaching a total of DM15 billion in the early 1980s, despite a slowing of each country's overall foreign trade.

The economics of inter-German relations was even more impor-

2. Fritz Stern, "Germany in a Semi-Gaullist Europe," *Foreign Affairs* 58 (Spring 1980): 885.

3. Quoted in "Hamburg between East and West," *Economist*, February 1, 1958, p. 412.

tant for the GDR. Along with the increase in trade between the two German states, East Germany benefited from a steady flow of West German credits and from its participation in the duty-free structure of the European Community. Also, the GDR took in several hundred million dollars a year in hard currency from the money exchanged by West Germans visiting the GDR and from cash payments made by the FRG for the release of East German political prisoners.[4] This expanded Deutschlandpolitik also brought the GDR political benefits in the form of a vast improvement in its international status.

By the early 1980s, the widespread commitment in both Germanies to a continuation of this Deutschlandpolitik was most evident in the changed attitudes of two groups in the FRG and GDR which originally opposed it: the CDU/CSU in the FRG and the East German leadership itself. As we noted in chapter 4, the CDU/CSU vilified Willy Brandt and the Social Democrats for signing the Eastern treaties with Poland and the USSR, thereby tacitly accepting the territorial status quo in Central Europe. The CDU/CSU claim that the treaties foreclosed any possibility of German reunification within the pre-1937 borders resulted in a bitter ratification debate over the treaties from 1970 to 1972. As late as 1980, Franz Josef Strauss of the CSU asserted that if he were elected chancellor, one of the first steps of his government would be the renegotiation of the Eastern treaties in order to allow eventual German reunification.[5] Yet so broad was the domestic consensus in the FRG over the necessity of continuing the Deutschlandpolitik that Strauss quickly dropped any further mention of reversing West German policy. When the CDU/CSU did come to power in 1982, the government of Helmut Kohl chose to continue the policies of his Social Democratic predecessors practically unchanged. And Strauss himself recognized the domestic political benefits of supporting inter-German relations when, during the height of the Euromissile controversy in 1983, he helped negotiate a new $400 million West German loan to the GDR.

No less striking was the reversal of the East German attitude toward inter-German relations. In 1970–71 the East German leader Walter Ulbricht had to be pressured by the Soviet Union to accept Brandt's "opening to the East." Ulbricht was primarily concerned that an improvement in Soviet–West German relations could leave

4. *Die Zeit,* January 4, 1980, p. 2. For more on the cash payments made by West German governments for East German émigrés and political prisoners, see John Ardagh, *Germany and the Germans* (New York: Harper & Row, 1987), pp. 377–78.

5. *Frankfurter Allgemeine Zeitung,* February 25, 1980, p. 4.

the GDR politically isolated; therefore he demanded that the FRG accord the GDR legal recognition as a separate sovereign state (as opposed to Brandt's purposely ambiguous formulation of "two German states in one nation") before relations between the two could be improved.[6] The Soviet Union, however, was not willing to let Ulbricht's demand block progress in East–West détente (the Moscow and Warsaw treaties, the Berlin Quadripartite Agreement, and the SALT talks). Ulbricht's continued intransigence led to his removal in May 1971 and replacement by Erich Honecker. Moreover, despite Ulbricht's fear that West Germany's refusal to extend formal recognition of the GDR's sovereignty would perpetuate East Germany's political isolation, the GDR's international standing greatly benefited from more than a decade of improved inter-German relations.

By the 1980s, both German states had thus developed a strong stake in the continuation of a broad-based Deutschlandpolitik. From their trading relations to environmental and transportation issues, from humanitarian concerns to the joint discussion of security issues, the two German states were reluctant to permit even the sharp downturn in superpower relations after Afghanistan, the Polish crisis, and the Euromissile debate to constrain their relationship.[7]

Concepts of Ideology and Nation in the Two Germanies

Despite their common interest in continuing Deutschlandpolitik, of course, the two German states pursued fundamentally different objectives. Up until Honecker's fall in 1989, these differences were rooted in the opposing social systems and bloc allegiances of the FRG and the GDR. Yet this conflict of ideology between the Germanies was attenuating even before 1989 (more for the FRG than for the GDR), especially in the early 1980s, when each German state began to emphasize its own historical legitimacy as the true successor of the German nation of the eighteenth and nineteenth centuries. Changes in both the domestic politics and the external relationships

6. West Germany has never formally recognized the territorial sovereignty of the East German state under international law. The preamble of the West German Basic Law (Grundgesetz), enacted in 1949, states that the law applies not only to the Länder of the FRG but also to "those Germans to whom participation was denied," and that "the entire German people is called on to achieve by free self-determination the unity and freedom of Germany." See Louise W. Holborn, et al., eds., *German Constitutional Documents since 1871* (New York: Praeger, 1970), p. 18.

7. See Eberhard Schulz, *Die deutsche Nation in Europa* (Bonn: Union Verlag, 1982).

of the FRG and the GDR were producing a new dialectic between ideology and nation, with interesting ramifications for the process of German reunification in the 1990s.

To summarize the point briefly, in the 1950s and 1960s the sociopolitical structures of the FRG and the GDR were shaped largely by the East–West ideological competition.[8] As the two German states were largely the creations of their respective superpower allies, the FRG and the GDR were subjected for years to a process of system dominance, in which external and internal security concerns were effective regulators of the political system.[9]

To a great extent, this "double security complex" remained the dominant feature of East German politics up through 1989, given the need of the ruling Socialist Unity Party (SED) to base its legitimacy on the socialist ideology of Marxism-Leninism and on its fraternal ties to the Soviet Union and the other members of the East bloc. The evolution of Deutschlandpolitik and greater contacts with the FRG actually increased the importance to the SED of stressing the centrality of socialist ideology as an underpinning for East German society. As Hermann Axen, a leading member of the SED politburo, noted at the time, "relations between the GDR and the FRG are characterized not by commonality but by unbridgeable differences, by irreconcilable differences between socialism and capitalism."[10]

Thus East Germany's policy in the 1980s reflected the country's two identities, one derived from a Soviet-inspired, socialist ideology and the other a continuation of the historical German nation. The SED's attempt to claim the inheritance of all that is "good" in German history will be discussed more fully below. For now, it is sufficient to note that the GDR regime faced the difficult task of reconciling these quite different bases of East German legitimacy, especially with the changes occurring in the Soviet Union under Mikhail Gorbachev. This dichotomy was apparent in the regime's conduct of Deutschlandpolitik, as Honecker sought to improve the stability of the SED regime yet also to give it a measure of economic and political independence from Moscow. One means of doing so

8. See especially Rudolf Schuster, *Deutschlands staatliche Existenz in widerstreit politischer und rechtlicher gesichtspunkte: 1945–1963* (Munich: Oldenbourg, 1963).

9. For more on the interaction of foreign policy and domestic politics in the FRG and GDR, see Joseph Joffe, "Society and Foreign Policy in the Federal Republic" (Ph.D. thesis, Harvard University, 1975); and Hans-Adolf Jacobsen, Gert Leptin, Ulrich Scheuner, and Eberhard Schulz, eds., *Drei jahrzente Aussenpolitik der DDR* (Munich: Oldenbourg, 1979).

10. Quoted in Klaus Bölling, *Die fernen Nachbarn* (Hamburg: Stern, 1983), p. 203.

was to strengthen its political and economic ties with the FRG, yet this move entailed the danger of spreading "capitalist and bourgeois" influences that could undermine the SED's socialist ideology.

In the Federal Republic, the dichotomy between ideology and nation had shifted much further in the direction of the latter. Initially, domestic politics in the FRG were characterized by a strident anticommunism that the Adenauer government was able to exploit effectively against both the opposition Social Democrats and the East German regime (e.g., the Hallstein Doctrine, whereby the FRG threatened to sever relations with any country that recognized the GDR). In tandem with the FRG's growing economic prosperity, anticommunist sentiments replaced German nationalism as a unifying ideology that brought political benefits both domestically, in terms of citizen identification with the Federal Republic, and externally, in the FRG's integration within the Western alliance.[11]

Beginning in the mid-1960s, however, the onset of détente began to reduce the effectiveness of anticommunism as a domesti: political tool in the FRG. By the time Helmut Schmidt came to power in 1974, ideology as a basis of West German foreign policy was being overshadowed by a new West German assertiveness based on national self-interest.[12] As was demonstrated in 1981, when the Schmidt government's attempt to brand members of the peace movement as communist sympathizers backfired with the West German public at large, anticommunism was no longer a unifying force in domestic politics.[13]

Competing concepts of German national identity appeared, from the Gaullism of the conservative right to the diffuse cultural nationalism of the radical left and the Greens. In the 1983 election, the SPD

11. See Wolf-Dieter Narr, "Social Factors Affecting the Making of Foreign Policy," in Karl Kaiser and Roger Morgan, eds., *Britain and West Germany: Changing Societies and the Future of Foreign Policy* (London: Oxford University Press, 1971).

12. As usual, Fritz Stern has put it best, noting that Schmidt "found his role of worldwide authority as natural to his temperament as Adenauer had found his role as reconciler with the West or Brandt his position of contrite authority vis-à-vis the East." See his "Germany in a Semi-Gaullist Europe," p. 875. See also the various essays that examine concepts of German identity in "Thema: Nation and nationale Frage," *Neue Gesellschaft*, August 1982.

13. In August 1981 Schmidt was very critical of the peace movement, saying that it was an "instrument that would come in handy for the Soviet leadership": quoted in *Frankfurter Allgemeine Zeitung*, August 31, 1981. By October, however, Schmidt had moderated his criticism, saying that only a minority in the movement "want to persuade us that Soviet missiles serve peace, whereas American missiles serve war": quoted in *Foreign Broadcast Information Service* (hereafter *FBIS*): *Western Europe*, October 13, 1981, p. J3.

sought to capitalize on this growth in German self-consciousness (deutsche Selbstbewüsstsein) with its main electoral slogan, "In the German Interest" (Im deutschen Interesse). Yet a further variant of this effort to promote German interests was the pan-European security proposals of Hans-Dietrich Genscher and the FDP.

Concepts of how to promote West German security have existed throughout the postwar period; what was new in the 1980s was a greater sense of deutsche Patriotismus, of the need to give increased priority to German interests in the context of both Deutschlandpolitik specifically and West German foreign policy in general. What makes this development so important for the 1990s is that the emerging reality of German reunification could sharpen even further the trade-offs inherent in the FRG's three foreign policy spheres: the Atlantic, the European, and the Eastern.[14]

THE FRG'S "GERMAN" INTERESTS

Given the fragmentation of FRG domestic politics in the 1980s, "the German interest" came to be defined quite variously across the West German political spectrum. From the neutralist policies of the Greens to the stark nationalism of the right-wing Republikaner Party, there emerged a variety of proposals for the FRG's conduct of its Deutschlandpolitik with the GDR.

As we've noted, the government of Helmut Kohl and the more moderate elements of the CDU/CSU fully supported a continuation of inter-German relations following their accession to power in 1982. Not only had Deutschlandpolitik become a major component of CDU foreign policy; the Kohl government's deviation from long-standing CDU policy on several important issues related to Deutschlandpolitik in the 1980s testified to the widespread desire of West Germans for continual improvement in inter-German relations.

One shift occurred in 1984–85 when the Kohl government returned a number of East German citizens to the GDR after several hundred refugees, in a precursor of the flight of East Germans to the FRG in 1989, sought sanctuary in West German embassies in Prague, Budapest, Warsaw, and Bucharest.[15] At first the affair was highly embarrassing

---

14. David Calleo, *The German Problem Reconsidered: Germany and the World Order, 1870 to the Present* (New York: Cambridge University Press, 1978), p. 177.

15. An account is given in Ardagh, *Germany and the Germans*, pp. 371–78.

for the GDR, as the asylum seekers included the niece of GDR Prime Minster Willy Stoph and her family. In that case, negotiations between Bonn and East Berlin produced an agreement whereby the family left the Prague embassy and returned to the GDR with the promise of exit visas to the West (which were soon forthcoming). Yet this precedent produced a flood of East Germans into FRG embassies in Eastern Europe (150 East Germans held out in the Prague embassy for three months in the fall of 1984), and the Kohl government finally felt the need to condemn the practice publicly (via West German television to the GDR) in order to minimize tensions with Honecker.[16] Although most of the refugees ultimately received exit visas after returning to East Germany, some did not, and the affair led to a good deal of criticism of Kohl from CDU/CSU conservatives, who saw the chancellor as caving in to the GDR and undercutting provisions of the FRG constitution which permit automatic FRG citizenship to those East Germans who make it to West Germany (in this case, West German embassies).[17]

A second change took place in June 1985 when Kohl appeared at the annual rally of Silesian refugees, a group that advocates German reunification within pre-1937 borders, and gave only lukewarm support to their claims.[18] Though Kohl was the first chancellor in twenty years to appear at the Silesian rally, he was not warmly received for noting both the domestic and external difficulties of reopening the territorial question. At the time, of course, most West Germans believed that German reunification was still decades away (a 1985 poll showed that only 7 percent of West Germans thought it would ever come). Nonetheless, Kohl consistently gave higher priority to inter-German relations than to the reunification interests of many members of his own party.[19]

16. Though the Kohl government sought assurances from the GDR that these people would be allowed to emigrate eventually, not all were allowed to do so. For a report on those East Germans who occupied the West German embassy in Prague in late 1984 and who were allowed to emigrate to the FRG, see *FBIS: Western Europe*, August 29, 1985, p. J3.

17. Although the West German Basic Law grants citizenship to Germans in both the FRG and the GDR, and though international law considers national embassies in foreign countries to be sovereign territory, it is not legal under international law for embassies to provide this type of haven.

18. The West German Federation of Expellees (Bund der Vetriebenen) has 2 million members, and was founded in 1950 to represent the 12 million Germans expelled from pre-1937 German territory and other parts of Eastern Europe following World War II.

19. *Die Zeit*, June 28, 1985, p. 6.

Even major spy scandals, such as the Hans Joachim Tiedge affair in 1985, could not disrupt the orderly expansion of inter-German relations. The revelation that Tiedge and several other members of the FRG's counterintelligence service were East German double agents resulted in severe domestic criticism of the Kohl government. Yet there was little sentiment for retaliating by curtailing inter-German relations, and even Franz Josef Strauss noted that "relations with the GDR...cannot be made dependent on whether they're sending over spies and agents."[20] East Germany, for its part, played down its intelligence coup and continued to demonstrate its interest in negotiating new accords with the FRG on transportation and cultural issues.[21]

Also, the mid-1980s saw a steady continuation of West German loans and credit to the GDR to foster inter-German trade. The $400 million loan involving Strauss in 1983 was followed by others, including one for $2 billion in 1988 to facilitate trade in the energy and high-technology sectors. Moreover, the CDU/CSU continued to negotiate the release of dissidents from the GDR, in large part through cash payments to the East German government.

As the originators of West Germany's Ostpolitik, the Social Democrats remained deeply committed to preserving and expanding the gains of inter-German relations. The problem for the SPD in the mid-1980s, however, was that of reconciling its commitment to improved relations with the East and its support for NATO and the Western alliance. The SPD concept of an East-West "security partnership" and of a "special role" for the two Germanies in constructing a new European security framework raised fears, especially in the United States and France, that the SPD was seeking a quasi-neutralist third way between the two superpowers. Especially during the 1983 and 1987 election campaigns, statements by such left-wing SPD leaders as Oskar Lafontaine and Erhard Eppler emphasized German national interests that at times conflicted with broader Western alliance interests. For many in the West the appearance in September 1985 of a draft SPD report on security which called for a "European peace order" and SPD discussions with the East German SED on chemical and nuclear-weapons-free zones covering the two

---

20. Quote in *Die Zeit*, September 6, 1985, p. 1. Western estimates were that some 3,000 East bloc agents were operating in the FRG at the time, about two-thirds of them East German.

21. *FBIS: Western Europe*, August 23, 1985, p. J5.

Germanies called into question the party's commitment to the FRG's role in NATO.[22]

Nationalist strains in the Green party and the peace movement in the mid-1980s were more complex, given the various shades of cultural chauvinism, romantic idealism, and radical antiestablishmentism existing on the West German left.[23] As Richard Löwenthal has pointed out, the ideological diversity of the Greens allowed the movement to win support from a broad segment of the postwar successor generation, yet handicapped it from developing and implementing a coherent political strategy.[24] For this reason the Greens were more successful in pushing single-issue topics at the district and regional levels than they were in influencing party politics and security issues at the national level.

What was less certain was the extent to which concepts of German identity being formed by members of the successor generation might be translated into political strategies once this generation moved into positions of influence in the 1990s. Ronald Inglehart maintained that the "post-materialist" values of the successor generation in Western Europe on defense and nuclear weapons issues were not being ameliorated by the effects of aging and the processes of socialization. For Inglehart, polling data demonstrated that a commitment to nuclear disarmament and new security arrangements in Europe was increasing among people born after 1945.[25] Accordingly, members of the Green party issued a steady stream of alternative security proposals, including calls for nonprovocative defense postures and passive resistance strategies (*Sozialvertidigung*) based on the demilitarization of West Germany.

At the time, these proposals generated little support among the West German public. Most West Germans continued to support NATO as important for FRG security, and many analysts concluded that it would take extreme changes in the European order to make

22. The draft was authored by Andreas von Bülow, chairman of an SPD security commission, and titled "Strategie vertrauensschaffender Sicherheitsstrukturen in Europa: Wege zur Sicherheitspartnerschaft" (Bonn: SPD, 1985). For more on the SPD-SED discussions on chemical weapons, see "Chemische Abrüstung: Modell für eine chemiewaffenfreie Zone in Europa," *Politik*, no. 6 (Bonn: SPD, July 1985).

23. See, for example, Wilhelm P. Burklin, *Grüne Politik: Ideologische Zyklen-, Wahler- und Parteiensystem* (Opladen: Westdeutscher Verlag, 1984).

24. Richard Löwenthal, "Reflections on the 'Greens': Roots, Character, and Prospects," *German Studies Newsletter* (Harvard University, Center for European Studies), February 1985.

25. Ronald Inglehart, "Generational Change and the Future of the Atlantic Alliance," *PS* 17 (Summer 1984).

these alternative security concepts more politically acceptable in the FRG.[26]

By late 1989, of course, such changes were sweeping across the continent. In a matter of months, as first Hungary, then Czechoslovakia, and finally East Germany itself opened their borders to the West, the prospect of German reunification rushed to the top of the East–West political agenda. In West Germany, Chancellor Kohl issued a ten-point plan for reuniting the two Germanies. In East Germany, demonstrators massed weekly in Leipzig and other major cities in late 1989 and early 1990 to call for reunification.[27]

Given the tremendous political and economic challenges facing the East European reform movements, it remains to be seen how the issue of German reunification will be played out. What is not in doubt is that its emergence as a priority issue in East–West relations has greatly accelerated the convergence of concepts of German identity and patriotism in the FRG with similar sentiments in the GDR. For the first time in the postwar period, the concept of the German nation became as important as the nation-state identities of the FRG and the GDR for citizens on both sides of the Elbe.

The "German" Interests of the GDR

The increased attention being given to questions of German identity in the FRG had its counterpart as well in the GDR, and was likewise partly the result of the maturation of a generation that did not bear direct responsibility for the horrors of Nazism. Society in both West and East Germany, shaped as it had been since 1945 by American and Soviet influences, was no longer so inhibited in seeking roots in German history before the rise of the Third Reich. In the early 1980s especially the two German states almost competed to see which one could more grandly commemorate such high-water marks of German history as the reign of Frederick the Great and the five hundredth anniversary of the birth of Martin Luther.

The occurrence of such events in West Germany was certainly noteworthy, and represented an acceleration of the process of

26. A position taken by Christoph Bertram in his "Strategic Defense and the Western Alliance," in Franklin A. Long, Donald L. Hafner, and Jeffrey Boutwell, eds., *Weapons in Space* (New York: Norton, 1986).

27. For an analysis of the prospects for reunification, see Gordon A. Craig, "A New, New Reich?" *New York Review of Books*, January 18, 1990.

"overcoming the past" (*Bewältigung der Vergangenheit*). That they occurred in East Germany, where the state for so long maintained a policy of "renunciation of the past" (*Ablehnung der Vergangenheit*), was nothing short of extraordinary. Since 1945 the ruling Socialist Unity Party (SED) had sought to base the very legitimacy of the GDR on a renunciation of any links with Germany's feudal, bourgeois, and fascist past. In addition, the leadership of the GDR had excoriated the FRG for being the repository of those prefascist tendencies (e.g., Bismarck and Prussian Junkerism) that produced Hitler, and denied the legitimacy of German Protestantism (i.e., Lutheranism) in a Marxist-Leninist society.

To be sure, the eagerness with which the GDR promoted a sense of continuity between pre-Hitlerite Germany and East German society was undeniably politically motivated. As one GDR official put it, this revisionism was a form of "ideological class warfare," designed in part to strengthen the legitimacy of the socialist East German state.[28] In seeking to appropriate (or expropriate, as the case may be) all that was "good" in pre-Nazi German history, the SED leadership tried to maintain a clear differentiation between East German society and that of the FRG. Nonetheless, the fact that both the FRG and the GDR were plowing the common ground of German history and culture was significant in making the German nation a legitimate symbol of allegiance for all Germans.

The difficulty for the SED in the 1980s was that this increased emphasis on the GDR as a "German" as opposed to a "socialist" state served to undermine the legitimacy of the East German regime. In part this development was the result of a growing bond between members of the peace movements in the two Germanies, which accelerated the alienation of East German youth from the centralized GDR society.[29] The situation was exacerbated in 1985 when Mikhail Gorbachev instituted his policies of *glasnost* and *perestroika* in the Soviet Union, and the SED consciously sought to limit their appeal in the GDR. Certainly there was little hint before 1989 that such disaffection could so swiftly topple the Honecker regime.[30] Yet when

28. Quoted in Michael Stürmer, "Quest for National Identity," *German Comments: Review of Politics and Culture,* April 1983, p. 53.

29. For a particularly good analysis, see Joyce Marie Mushaben, "Anti-politics and Successor Generations: The Role of Youth in West and East German Peace Movements," *Journal of Political and Military Sociology* 12 (Spring 1984).

30. Most political observers would have agreed with the analysis found in C. Bradley Scharf, *Politics and Change in East Germany* (Boulder Colo.: Westview Press,

these factors were combined with pressing economic, social, and environmental problems, there was little doubt that the SED needed more than the mantle of "German" history and culture to support its claim to legitimacy.[31]

In both German states, then, domestic currents in the 1980s were posing new challenges to the political structures that had evolved in the postwar period. In the case of the FRG, the domestic challenges posed by the Greens and the rise of the right-wing Republikan Party signaled an end to thirty years of domination of FRG party politics by the CDU/CSU, SPD, and FDP. Although changes at the grass-roots level in East Germany were far less visible, important dissident currents in the fledgling East German peace movement, the Protestant churches, and other sectors of society were gnawing at the edges of SED authority and legitimacy. As the INF dispute heated up in the early 1980s, both the Kohl and the Honecker governments sought to deflect domestic criticism through appeals to the "German national interest."

"In the Name of the German Nation"

Increasingly as East–West relations deteriorated and fears of nuclear war increased in the early to mid-1980s, both German governments promoted their policies as the best way to protect the interests not only of their individual states but of the German nation. Such claims had long been official West German policy, embedded as they were in the Basic Law (Grundgesetz) on which the FRG was founded, but now they appeared in the vocabulary of the East German government for the first time.

The tendency to claim responsibility for the well-being of all Germans was to be expected from the Christian Democratic government of Helmut Kohl, which is heir to the *Alleinvertretungsanspruch* (claim of sole representation) tradition of Konrad Adenauer. The assumption of such a responsibility by the East German government, however, represented a reversal of more than a decade of

---

1984), which accented the "integrative" nature of East German society; see chap. 6 especially.

31. For example, just days after East German representatives signed a CSCE agreement on human rights in Vienna, East German police forcefully broke up a peaceful demonstration in Leipzig; see *Christian Science Monitor*, January 26, 1989, p. 6.

Abgrenzung (separation) policy, by which the GDR sought to distance itself from its capitalist, bourgeois neighbor. Throughout the 1970s, in direct opposition to Willy Brandt's claim of "two German states in one nation," East German officials had stressed the uniqueness of the "developing socialist nation" in the GDR and vehemently denied the legitimacy of the "unity of the nation." In seeking to construct a nationalist identity based on this "will to socialism," East German leaders rejected the concept of the German nation and the possibility of German reunification. Mention of all things German was deleted from the country's constitution, and the GDR at the stroke of a pen transformed itself from a "socialist state of the German nation" to a "socialist state of the workers and peasants."[32]

By the time of the SED's tenth party congress in April 1981, however, the GDR was once again stressing its German identity. Realizing that Marxism-Leninism alone would not suffice to promote a sense of East German nationhood, Honecker and the East German leadership declared that the GDR should now be thought of as a "socialist German nation." At about the same time, Honecker began to make vague references to a subject that had long been taboo— German reunification. In a speech to SED party functionaries in February 1981, Honecker cautioned that the terms "unification" and "reunification" were to be avoided. Nonetheless, no longer was it official SED doctrine that the German national issue would automatically lapse with time. In even raising the issue of a "union of two German states," which for Honecker would be "posed in an entirely new form . . . once the working people of the Federal Republic begin the socialist transformation of the FRG," the East German leadership essentially legitimized discussion of the German question in the GDR for the first time since the 1960s.[33] While East German policy necessarily concentrated on establishing a separate, albeit German, identity for the GDR, as opposed to actively seeking reunification, this weakening of Abgrenzung represented a shift to the German nation as an additional source of national legitimacy.

This process was taken a step further when, at the height of the Euromissile crisis in the fall of 1983, Honecker wrote a letter to Chancellor Kohl, "in the name of the German people," calling on the FRG to forgo deployment of the new NATO missiles and work

32. Gebhard Schweigler, *National Consciousness in Divided Germany* (London: Sage, 1975), chap. 2 especially.
33. Martin McCauley, "Power and Authority in East Germany: The Socialist Unity Party (SED)," *Conflict Studies*, no. 132 (July 1981), p. 11.

for a nuclear-free Europe.[34] In discussing the ramifications of the Euromissile issue for inter-German relations, Honecker referred to a "community of responsibility" between the FRG and GDR for safeguarding peace and ensuring that "war never again starts from German soil."[35] Within a few short years, the East German government had gone from seeking to extinguish all references to Germany to claiming that it was working for peace on behalf of the entire German people. Again, this switch was motivated primarily by short-run political considerations, aimed at persuading the West German people to reject the stationing of new nuclear missiles in the FRG. Also, East German references to the possibility of German reunification were predicated on the dissolution of West Germany's ties to NATO. These sentiments were shared by some members of the West German peace movement, and the GDR sought to exploit them.

The East German leadership was also concerned, however, that Soviet countermeasures to the NATO deployment, consisting of increases in the Soviet nuclear arsenal in the GDR, would not be particularly popular with the East German public. The SED position that the party, and not the fledgling and tightly constrained East German peace movement, had the better policy for reducing tensions in Central Europe was undercut by the deployment of the Soviet SS-21s and SS-23s on East German soil. At the time, Honecker made known (albeit obliquely) his displeasure with what he saw as a Soviet response taken at the expense of East German security.[36]

At a minimum, then, both German governments sought to insulate their relationship from the tensions between the superpowers.[37] For months before the actual deployment of the Euromissiles, East Berlin had been threatening the Federal Republic with what Honecker called a "political ice age" if deployment went ahead. Yet this threat

34. For the text of the letter as it was broadcast by East Germany's ADN International Service on October 9, 1983, see *FBIS: Eastern Europe*, October 11, 1983, pp. E1–E2.

35. See ibid., October 6, 1983 p. E3.

36. In a statement released the day after the signing of the INF Treaty in 1987, Honecker referred to East German anxieties about increased Soviet missile deployments in the GDR when he said: "We have never made it a secret that the deployment of additional nuclear weapons in both West and East was not welcomed with joy in our country." See *Statement by the General Secretary of the SED Central Committee and Chairman of the GDR Council of State, Erich Honecker*, December 8, 1987 (Berlin: Zeit im Bild, 1987), p. 9.

37. See Ronald Asmus, "The GDR and the German Nation: Sole Heir or Socialist Sibling?" *International Affairs*, Summer 1984, pp. 403–18.

was mainly bluff, as both German states were taking significant steps to ensure the continuation of Deutschlandpolitik. Honecker, for his part, ordered the removal of the automatic firing devices, a particularly noxious symbol of the separation of Germany, along the entire inter-German border, and reaffirmed that they would be removed even as he was justifying Warsaw Pact countermeasures to the NATO deployment.[38]

Over and above this desire of the two German states to insulate their relationship from superpower tensions, a new emphasis on common security concerns also appeared in the conduct of Deutschlandpolitik. This increased dialogue between the two German states on security issues in general and on nuclear weapons in particular reflected a growing interest in protecting the security of all Germans, while it also of course raised fears outside of Germany that the two states were compromising their bloc allegiances.

DEUTSCHLANDPOLITIK AND SECURITY ISSUES

At its inception in the early 1970s, Deutschlandpolitik focused primarily on issues of "low politics" (trade, transportation, energy and environmental concerns). More politically sensitive issues, such as West German recognition of GDR sovereignty, questions of German citizenship, access by West Germans to friends and family in the GDR, and the ability of East Germans to emigrate to the FRG, were central as well, but these matters were primarily indigenous German concerns. Only in the late 1970s did Deutschlandpolitik begin, slowly, to extend beyond the sphere of strictly German issues to include larger security and arms control issues that previously had been the domain of the two superpowers (nuclear arms control) or the NATO and Warsaw Pact alliances (conventional arms talks and confidence-building measures).

This process was given a marked impetus by the Schmidt-Honecker summit of December 1981, when the two heads of government agreed to try to formulate a joint initiative that would break the deadlock at the MBFR talks on conventional forces being held in Vienna.[39] This agreement was followed by meetings in early 1982 between West German Foreign Minister Hans-Dietrich Genscher and

38. Not surprisingly, the East German government reinforced its passive barriers along the inter-German border as it took down the automatic firing devices. See *FBIS: Eastern Europe*, October 6, 1983, p. E1.
39. Ibid., February 10, 1982, p. E2.

his East German counterpart, Oskar Fischer—a departure from the usual FRG practice of entrusting such contacts to its minister for inter-German affairs (in this case, Egon Franke). By the same token, the GDR had usually avoided participating in joint ventures with the FRG which went beyond issues of Deutschlandpolitik for fear of compromising its status as a sovereign state (the FRG still did not officially recognize the GDR as a legal, sovereign entity). But in this case, given the opportunity to deal directly with Genscher on an issue of such importance, East Germany overcame its hesitation.[40]

Though no dramatic proposals ultimately emerged from the web of contacts between disarmament officials of the two countries,[41] the process itself was noteworthy not only for inter-German relations but for foreign perceptions of those relations. As one West German editorial writer commented in evaluating Western reaction, these inter-German talks "trip alarm bells in foreign capitals, as the world believes it can live more safely if the Germans are quarreling rather than agreeing."[42]

Following the fall of the Schmidt government in October 1982, the Kohl government reduced both the scope and the visibility of these talks, but they continued nonetheless.[43] Alongside these government-to-government discussions, the Social Democrats in March 1984 initiated a series of talks with SED officials on the need for a chemical-weapons-free zone in Central Europe. At the conclusion of the fifth round of talks, in June 1985, the SPD and SED reached agreement on a draft proposal.[44] Seeing this as a concrete expression of the viability of its security partnership policy, SPD spokesmen said the proposal, which included provisions for on-site inspection by an international commission, could provide the basis for formal governmental negotiations.[45] Not surprisingly, the East German and

40. *Frankfurter Rundschau*, January 19, 1982, p. 3.

41. For example, in early 1982 the heads of the West and East German delegations held meetings at the UN International Disarmament Commission in Geneva and the MBFR talks in Vienna; see *FBIS: Western Europe*, February 10, 1982, p. U1, and *FBIS: Eastern Europe*, February 10, 1982, p. E2.

42. *Frankfurter Rundschau*, January 19, 1982, p. 3.

43. In February 1985, for example, Genscher and Friedrich Ruth, the FRG disarmament representative, held talks with Hermann Axen of the SED; see *FBIS: Western Europe*, March 4, 1985, p. J4.

44. K. H. Lohs, a member of the East German delegation, provides a summary of the GDR position in his "Pros and Cons of a Chemical Weapon–Free Zone in Europe: The Genesis of a Concept," paper presented to the 35th Pugwash Conference on Science and World Affairs, Campinas, Brazil, July 3–8, 1985.

45. *Die Zeit*, June 28, 1985, p. 1.

Czechoslovak governments proposed to the Kohl government in September 1985 that the three countries begin such negotiations. The Kohl government demurred, saying it did not want to complicate the ongoing Geneva disarmament negotiations on a global ban of chemical weapons. According to government spokesman Friedhelm Ost, the CDU position was that the Geneva talks should not "be circumvented through regional partial solutions," a polite way of dismissing the SPD-SED initiative.[46]

These direct negotiations by the SPD with the SED (i.e., with the East German government), which would have been an immense political liability in the 1950s, passed with little comment from the Kohl government. Yet the talks did raise political concerns within NATO (especially as the SPD was discussing American weapons) that the party was undermining the alliance through independent initiatives. When the SPD and SED went on to discuss the creation of a nuclear-weapons-free zone in Central Europe, fears were heightened within the Alliance that the SPD was embarked on a unilateral course that would undermine NATO cohesion. Then, in the summer of 1987, the SPD and SED produced a joint document titled "Conflicting Ideologies and Common Security," which stressed the need for "peaceful competition, nonviolent argument" between East and West. The paper went beyond military and security issues and addressed a wide range of social, environmental, and humanitarian concerns that, its authors wrote, "for German communists and Social Democrats . . . should lead to new common interests in the struggle for peace."[47]

For many observers, the appearance of a joint declaration of principles by "German communists and Social Democrats" (for the first time since 1919) was indicative of the SPD's unilateral approach in trying to implement its concept of a "European security partnership."[48] While the SPD's status as the opposition party obviously limited its influence, this type of SPD-SED dialogue at a minimum served to focus attention on common German concerns and, indirectly, maintained pressure on the Kohl government to safeguard German interests in the arms control sphere.

46. *FBIS: Western Europe*, September 17, 1985, p. J6.

47. "Conflicting Ideologies and Common Security," a joint paper of the Academy for Social Sciences attached to the SED Central Committee and the Basic Values Commission of the SPD (Bonn/Berlin, August 27, 1987), p. 8.

48. For a thoughtful critique of the SPD-SED paper, see Gerd Bucerius, "Aus der Vergangenheit nichts gelernt?" *Die Zeit*, September 18, 1987 (overseas ed.).

The importance of security issues within the conduct of Deutschlandpolitik was also evident in the unilateral actions of both German states to ensure the security of Germany as a whole. Government spokesmen in West Germany emphasized the distinct security benefits the FRG might gain by promoting stability in the GDR through trade, humanitarian efforts, and legal agreements. To those Western allies who criticized Ostpolitik for going too far, or for bestowing on the East German regime benefits that did not accrue directly to the East German people, many West Germans responded that it was in NATO's interest to reduce the likelihood of domestic unrest in East Germany and thus reduce a potential source of East–West conflict in Europe.[49]

West German officials also took an independent stance when NATO policy was seen as unnecessarily complicating FRG domestic politics and inter-German relations. In 1981, for example, the U.S. Army proposed to relocate American ground forces from the Kreuznach-Mannheim area to a base east of the Rhine, in order to improve operational mobility in carrying out NATO's forward defense strategy. Though the proposal was eminently sensible militarily, the FRG resisted, citing increased costs, domestic political reaction, and possible adverse consequences to the country's Ostpolitik.[50] This sensitivity to the effect on Deutschlandpolitik, shown by both SPD and CDU/CSU governments, was equally strong on the topic of fortifying the inter-German border with passive barriers in order to strengthen NATO's strategy of forward defense. While the FRG was the most strongly committed of all the allies to forward defense (the alternative being mobile operational strategies that would trade West German territory for time needed to counterattack), it nonetheless was difficult for West German governments to accept the building of passive antitank barriers that would visibly highlight the separation of the two German states.

Even more sensitive was the issue of altering the alliance's military doctrine to provide for deep counterattacks by armored forces into East Germany and Czechoslovakia. It was one thing for West Germany to sign on to the NATO strategy of Follow-On Forces

49. For the argument that Deutschlandpolitik provided real benefits for the East German people, as opposed to just increasing the legitimacy of the SED regime, see the interview with Günter Gaus in *Die Neue Gesellschaft*, August 1982; see also the rejoinder from Wolfgang Leonhard, "Was Günter Gaus übersieht," in ibid., October 1982.

50. *Frankfurter Allgemeine Zeitung*, September 3, 1981.

Attack (FOFA), adopted in 1984, which entailed improving the alliance's capabilities of interdicting second-echelon Warsaw Pact forces in Eastern Europe with aircraft and missiles. Even so, FOFA remained highly controversial in the FRG, and the subject of constant criticism by the SPD and Greens. It was quite another thing to contemplate West German and NATO ground troops attacking deep into East German or Czech territory, as called for by the U.S. Army's Air-Land Battle doctrine (not officially adopted by NATO).[51]

Another way the FRG took *gesamtdeutsch* (all-German) concerns into account in its security policies was seen in its attempts to influence French defense policy, especially French nuclear targeting options. In the mid-1980s, the Kohl government made known its desire to have a direct say in French nuclear weapons targeting strategy, particularly in regard to the new Hades tactical missile, which had a range of 200 miles and thus could strike targets in East Germany. As one West German official put it, "We want some sort of nuclear guarantee whereby France regards German territory, East and West, as its [Bonn's] own security area."[52] In a move that partially accommodated these concerns, all of the major political parties in France, save the communists, endorsed the concept of an "enlarged sanctuary," in which the territorial integrity of the FRG (though not of the GDR) was seen as vital to the security of France.[53] Of course, French governments also made it abundantly clear that targeting options and strategies for the country's nuclear deterrent would remain a distinctly national concern.

The position of the GDR in the Warsaw Pact obviously afforded it much less leeway in undertaking independent steps to maintain German security. Indeed, the very wording of the 1955 Warsaw Treaty placed greater constraints on East Germany than on any other East European member regarding the Pact's military structure and political decision making.[54]

51. On the concept of armored retaliatory strikes into East Germany, see Samuel P. Huntington, "Conventional Deterrence and Conventional Retaliation in Europe," *International Security*, Winter 1983/84. For a West German critique of this concept, see Eckhard Lubkemeier, "Deterrence, Détente, and Defense in Europe: How Not to Reform NATO's Strategy" (Bonn: Friedrich Ebert, May 1984).

52. "Bonn Seeks More Influence on French Nuclear Targeting," *Washington Post*, April 20, 1984.

53. See David Yost, "Franco-German Defense Cooperation," in Stephen F. Szabo, ed., *The Bundeswehr and the Future of Western Defense* (New York: Macmillan, forthcoming), and Stanley Hoffman, "France's Relations with West Germany," *German Studies Newsletter* (Harvard University, Center for European Studies, February 1985).

54. For example, the Russian, Polish, and Czech versions of the Warsaw Treaty

Yet, especially during the uncertainty caused by the transitions from Brezhnev to Andropov to Chernenko to Gorbachev in the early and mid-1980s, Erich Honecker was able to exercise some degree of flexibility in his dealings with the FRG. While Honecker did bow to Soviet pressure and cancel his summit meeting with Kohl scheduled for September 1984, the East German leader was able during that period to solidify his base in the SED Politburo and persuade Andropov to replace the overbearing Soviet ambassador to the GDR, Pyotr Abrassimov.[55] In addition, East Germany voiced its support for more independent policymaking within the Warsaw Pact. In March 1985, on the eve of the thirtieth anniversary meeting of the Warsaw Treaty Organization (WTO) to extend the pact, the SED newspaper *Neues Deutschland* reprinted an interview with Istvan Roska, the Hungarian deputy foreign minister, in which Roska defended independent policies within the Soviet bloc.[56]

A watershed in inter-German relations was then reached in September 1987, when Honecker made the first visit ever by an East German head of state to the FRG.[57] The meetings between Kohl and Honecker were not officially between heads of state, in deference to West German sensibilities about the sovereignty of the GDR. Yet the interest stimulated by Honecker's three-day visit, which included a visit to Honecker's birthplace (in the village of Neunkirchen, in the Saar region), left little doubt about the desire of both West and East Germans for continued expansion of inter-German relations. Indeed, less than nine months later, in May 1988, Kohl followed this visit by a low-key private visit to Dresden, which was all the more remarkable for the lack of publicity it generated.[58]

(art. 4) state that each country will lend "assistance to the victim of an attack with all means it deems necessary," while the German version states "with all means they [the other members] deem necessary." Also, the 1957 troop-stationing agreement between the GDR and the USSR differs from similar agreements with other WTO members in that the Soviet Union is given the sole right to determine the strength, deployment, and movement of Soviet forces in the GDR. While these differences ultimately have had little operational significance, given the traditional subservience of all WTO members to the Soviet Union, they are nonetheless interesting. See Boris Meissner, "The GDR's Position in the Soviet Alliance System," *Aussenpolitik* (English ed.) 35 (4th quarter 1984).

55. According to Klaus Bölling, who in 1982–82 was the FRG's permanent representative to the GDR, Abrassimov was disparagingly referred to as a "proconsul" by many East Germans for his heavy-handed treatment of GDR officials; see Bölling, *Die fernen Nachbarn*, pp. 251–63.

56. *New York Times*, March 7, 1985.

57. See *Die Zeit*, September 25, 1987.

58. *Economist*, June 11, 1988, pp. 50–51.

THE EAST GERMAN REVOLUTION

As the East European reform movements gathered momentum in 1988 and 1989, however, Honecker and the SED became increasingly alarmed about the threats these events posed to East Germany's economic gains and political stability. Honecker continued to be an outspoken critic of the Solidarity movement in Poland, and he was far less enthusiastic than the Poles and Hungarians about Gorbachev's perestroika. By January 1989 the SED was so unsettled by the possibility that the perestroika contagion might spread to East Germany that it took the remarkable step of banning the sale of a Soviet publication, the magazine *Sputnik*, because of its pro-perestroika views. That same month, Honecker uttered what turned out to be a gaffe of historical proportions when he claimed that the Berlin Wall "will still be standing in 50 or even 100 years."[59] Within ten months, of course, Honecker had been ousted from power, and by January 1990 the Berlin Wall was being dismantled.

The incredible rush of events that led to Honecker's downfall in 1989 and the prospect of multiparty elections in East Germany (scheduled for March 18, 1990) can only be summarized here. Suffice it to say that Honecker as much as anyone should have seen the handwriting on the wall when, in the spring of 1989, Hungary began to dismantle its barbed-wire border with Austria. Over the next several months, hundreds of East Germans used Hungary as an escape route to the West. Then, in August 1989, hundreds more East Germans repeated the events of 1984–85 by taking refuge in West German diplomatic missions in Budapest, Warsaw, and East Berlin and demanding political asylum in West Germany.[60] Pressure on the SED regime increased when its border with West Germany began to leak, and Honecker reached the point of no return in early October when Gorbachev, visiting East Berlin for the fortieth anniversary celebrations of the founding of the GDR, ruled out any Soviet assistance should Honecker decide to crack down on the increasingly massive pro-democracy demonstrations erupting throughout East Germany.[61]

Honecker himself was removed from power by the SED Central

---

59. Quoted in Daniel Hamilton, "Dateline East Germany: The Wall Behind the Wall" *Foreign Policy*, no. 76 (Fall 1989), p. 176.
60. See "Asylum in Hungary for East Germans," *New York Times*, August 6, 1989.
61. Gorbachev was quoted as telling Honecker that "if we are late [with reform], we will be punished." See *Economist*, October 14, 1989, p. 53.

Committee on October 18, 1989, and replaced by Egon Krenz, who on November 9 took the dramatic step of opening the Berlin Wall and allowing East Germans to cross freely into West Berlin and West Germany.[62] Yet Krenz, former party secretary for internal security, lacked credibility from the start and was widely seen as only an interim solution.[63] In December he was replaced by the mayor of Dresden, Hans Modrow, an SED reformer. Modrow faced the enormous problem of stemming the continuing flow of skilled East German workers to the West and managing a chaotic political situation characterized by massive public resentment against the SED and the rise of numerous opposition political parties.

The uncertainty facing East Germany in its attempt to shed forty years of centralized political and economic control and to implement multiparty elections was mirrored by events elsewhere in the East bloc in early 1990. In the Soviet Union, Gorbachev faced secessionist movements in the Baltic republics and ethnic warfare in Armenia and Azerbaijan.[64] Faltering economies threatened the political reform movements in Poland, Czechoslovakia, and Hungary. The GDR's situation was also complicated by events in West Germany, as right-wing nationalists called openly for a reunited Germany and a return to the pre-1937 borders and many West Germans became openly anxious about the ability of the FRG to absorb hundreds of thousands of East Germans and ethnic Germans from other East European countries.[65]

Summary

If there were any constants throughout the tumultuous changes taking place in Europe in 1989, they were these. First, the United States, the Soviet Union, Britain, and France were determined that

62. For a comprehensive collection of reporting on the events leading to the opening of the Berlin Wall, see "DDR Journal zur November Revolution: Vom Ausreisen bis zum Einreissen der Mauer" (Frankfurt: Tageszeitungsverlangsgesellschaft, 1989).

63. To his credit, Krenz reportedly flew to Leipzig in October to block an order from Erich Honecker to East German police to fire on demonstrators, saying that "a Chinese solution could not be tolerated." See *New York Times*, January 23, 1990, p. A10.

64. See "Azerbaijan Vows to Secede if Soviet Troops Stay," *New York Times*, January 23, 1990, p. A1.

65. Hartmut Koschyk, the general secretary of the West German Federation of Expellees, predicted that attempts to block German reunification could unleash a nationalist backlash in both German states; see *Financial Times*, January 10, 1990.

moves toward German reunification would take place within an integrated security framework, be it the EC, the CSCE, or some other entity. The palpable nervousness of Germany's neighbors at the prospect that German unity would take on a life of its own initiated a diplomatic chain reaction aimed at "managing" the future course of inter-German relations.[66] Whether such efforts will succeed in constraining the independence of the FRG and GDR in this regard was very much an open question.

And second, in the midst of these political upheavals in the East, there was the continued existence on German soil of hundreds of thousands of U.S. and Soviet troops and thousands of nuclear weapons. In contrast to the abnormal but stable situation of the previous four decades, Europe once again faced the possibility, however remote, that domestic unrest could spark an international conflict.

Whatever the course of political reform in the Soviet Union and Eastern Europe, no country would benefit from the development of political chaos into armed conflict in Central Europe. Thus, despite the vastly changed political environment, the validity of Stanley Hoffmann's assertion still holds: The existence of nuclear weapons has meant that an "internalized imperative of survival" (of the nation-state) must now be balanced with those external threats that heretofore have constrained the nation-state, yet rarely threatened its very existence.[67]

During the 1980s an increase in this "internalized imperative of survival," coupled with groping attempts to find a new German identity, increased the symbolic importance of the German nation as a binding element between the FRG and GDR. In the 1990s the FRG and GDR may well have an opportunity to realize the concept of a German nation by establishing a new German state. The manner in which they do so will have much to say about the outcome of the German nuclear dilemma.

66. Soon after the Berlin Wall was opened on November 9, 1989, representatives of the United States, the Soviet Union, France, and Britain convened a four-power meeting in Berlin for the first time in almost two decades.

67. Stanley Hoffmann, "Terror in Theory and Practice," in his *State of War: Essays on the Theory and Practice of International Politics* (New York: Praeger, 1965), p. 252.

[7]

The German Nuclear Dilemma
in the 1990s

In an April 1987 article in the *New York Times*, Helmut Schmidt wrote: "It is unrealistic to believe that West German soldiers would fight after the explosion of the first couple of nuclear weapons on West German soil; the West Germans would certainly not act any more fanatically or suicidally than the Japanese did after Hiroshima and Nagasaki."[1]

This is a powerful indictment of West German reliance on nuclear deterrence, coming as it does from someone of Schmidt's stature, a former chancellor and defense minister who is arguably the Federal Republic's foremost expert on the political and military dimensions of nuclear weapons. And it goes to the heart of the current debate within the Western alliance (especially in West Germany) as to whether the credibility of nuclear deterrence has been fatally eroded by doubts over the military utility of ever using nuclear weapons in combat.

To the extent that Schmidt is skeptical of actually using nuclear weapons for military defense, his sentiments are no different from those he has articulated over the span of a forty-year involvement with West German security policy. Even in the early 1960s, Schmidt disparaged a NATO policy that called for early first use of tactical nuclear weapons to defend West German territory, noting that "those who think that Europe can be defended by the massed use of such weapons will not defend Europe, but only destroy it."[2]

---

1. *New York Times*, April 29, 1987.
2. Helmut Schmidt, *Defense or Retaliation: A German View* (New York: Praeger, 1962), pp. 100–101.

Schmidt has long been a forceful advocate of the deterrent value of nuclear weapons, however, both in the military sense of preventing an East–West conflict and in the political sense of reducing Soviet leverage and coercion vis-à-vis Western Europe. Indeed, deterrence in both its military and its political dimensions is at the core of Schmidt's belief in the need for a stable balance (Gleichgewicht) between East and West, a belief first articulated in the 1950s and prominently put forth as the rationale for NATO's INF decision in 1979.

This inherent tension of nuclear deterrence, that to be credible it must rest on the threat to actually use nuclear weapons for defense, has been a source of continued debate during the postwar period and represents the core of the German nuclear dilemma. Schmidt's 1987 remarks, however, go beyond his earlier statements in calling into question any military utility whatsoever in the use of nuclear weapons. If the West German Bundeswehr is likely to disintegrate after only a few nuclear weapons have been used, the strongest component of NATO's conventional deterrent vanishes, and with it the possibility of an effective conventional defense of Western Europe. Logically, if Schmidt is correct, the NATO threat to use nuclear weapons is an empty one and calls into question the twin alliance goals of deterrence and defense.

It is true, of course, that logic and rationality have never been strong points of nuclear deterrence theory (Richard Nixon remarked that not knowing whether an adversary might be crazy enough to use nuclear weapons is what gives deterrence its ultimate credibility). For a country such as West German, however, irrationality and incalculability cut both ways. No other country is at such grave risk from the possible use of nuclear weapons in an East–West conflict, yet no major power is so highly dependent on the actions and decisions of others. Since 1949, this has been the crux of the German nuclear dilemma. Although this dilemma has been managed successfully for forty years, events in recent years have conspired to cast doubt on whether the Germans will be content to play the deterrence game by the old rules.

THE SYMBOLISM OF 1989

Indeed, one could question whether the old rules even apply. By early 1990, Poland, Hungary, and Czechoslovakia had won Gorbachev's acceptance of the complete withdrawal of Soviet troops within two years at most, calling into question the very existence of the Warsaw Pact. Nor was NATO immune to such changes, as some member governments voiced the possibility of withdrawing their forces from West Germany.

In other respects as well, 1989 was a year rich in symbolism, containing as it did several highly significant anniversaries for West Germany, the Western alliance, and the nuclear age. That year marked the fiftieth anniversary of the discovery of atomic fission and the outbreak of World War II; the fortieth anniversary of the creation of the two German states, as well as of the first Soviet atomic detonation; the thirtieth anniversary of Bad Godesberg and the acceptance by West Germany's Social Democrats of the basic tenets of the Western alliance; the twentieth anniversary of Willy Brandt's initiation of Ostpolitik; and the tenth anniversary of the NATO INF decision.

Each of these events was a significant way station in the postwar evolution of the German nuclear dilemma, representing as it did one of the three policy dimensions (foreign, domestic, and nuclear) in which German security options have been framed. Moreover, as we've seen, these three policy areas had undergone major changes even before the outbreak of the East European revolutions in 1989. In foreign policy, for example, West Germany had to manage challenges to its Ostpolitik (perestroika) and equally demanding challenges to its West European interests (the 1992 internal market program of the European Community) and its Atlantic interests (burden-sharing and trade issues with the United States). Domestically, the fragmentation of party politics and an increased commitment to safeguarding German national interests had widened the parameters of the West German security debate. Finally, in nuclear policy, both the public and policymakers were engaged in a fundamental reevaluation of the military and political roles of nuclear weapons.

It remains to be seen in what ways the emergence of the German reunification issue will fundamentally alter the terms of the German nuclear dilemma. Much will depend on the fate of Gorbachev's attempts to restructure Soviet society in the face of centrifugal ethnic and nationalist challenges and the success or failure of the East European reform movements. These factors in turn will influence heavily the pace of German unity, and concomitantly, the nature of West Germany's relationship with Western Europe and the United States. Despite all this uncertainty, we can safely say that NATO nuclear policy and the German nuclear dilemma will not be accorded the benign neglect it received during much of the 1960s and 1970s.

If the specifics of West German policy regarding the German nuclear dilemma remain necessarily speculative, the dynamics of change shaping that debate are all too clear. At the heart of this dynamic is the relationship between issues of external security and domestic legitimacy, and it is this synergism that is essential to an understanding of the range of policy alternatives for managing the nuclear dilemma which may be available to German policymakers in the 1990s.

THE FOREIGN POLICY DIMENSION

The events of 1989 signaled the end of the postwar "abnormality," as Raymond Aron called it, of the division of Europe, and a return to European security policies based more on national interest.[3] The dismantling of the dividing line between East and West seemed certain to give greater scope for the articulation of German national interests, though constraints will still exist as the FRG seeks to sort out its priorities regarding its Atlantic, West European, and Eastern spheres of influence.

The fundamental issue here is the extent to which the pace and prospects of German unity affect the FRG's relations with the United States, the Soviets, and its European neighbors, as well as its membership in NATO and the European Community. On the assumption that strict Stalinist control will not again be imposed on Eastern Europe, West German foreign policy cannot help giving priority to German unity at some expense to its traditional postwar Atlantic and West European interests.

In regard to the Atlantic sphere, a wide range of political, military, and economic issues in U.S.–German relations were immediately influenced by the opening of the Berlin Wall and strengthening ties between the two Germanies. Politically, Washington and Bonn evinced different agendas regarding the prospects of German reunification. Whereas the Bush administration was supportive in general though cautious as to timing, the Kohl government was not hesitant about

3. In 1957 Aron noted that he preferred the "abnormal" division of Europe, which was at least clear-cut, to a more "equivocal" situation in which a reunited Germany could once again cause instability in Central Europe. Aron added that he found himself "for once, by accident and with deep regret, on the side of the statesmen."

setting out a concrete agenda for bringing the two Germanies together, as the chancellor did in his ten-point plan to the Bundestag on November 28, 1989.[4] As epitomized by the convening of the first four-power meeting in Berlin in twenty years, the United States found itself sharing doubts with France, Britain, and the Soviet Union about the prospect of unilateral German reunification efforts.

Indeed, some Americans openly raised the specter of the Third Reich in voicing their fears about the implications of German reunification. Writing in the *Wall Street Journal*, the historian Arthur Schlesinger cautioned that "by the turn of the century, a unified Germany, the most powerful and dynamic state in Europe, may be demanding Lebensraum—a revision of its eastern borders, a new Anschluss with Austria, a new outreach to German-speaking minorities in neighboring countries."[5]

While not as explicit as Schlesinger in spelling out the dangers of a reunified Germany, Western policymakers nonetheless made plain their preference for an evolutionary reunification process in which a reunified Germany was inextricably set in an integrated European framework. As outlined by Stanley Hoffmann, such a process would entail the creation of confederal structures in the two Germanies, a strengthening of the institutional authority of the European Community, formal acceptance by the FRG and GDR of the German-Polish border, and a continuation of East–West arms control limitations which could ultimately lead to a pan-European security system.[6]

Over the near term, there was little doubt that military and economic issues in U.S.–FRG relations were being greatly affected by the reappearance of the German Question. Even before 1989, tensions had reappeared in economic policy between Washington and Bonn, as U.S. budget deficits and domestic debate over American military strategy were raising serious questions about the role of U.S. forces in Europe.[7] In the 1990s, the possible dissolution of the

4. For excerpts from the text of Kohl's ten-point plan, see "Speech by Chancellor Helmut Kohl in the German Parliamentary Debate: Policy Towards Germany, November 28, 1989," in *Survival* 32 (January/February 1990): 86–87.

5. Arthur M. Schlesinger, Jr., "Germany's Fate Will Determine Europe's," *Wall Street Journal*, December 21, 1989.

6. Stanley Hoffmann, "A Plan for the New Europe," *New York Review of Books*, January 18, 1990.

7. For more on the burden-sharing issue, see U.S. Congress, House, Armed Services Committee, *Report of the Panel on Burden-Sharing* (Washington, D.C.: Government Printing Office, 1988); and James B. Steinberg, "Rethinking the Debate on Burden-Sharing," *Survival* 29 (January/February 1987).

Warsaw Pact, or even a greatly reduced Soviet military presence in Eastern Europe, could well call into question NATO's very raison d'être. Yet given that NATO was originally created to contain German as well as Soviet power, strong pressure will be felt in the United States and elsewhere (not least in the Soviet Union) for maintaining the integration of West German armed forces in a multinational framework, be it NATO or some modern variant of the European Defense Community.

Many analysts were predicting that the opening of Germany's traditional "hinterland" in Eastern Europe would propel the FRG to becoming the dominant economic power of the 1990s. At the same time, there was a sobering realization that tremendous financial investment, perhaps on the order of DM500 billion over a ten-to-fifteen-year period, would be necessary to restore "East Germany's ramshackle infrastructure . . . and catastrophic state of the environment."[8] What was certain, however, was that a faltering U.S. economy, the prospect of the European Community's internal market program, and a West German economy well positioned to exploit new commercial markets in Eastern Europe could combine to introduce new tensions in U.S.–FRG relations.

Given that security is coming to be defined as much in economic as in military terms, the EC 1992 issue is perhaps most symptomatic of the trade-offs that West Germany will face in its three foreign policy spheres in the 1990s. Before 1989, the FRG was one of the strongest supporters of the EC plan to create a unified market with a total population of 323 million people and a total GDP of $4.6 trillion.[9] The emergence of German reunification as a short-term possibility, however, threw into sharper relief West German hesitations about the possible loss of national independence to the EC bureaucracy in Brussels. It also exacerbated existing tensions between the FRG and its two major EC partners, France and Britain, on the preferred political outcome of the EC 1992 program.

The French government of François Mitterrand, for instance, viewed EC 1992 as constructing a tightly integrated Western Europe that could both promote economic growth and contain West German political power. The British government of Margaret Thatcher, by contrast, continued to prefer the concept of a "common Atlantic

8. "Putting the Jigsaw Back Together," *Financial Times*, January 12, 1990, p. 10.
9. For more on the EC 1992 program, see Michael Calingaert, *The 1992 Challenge from Europe* (Washington, D.C.: National Planning Association, 1988).

house," where Britain could enjoy the benefits of both EC member-ship and its special relationship with the United States.[10]

With German unity seemingly a short-term option, tensions can only increase between both of these visions and the prospect of a reunited Germany of 80 million people in the center of Europe. As many West Germans had noted before the events of 1989, the obligations inherent in the FRG's role in NATO and the European Community could not be easily reconciled with the dynamics of German reunification.[11]

In essence, then, the EC 1992 program is a concrete example of the trade-offs facing the Federal Republic in its Atlantic, West European, and Eastern spheres. EC developments will not be occurring in a vacuum, of course, but will be directly relevant to changes within NATO and Eastern Europe. And the way FRG policymakers respond to these challenges will both reflect and be influenced by developments in West German domestic politics.

GERMAN DOMESTIC POLITICS

The domestic bases of West German security policy, already com-plicated in the 1980s by the fragmentation of German party politics, were roiled further by the events of 1989. For the time being, a majority of West Germans continue to support the United States and NATO as the main guarantors of German security. Yet the mounting influence of Deutschlandpolitik on West Germany, especially with elections scheduled in both the FRG and GDR in 1990, introduced a qualitatively new element into the equation.

Indeed, the dismantling of the Berlin Wall had the effect of exacerbating precisely those issues, such as the economy, foreign émigrés, unemployment, and housing, that had already led to a

10. See the article by Christoph Bertram in *Die Zeit*, August 12, 1988.

11. In 1988, for example, Egon Bahr of the SPD criticized the "hypocrisy" of those in the CDU/CSU who advocated German reunification while ignoring the implications for West German sovereignty of the EC 1992 program; see *Die Zeit*, August 12, 1988. Yet in 1990, the Republikan Party was seeking to contest elections in both the GDR and the FRG on a platform that gave precedence to German unity over European unity and called for a return to Germany's pre–1937 borders. As Franz Schönhuber remarked, "We are the genuine advocates of reunification—the others are only cheap imitations": quoted in *Die Zeit*, January 26, 1990, p. 2. For a good analysis of the trade-offs between EC integration and German reunification, see Marion Gräfin Dönhoff, "Von der Geschichte längst überholt: Wiedervereinigung oder europäische Union—keine Alternative mehr," *Die Zeit*, January 27, 1989.

fragmentation of FRG party politics. In early 1989, for example, the Christian Democrats suffered major defeats in Land elections held in West Berlin and Frankfurt. In both cases, ruling CDU governments were voted out of office and replaced by SPD-Green coalitions. In scenarios with ominous implications for the 1990 national election, the SPD and Greens were able to form a government only because of the stunning success of right-wing nationalist parties and the failure of the FDP to win the required 5 percent of the vote necessary for parliamentary representation.

In the January 1989 election in Berlin, for instance, the CDU government of Mayor Eberhard Diepgen lost support to the ultrana-tionalist Republikan Party, which won seats in both the Berlin parliament and the Bundestag for the first time, with 7.5 percent of the vote. Many analysts thought this slippage in support for the CDU was due mainly to local conditions in Berlin, in particular a conservative backlash over the social problems caused by the large number of émigrés and foreign workers in the city.[12] Yet the protest vote that put the Republikans into office represented yet another indication of the growing electoral salience of German national interests—in this case, voters' resentment at the competition for jobs and housing posed by "ethnic German" refugees (many of whom speak little or no German) arriving from Poland and the Soviet Union.[13]

Yet the election in Frankfurt in March 1989 demonstrated the pervasiveness of the refugee issue in particular and voter dissatisfaction with the CDU in general. Support for the local CDU plummeted from 49 percent in 1985 to 36 percent, in large part because of the emergence of yet another right-wing party, the National Democratic Party (NDP), which won 6.6 percent of the vote. The Free Democrats again failed to win 5 percent of the vote, and the SPD and the Greens were able to form a "Red-Green" coalition with 40 percent and 10 percent of the vote, respectively.[14] In the weeks following, opinion polls revealed the obvious when 64 percent of respondents nationwide (and 70 percent of CDU supporters) voiced their displeasure with Helmut Kohl's leadership.[15]

12. The CDU's share of the vote fell to 38 percent (from 46 percent in the 1985 election); see *Economist*, February 4, 1989, p. 44.

13. The strength of the Republikans' showing in Berlin took almost everyone by surprise, including the noted weekly *Die Zeit*, which on February 3, 1989, a few days before the elections, asserted that "the Union [CDU] and the Free Democrats are counting on the continuation of their coalition."

14. *Kieler Nachrichten*, March 13, 1989.

15. See "Polls Say Kohl Is in Political Trouble," *New York Times*, March 30, 1989.

It was true that by early 1990 Kohl and the CDU/CSU had ridden the crest of West German euphoria over events in East Germany and reestablished their position as favorites to win the December 1990 election.[16] Yet growing West German resentment over the flood of East German refugees into the FRG and the possibility of serious setbacks to the East European reform movements could easily undermine Kohl's position. Moreover, Kohl was facing a formidable SPD opponent in Oskar Lafontaine, who became the SPD candidate for chancellor after easily winning reelection in January 1990 as premier of the Saarland. A witty and adroit campaigner, Lafontaine appealed to moderate German voters and blunted the appeal of the right-wing Republikan Party by calling for measures to stem the flow of East Germans into the FRG.[17]

Thus Kohl faced challenges from both a reinvigorated SPD on his left and the emerging right-wing Republikans. The latter threat could be especially strong in cities with large émigré populations, such as Berlin and Frankfurt, as well as in Bavaria now that Franz Josef Strauss has passed from the scene. For four decades Strauss attracted right-wing voters to the Bavarian-based CSU, and it is quite possible that without him the CSU (and thus the CDU/CSU coalition) may well lose voters to the Republikan Party and its dynamic leader, Franz Schönhuber, a television personality and former member of the SS.

Along with the "Strauss factor," analysts such as Joachim Fest have suggested that the growth of the nationalist far right in West Germany is a predictable reaction to the rise of the leftist Greens in the early 1980s—on the theory that one political extreme begets another. And Fest and others have noted that the weakening of the external threat to the FRG in the Gorbachev era has made domestic political extremism more palatable to German voters.[18]

A second consequence of this weakening of the threat from the

16. In a January 1990 poll, 41 percent of West German voters preferred the CDU/CSU, while 39 percent supported the SPD. The FDP and Greens each garnered 7 percent, while the Republikan Party was the first choice of 4 percent of the voters. See *New York Times*, January 29, 1990, p. A10.

17. Lafontaine advocated terminating the subsidy benefits that East Germans received upon arriving in the FRG and called on East Germans to stay home and build "democratic socialism" in the GDR. For more on SPD policy toward the GDR, see "Deutsche Träume, deutsche Sorgen," *Die Zeit*, December 29, 1989, p. 9.

18. The historian Arnulf Baring drew similar conclusions, believing that many West Germans were overestimating their capability to replace "their western orientation with an eastern one without risk and without danger to harming the American base on which the federal republic to this day stands." See *Economist*, March 4, 1989, pp. 43–44.

East is the growing tension in public opinion between continued support for the FRG's Western ties on the one hand and dwindling support for the Western nuclear deterrent on the other. Polling data in 1988 showed only 9 percent of the public supporting the NATO Flexible Response doctrine (defined as conventional forward defense with the possible first use of NATO nuclear weapons), while 79 percent favored the removal of all nuclear weapons from West Germany.[19]

This tension is likely to dominate the domestic debate on security issues, no matter which party is in power. As Volker Rühe, a leading CDU/CSU expert on security, has noted, "It is no longer possible to ignore the political fact that deterrence is being criticized in the FRG not only by the Left but by the Right and by people who have traditionally been in favor of the strategy of nuclear deterrence, and because of the structures [i.e., short-range nuclear weapons] that will be left in place by the INF Treaty."[20]

Over and above the growing public disquiet with nuclear deterrence, other factors, such as economic and demographic constraints on West Germany's armed forces, will sharpen the German domestic debate on security. An especially prominent issue involves the FRG's falling birth rate and its effect on the active-duty strength of the Bundeswehr. It is estimated that in the absence of corrective measures, such as an extension of military service for conscripts, all three services, but especially the army, will suffer serious declines in numbers of active-duty troops and noncommissioned officers in the 1990s.[21]

By 1988, the prospect of troop shortfalls had already led to a restructuring of West German combat forces and a greater reliance on reservists to man front-line divisions.[22] Then, in the spring of

19. Cited in Gwyn Prins, "Theatre Nuclear Issues," paper presented at an American Academy of Arts and Sciences conference on conventional forces in Europe, held December 17–18, 1988, in Cambridge, England, p. 2, and *Frankfurter Allgemeine Zeitung*, July 22, 1988.

20. *Süddeutsche Zeitung*, January 21, 1988; cited in Ronald D. Asmus, "West Germany Faces Nuclear Modernization," *Survival* 30 (November/December 1988): 513.

21. The number of young West Germans applying for conscientious objector status in the late 1980s was more than 70,000 annually, or 20 percent of the available manpower pool. When this figure is considered in combination with the decreasing numbers of eligible draftees, the number of active-duty troops in the West German army is expected to fall from 341,000 in 1989 to 324,000 by 1994. See *Economist*, January 14, 1989, pp. 46–48.

22. According to the FRG's "Bundeswehr 2000" plan, reserve battalions will make up a greater proportion of the Bundeswehr's thirty-six active-duty brigades, thus

1989, the issue of extending the length of conscription came to a head when the Kohl government did an abrupt about-face and canceled plans to extend military service from fifteen to eighteen months.[23]

The West German debate over conscription in 1989 was symptomatic of the growing influence of domestic political concerns in the making of FRG security policy. The Kohl government had continually reassured its NATO partners that it would implement the eighteen-month conscription policy, originally proposed in October 1984, to compensate in part for shortfalls in Bundeswehr active-duty strength. As late as February 1989 the chancellor asserted in an interview with the *Financial Times*: "I have said that the 18-month service time will not be changed. We have promised to NATO to put up a certain number of soldiers, and this will be adhered to. Our friends and partners can rely on us."[24]

Within two months, however, Kohl succumbed to pressure from both Genscher and the SPD opposition and canceled the extension of conscription. At the time, the Kohl government was under considerable pressure on several fronts (the Lance nuclear modernization debate, government tax policy, internal disarray in the CDU/CSU/FDP cabinet), and the chancellor had been further weakened by the election setbacks in West Berlin and Frankfurt. Nonetheless, in a scene reminiscent of President Carter's handling of the neutron bomb issue, Kohl was highly embarrassed, and his NATO allies were more than a little irritated, by this policy reversal.

As for defense budgets, the Bonn government and the Bundeswehr will be faced with difficult choices when it comes to funding weapons modernization, infrastructure improvements, ammunition stocks and spares, and the like.[25] Given a similar debate in the United States over military spending and increased public interest in a possible "peace dividend" from cutbacks in defense budgets, the potential exists for a sharpening of the U.S.–FRG burden-sharing debate.

---

decreasing active-duty manning levels from the current 90 percent to between 50 and 70 percent; see Wolfgang Flume, "Forward Defence with Fewer Standing Forces," *Military Technology*, April 1988, pp. 34–40.

23. For more on the Kohl decision and French anxieties about West German security policy, see *Economist*, April 22, 1989, pp. 46–47.

24. Quoted in "CDU Conscription Decision Could Prompt Change in West German Defence Policy," *Financial Times*, April 24, 1989.

25. See Christoph Bertram, "Arme Bundeswehr," *Die Zeit*, January 27, 1989.

By itself, this coming together of shifts in public and official attitudes regarding nuclear weapons with social and budgetary pressures on West German defense budgets and the Bundeswehr would present major policy problems. When these considerations are combined with the momentous implications of German reunification and the formation of new European security arrangements, the security choices facing the FRG will be thrown into even sharper relief.

From being one of the most visible and controversial East–West issues throughout the 1980s, the nuclear weapons debate was quickly overshadowed in 1989 by events in Eastern Europe and the Soviet Union. As we noted earlier, however, the existence of thousands of U.S. and Soviet nuclear weapons in the two Germanies, in addition to more than a half-million American and Soviet troops, is certain to complicate whatever efforts emerge to refashion the European security system.

Certainly one major influence on the German nuclear dilemma will be the extent to which the United States and the Soviet Union follow up the INF Treaty with major agreements on strategic nuclear forces and European theater nuclear weapons. The prospects of substantial reductions in U.S. and Soviet forces under a START agreement have major implications not only for the U.S. nuclear guarantee but for French and British nuclear forces and West Germany's relationship with all three nuclear powers.

As in the EC 1992 issue, the FRG's Atlantic, West European, and Eastern interests converge in the arena of U.S.–Soviet arms control. The shock waves generated by the 1986 Reykjavik summit, with its prospect of the dismantling of the U.S. nuclear umbrella, still reverberate in the West German domestic debate. In practical policy terms, however, the FRG continues to have only limited influence on superpower arms control efforts. The more important arena is that of NATO nuclear policy, especially as the 1987 INF Treaty focused increased attention on those short-range weapons that most threaten the two Germanies.

From 1987 to 1989, the most pressing NATO issue involved the modernization and replacement of the short-range Lance missile.

NATO's 1983 Montebello decision, which coupled the withdrawal of 1,400 nuclear warheads with plans for modernizing remaining NATO nuclear forces, led to plans to replace the Lance by the mid-1990s. In the wake of both the INF Treaty and Gorbachev's announcement in December 1988 of unilateral reductions of Soviet conventional and nuclear forces in Eastern Europe,[26] however, West German opposition to a Lance replacement had grown considerably by 1989. Accordingly, Chancellor Kohl preferred to delay a Lance decision, preferably until after the 1990 election, while Genscher stressed the need for exploring arms control options on short-range systems, noting that "there is an urgent need for a Western negotiating position on short-range missiles . . . [which] are, in any case, of least importance for deterrence."[27]

This West German preference for delaying a Lance decision was stridently opposed by others in NATO, especially by Prime Minister Margaret Thatcher. Tensions between London and Bonn deepened considerably as Thatcher twice traveled to West Germany in an attempt to persuade Kohl to support a Lance modernization decision at the NATO heads-of-government meeting on May 29–30 in Brussels. Newly elected president George Bush used more quiet methods of persuasion to prevent an open rift in the alliance, but to no avail. Prospects for the NATO summit seemed bleak indeed, given the stalemate over Lance modernization, Kohl's refusal to extend military conscription, and mounting public criticism of NATO for

26. In a speech at the United Nations on December 7, 1988, Gorbachev startled the West by announcing that the Soviet Union would unilaterally withdraw six tank divisions, 50,000 troops, and 5,000 tanks from Eastern Europe as part of a larger reduction of Soviet armed forces amounting to 500,000 men. What made the offer especially significant was Gorbachev's promise to withdraw assault landing troops and assault river-crossing units, moves that would reduce Soviet capabilities for mounting short-warning attacks against NATO. For the text of Gorbachev's speech, see "Mikhail Gorbachev—United Nations Address" (released by Novosti Press Agency in London, December 8, 1988), pp. 19–22 especially. By late 1989, reports indicated that the Soviet withdrawals were being implemented on schedule, although one congressional report noted that remaining Soviet divisions in Eastern Europe were receiving additional quantities of artillery and antitank weapons; see U.S. Congress, House, Committee on Armed Services, *Status of the Soviet Union's Unilateral Force Reductions and Restructuring of Its Forces* Committee on Armed (Washington, D.C. October 16, 1989).

27. Quoted in *Nordwest Zeitung*, November 7, 1988; cited in *German Tribune*, December 4, 1988, pp. 4–5. Chancellor Kohl stressed his preference for a delay during a meeting in Bonn with Secretary of State James Baker in February 1989; see *New York Times*, February 14, 1989, p. A8.

failing to respond substantively to Gorbachev's initiatives in reducing Warsaw Pact forces.[28]

To the surprise of many observers, President Bush pulled a rabbit out of his hat at the NATO summit by adroitly combining a new U.S. initiative for the Vienna talks on CFE (conventional forces in Europe) with a compromise on the Lance issue.[29] The latter consisted of NATO's agreement to propose negotiations on short-range missiles in Europe, with the caveat that such talks would not begin until after an agreement on conventional forces had been signed.

Despite this last-minute compromise, the Lance controversy demonstrated widespread German opposition to what was seen as NATO's overreliance on nuclear weapons that could be used only on German (East and West) territory. This was especially the case in regard to the more than 1,500 nuclear artillery shells in the NATO arsenal. From the SPD on the left to the CSU on the right, West Germans increasingly supported a great reduction in this nuclear artillery capability, if not its elimination.

The parties differed in their support for increased deployments of new longer-range systems (air- and sea-launched cruise missiles and air-delivered SRAMs—short-range attack missiles) that could bolster deterrence by threatening Warsaw Pact targets deep in Eastern Europe. Such CDU/CSU officials as Defense Minister Rupert Scholz, Alfred Dregger, and Volker Rühe argued that such systems were needed to take up the slack left by the INF Treaty ban on ground-based missiles with ranges greater than 500 kilometers. Dregger said bluntly, "We want to know whether and with which air- and sea-launched systems the United States is prepared to maintain intermediate-range deterrence."[30]

Genscher, by contrast, voiced firm opposition to introducing new nuclear systems that would contravene the spirit of the INF Treaty: "Any attempt to introduce a replacement for medium-range nuclear missiles where they are not banned by treaty arrangements would undermine the first nuclear disarmament agreement in history."[31] The SPD and Greens, not surprisingly, were even more opposed to

28. See Theo Sommer, "Rakaten-wider deutschen Willen?" *Die Zeit*, May 5, 1989, p. 1.

29. As the *Economist* noted (June 3, 1989, p. 47), the effect of President Bush's proposals at the NATO summit "was electric. Mr. Bush was immediately transformed from a do-nothing president into an imaginative statesman."

30. Quoted in Asmus, "West Germany Faces Nuclear Modernization," p. 505.

31. *German Tribune*, December 4, 1988, pp. 4–5.

implementing the modernization portion of the NATO Montebello agreement.

There is little likelihood that the Lance compromise will survive in a context of continuing reform movements in Eastern Europe and strengthening ties between the two Germanies. The same might even be said of NATO's flat rejection of a "third zero," the total elimination of short-range missiles in Europe. NATO might well eventually agree to reduce its nuclear artillery substantially in order to gain its members' agreement to deploy a limited number of long-range theater nuclear systems (U.S. sea- and air-launched strategic cruise missiles and SRAMs) as the next generation of the NATO deterrent.

Much will depend, of course, on the outcome of the December 1990 election in West Germany. Should the SPD come to power in 1990, as part of a grand coalition with the CDU/CSU (in the event that the FDP falls below the 5 percent threshold), in coalition with the Greens (less likely, though still possible), or even in tandem with the FDP, then FRG support for the Lance compromise or new deployments is highly problematic.[32] Yet even the continuation of the CDU/CSU/FDP government does not ensure West Germany's consent to new deployments, especially as the continued presence of U.S. and Soviet nuclear weapons on German territory raises serious questions about the pace and outcome of German reunification.

WHITHER THE GERMAN NUCLEAR DILEMMA?

It is hardly an understatement to say that the German nuclear dilemma was transformed by the events of 1989. The world was stunned by the sight of massive, nonviolent public uprisings sweeping across Eastern Europe. With the exception of the bloody conflict in Romania, the communist parties in Eastern Europe—Poland, Hungary, Czechoslovakia, Bulgaria, and East Germany—were brought

---

32. The possibility that the FDP might attempt to form a coalition government with the SPD following the December 1990 election gained credence in January 1990 when the FDP advocated security policies similar to those of the SPD. For example, the FDP called for reducing the Bundeswehr to 350,000 troops, limiting conscription to one year, and rejecting any modernization of NATO short-range missiles; see "Weniger Wehr," *Die Zeit*, January 26, 1990, p. 1. For more on SPD security policies, see Egon Bahr, Andreas von Bülow, and Karsten Voigt, *European Security 2000: A Comprehensive Concept for European Security from a Social Democratic Point of View* (Bonn: SPD, June 1989).

down by the combined might of workers, students, and intellectuals marching in the streets.

By early 1990, however, the outcomes of East European revolutions were anything but certain. Both Romania and Yugoslavia teetered on the brink of new outbreaks of violence, while the reform movements elsewhere in Eastern Europe struggled in the face of political and economic chaos. In East Germany, the continued flight to the West of almost 3,000 East Germans a day was draining the country of critically needed skilled labor. Most important of all, the survival of Gorbachev, perestroika, and the USSR itself was called into question by ethnic violence in Azerbaijan, Armenia, and Tadzhikistan, moves toward independence in the Baltic republics, a disintegrating Soviet economy, and the declared willingness of the Communist Party to relinquish its "leading role" in Soviet society. Following the initial euphoria over the events of 1989, many Westerners were increasingly skeptical that the Soviet Union could survive perestroika,[33] and were fearful that Eastern Europe would regress to the cauldron of nationalist and ethnic rivalries of the years before World War I.

This uncertainty over the fate of Mitteleuropa and the role to be played by the United States and the Soviet Union as a new European security situation develops has added a new dimension to the German nuclear dilemma. By early 1990, political events were running far ahead of the attempts of diplomats and arms control negotiators to construct a stable framework for managing the transition to a new era. In a period when electricians (Lech Walesa), playwrights (Vaclav Havel), and former SS officers (Franz Schönhuber) had emerged as political leaders, an air of unreality permeated day-to-day events.

Writing in the mid-1970s, Catherine Kelleher noted that before 1966 the phrase "Germans and nuclear weapons . . . provided a central, continually provocative stimulus in all East–West political discourse." By the mid-1970s, however, "the silence prevailing about German

---

33. In January 1990 the journal *Daedalus* published "To the Stalin Mausoleum," by an anonymous author, "Z," which expressed a profound skepticism of Gorbachev's chances of success. The article was excerpted under the title "The Soviets' Terminal Crisis" in the *New York Times* on January 4, 1990, and immediately became something of a media sensation in the United States, in large part because of the anonymity of its author, who turned out to be Professor Martin Malia of the University of California, Berkeley. See *Daedalus*, Winter 1990, and "A Scholarly Mystery: 'Z' Writes Darkly of Communism, but Who Is 'Z'?" *New York Times*, January 12, 1990.

ambitions or technical potential for imminent production of nuclear weapons [was] all but deafening."[34]

From the vantage point of 1990, the possible acquisition of nuclear weapons by Germany, whatever form it ultimately takes, still seems highly implausible. The web of domestic political constraints, Germany's previous acceptance of international legal prohibitions, and most important, the outright angst among Germany's neighbors in regard to an independent German nuclear capability argue against such an outcome.

Yet, in early 1989 the disintegration of the Iron Curtain and a Soviet military retreat from Eastern Europe seemed equally implausible. Thus, despite the uncertainty as to how the security map of Europe will evolve in the 1990s, it is worth exploring three major alternative ways in which the German nuclear dilemma might develop.

Neutralism and the Denuclearization of Germany

One possibility, highly dependent on the pace and form of German reunification, is the creation of a neutral and denuclearized Germany as part of a pan-European security system superseding NATO and the Warsaw Pact. Positive steps in this direction were taken in January 1990 when Gorbachev acknowledged the inevitability of German reunification and East German Prime Minister Hans Modrow dropped the SED's resistance to reunification and proposed that negotiations begin to create a neutral and nonaligned Germany.[35] While major differences remained between the FRG and GDR in regard to the political and military status of a reunified Germany, the prospects for such an outcome were considerably enhanced by the new Soviet position and by President Bush's proposal for accelerated withdrawals of U.S. and Soviet forces in Europe.[36]

It is possible that a neutral reunified Germany could emerge in tandem with a new European security system based on the thirty-five member CSCE framework initiated by the Helsinki process. In

34. Catherine McArdle Kelleher, *Germany and the Politics of Nuclear Weapons* (New York: Columbia University Press, 1975), p. 1.

35. *New York Times*, February 2, 1990, p. A1.

36. As Modrow and Gorbachev were meeting in Moscow, President Bush, in his State of the Union address to Congress, proposed to drop the ceiling for U.S. and Soviet troops in Europe from 275,000 to 225,000; see *New York Times*, February 1, 1990, p. A1.

conjunction with partial or total withdrawals of U.S. and Soviet troops from Europe, the size and disposition of national military forces would be constrained throughout Europe. In all probability, a CSCE framework would also entail the restructuring of military forces with the aim of sharply reducing Europe's offensive capabilities and imposing constraints on the ability of the United States and the Soviet Union to redeploy troops to Europe on short notice.

One key variable in this scenario is the role that would be played by nuclear deterrence in a pan-European security system. Important issues here involve the future nuclear force structures of the Soviet Union and the United States, and particularly of Britain and France. Will the U.S.–Soviet START talks lead to cuts of up to 35 percent in superpower nuclear systems, and will follow-on START negotiations bring added pressure on Britain and France to subject their nuclear forces to multilateral arms reductions efforts?

As we've noted often, the issue of arms control limits on third-country nuclear forces has been continually deferred throughout the postwar period. Yet a European security framework based on CSCE, in which Germany is reunified but substantially demilitarized, will coexist uneasily with the continued presence of two formidable European nuclear powers. It is hard to imagine that an economically strong Germany would continue to accept limits on its military forces, whether conventional or nuclear, which do not apply equally to the other European members of the CSCE system. Yet it is equally difficult to imagine that Britain and especially France would agree to abolish their nuclear forces entirely, even in the event that the United States and the Soviet Union adopt "minimum deterrent" force postures of several hundred or a thousand nuclear systems.

Another major obstacle to a CSCE collective security system is the potential for a return to traditional nationalist rivalries in Eastern Europe. Despite the proposal by Vaclav Havel of Czechoslovakia for a mutual security pact between his country, Poland, and Hungary, it is doubtful that such arrangements would be any more successful in providing long-term stability than such previous efforts as the "Little Entente" between the two world wars.[37] The nationalist and ethnic pressures that will continue to plague Yugoslavia, Romania, and

37. From 1920 to 1939, the "Little Entente" between Czechoslovakia, Romania, and Yugoslavia was somewhat successful in relaxing tensions between its three members, but was powerless in the face of the aggressive designs of Nazi Germany and Stalinist Russia. See Hugh Seton-Watson, *Eastern Europe Between the Wars, 1918–1941* (New York: Harper Torchbooks, 1967), pp. 364–365.

other territories in Eastern Europe make it difficult to imagine a stable Eastern Europe that is flanked on one side by a still militarily strong Soviet Union (or Russia) and on the other by a neutral, demilitarized Germany.

This problem would become especially acute should the Soviet Union ever feel the need to reassert itself militarily in European affairs. One can only conjecture what the Soviet Union will look like in a few years or a decade. But whether the Soviet Union remains essentially intact or a Great Russian Federation develops out of a disintegrated Soviet empire, Russian military power will continue to be the dominant force in the region.

If this type of CSCE-based system is to work, the United States and the Soviet Union will have to continue to play some role, however diminished, in guaranteeing its stability. The issue is how their involvement can be meshed with a reunified Germany on the one hand and the nuclear status of France and Britain on the other. The creation of an integrated European army, such as the European Defense Community proposed in the 1950s, might be sufficient to deter nationalist rivalries from breaking into military conflict. Yet the problems of a security vacuum in Eastern Europe and disparities in nuclear capabilities would still exist as potential sources of instability.

GERMANY AND A EUROPEAN NUCLEAR DETERRENT

Given the inherent uncertainty over the role Soviet military power will play in European affairs over the next decade, an alternative framework could involve a more integrated West European military structure based on a multilateral European nuclear force. Over the years, many variations of a European deterrent have been discussed, usually during periods when Europeans' anxieties over the credibility of the United States' commitment have been at their peak.

In 1957, for example, the shock of *Sputnik* and perceptions of growing Anglo-American nuclear cooperation led France, Italy, and Germany to investigate joint production agreements covering conventional and possibly nuclear weapons. These so-called F-I-G discussions were abandoned when de Gaulle returned to power and accelerated France's independent nuclear program, but Franz Josef Strauss did raise some eyebrows in 1958 when he responded to British criticism of the F-I-G venture by saying: "I can guarantee that for three, four, or even five years there will be no German nuclear weapons. After that, however, if other states, especially France, produce their own atomic bombs, Germany could also be dragged in."[38]

The negotiations in the 1960s over creating a jointly manned multi-lateral nuclear force (MLF) were the next attempt to "Europeanize" a portion of NATO's nuclear deterrent. In the end, however, this option was blocked by the Americans' preference for maintaining centralized control of NATO's nuclear capability, especially in the light of France's acquisition of nuclear weapons. The demise of MLF was followed in 1966 by the McNamara initiative to create a NATO Nuclear Planning Group (NPG), in which West Germany has from the first played a substantive role.

One consequence of this expanded West German role in the NPG over two decades has been a great increase in the FRG's expertise in nuclear planning. In the event that U.S. nuclear forces are withdrawn from Europe, the FRG (or a reunified Germany) may demand equality within a Franco-German-British nuclear force. It is possible that, as NATO diminishes as a military alliance, a new West European security union may develop, based on some combination of the military ties already forged by the European members of NATO within the Independent European Programme Group (IEPG) and the growing foreign policy coordination carried out under the EC's auspices.

In the event that a reunified Germany does not slow the process of EC integration and that a West European security constellation develops, it is possible to imagine a multilateral European nuclear force that would provide a measure of deterrence in conjunction with U.S.–based strategic forces. Yet such a force will evolve only over time. Despite France's flexibility in the 1980s in consulting the FRG on nuclear issues, serious obstacles remain in the way of joint operational control of French nuclear forces. Even greater obstacles exist in the case of Britain, given the long-standing Anglo-American nuclear relationship.[39]

Yet the alternative could well be either a totally demilitarized and denuclearized Germany, leading to a power vacuum in central Europe, or an independent German nuclear force, with equally ominous implications. In either case, France and Britain may well

38. Interview in *Daily Mirror* (London), April 2, 1958; quoted in Kelleher, *Germany and the Politics of Nuclear Weapons*, p. 150.

39. See especially Peter Malone, *The British Nuclear Deterrent* (New York: St. Martin's Press, 1984).

tolerate the surrender of national sovereignty in creating a European nuclear force that could constrain German nuclear capabilities.

Much will depend on how the United States' military commitment to Europe evolves over the coming years, and the political costs that Germany incurs in contemplating an alternative to forty years of relying on the U.S. nuclear guarantee. Certainly the U.S. nuclear deterrent will remain far more substantial and credible than the British and French deterrents, with or without German involvement. By the same token, the potential liability of relying on a strong if not always consistent American guarantee will be overshadowed by the specter of an independent German nuclear program.

AN INDEPENDENT GERMAN DETERRENT

The most extreme option of all, of course, is an independent German nuclear force. Despite the nightmare quality of such a vision, both for Germany's neighbors and for many Germans themselves, Germany's acquisition of nuclear weapons at some point in an uncertain future cannot be ruled out.

It is conceivable that such a force might come into being through bilateral arrangements between the United States and Germany. The United States would provide warheads and delivery systems either directly or through licensed coproduction, in much the way it does now to the United Kingdom. Having hosted the world's third largest nuclear arsenal for more than thirty years, Germany certainly has both the technical and the operational expertise to handle such a role.

The obstacles to such an option are, of course, enormous. In addition to violating German legal obligations under the 1954 London/Paris accords and the Non-Proliferation Treaty, such moves would subject Germany to a storm of political criticism from all directions. No matter what the future holds for the Soviet Union, it is difficult to imagine any Soviet/Russian leader tolerating the prospect of a nuclear Germany. The same can be said of the Poles, Czechs, French, Dutch, and other European victims of past German aggression. Moreover, and perhaps most important, such a move would be extremely counterproductive to German political and economic interests throughout Europe, but especially in an Eastern Europe where Germany hopes to become the dominant economic force.

Accordingly, it is hard to imagine any situation, short of an extreme crisis, in which German policymakers would be interested in openly deploying an independent nuclear force. At a time when the military utility of nuclear deterrence has been called into question, and given the geographical vulnerability of Germany to nuclear attack, Germany's acquisition of a *force de dissuasion* against the nuclear might of the Soviet Union would probably be both strategically irrelevant and politically counterproductive.

Yet what of the possibility that Germany might develop the necessary nuclear infrastructure, à la Israel, to permit rapid deployment of nuclear forces should an extreme crisis develop? The point has been made, more often in the past than at present, that the FRG does have the option of seeking a "threshold capability" that would allow the country to assemble a nuclear force rapidly in a national emergency. With a civilian nuclear program generating enough enriched uranium and plutonium for the manufacture of dozens or hundreds of nuclear warheads, this option is technically viable. In a world of tens of thousands of nuclear weapons, however, the military and political utility of such a capability remains dubious at best. Admittedly, the situation will be different after the United States and the Soviet Union reduce their nuclear weapons to a few hundred. Before that happens, however, the East–West and European security frameworks will have changed so greatly that any German decision to "go nuclear" would have to be evaluated in the light of extant circumstances.

A final point about the prospects for an independent German nuclear force is the current widespread domestic opposition to such an option. Such feelings extend across the West German political spectrum, and among the East German public as well. Circumstances will surely change over the coming years, and Arthur Schlesinger's fears of a German "desire for national vindication" may yet be realized. In the absence of truly cataclysmic changes to the European order, such as the onset of economic depression and the reemergence of an overt Soviet/Russian military threat, it seems unlikely that such desires will express themselves in the acquisition of nuclear weapons. What is more probable is that a German nationalism that has been truncated for forty-five years will express itself politically, culturally, and above all economically, rather than militarily.

SUMMARY

Ultimately, the evolution of the German nuclear dilemma in the 1990s will depend on the interaction between major shifts in Germany's three primary foreign policy spheres and changes in domestic attitudes regarding nuclear weapons. In the postwar period, as we know, the FRG sought to ensure its military and economic security through its Atlantic (NATO) and West European (EC) relationships while retaining a fair measure of independence in its Eastern policies (Ostpolitik). Before 1989, West Germany's dependence on the U.S. and NATO nuclear guarantees, despite the sometimes stormy complications it produced for the country's Ostpolitik, was a necessary element of FRG policy.

On the threshold of the 1990s, however, major changes loomed in all three of the FRG's foreign policy spheres. The European security system that was enshrined at Yalta in 1945 had all but crumbled, promising a major reorientation of the NATO alliance. Similarly, the EC 1992 program was recasting the FRG's economic and political relationships with its West European allies. Most important of all, the emergence of German reunification as a top East–West issue was changing the way Bonn policymakers formulated not only their Eastern policy but their Atlantic and West European policies as well.

Adding to the uncertainty over the evolution of the German nuclear dilemma were the fundamental changes taking place in West Germany's domestic politics and the growing political links across its eastern border. It remains to be seen how a new identity for the German nation will be fashioned in the center of Europe.[40] Much will depend on how the security interests of the Germans are reconciled with those of their European neighbors, the United States, and the Soviet Union.[41] What is not in doubt, however, is that new initiatives will be needed to resolve the tensions inherent in the German nuclear dilemma as Europe seeks to transcend the "abnormality" of East–West divisions and create a durable security framework for the twenty-first century.

40. For an insightful analysis of German aspirations, past and present, in Eastern Europe, see Timothy Garten Ash, "Mitteleuropa?" *Daedalus*, Winter 1990.

41. See Egon Bahr, *Zum europäischen Frieden: Eine Antwort auf Gorbatschow* (Berlin: Siedler, 1988).

Select Bibliography

WEST GERMAN GOVERNMENT PUBLICATIONS

Abrüstung und Rüstungskontrolle: Dokumente zur Haltung der Bundesrepublik Deutschland. Bonn: Auswärtiges Amt, 1981.

Aspekte der Friedenspolitik: Argumente zum Doppelbeschluss des Nordatlantischen Bundnisses. Bonn: Presse- und Informationsamt der Bundesregierung, 1981.

Deutscher Bundestag: Stenographischer Berichte. Bonn: Deutscher Bundestag.

Government Bulletin. Bonn: Presse- und Informationsamt der Bundesregierung.

Die nuklearen Mittelstreckenwaffen: Modernisierung und Rüstungskontrolle. Bonn: Federal Minister of Defense, 1980.

The Role of the Federal Republic of Germany in NATO. Bonn: Federal Minister of Defense, 1982.

White Paper: The Security of the Federal Republic of Germany and the Development of the Armed Forces. Bonn: Federal Minister of Defense, 1976, 1979, 1983, 1985.

Woche im Bundestag: Parlaments-Korrespondenz. Bonn: Presse- und Informationszentrum des Deutschen Bundestages.

WEST GERMAN POLITICAL PARTY DOCUMENTS

Social Democratic Party

"Dokumente: Beschlüsse zur Aussen-, Deutschland-, Friedens- und Sicherheitspolitik. In *SPD Parteitag Berlin, 1979.* Bonn: Vorstand der SPD, 1979.

"Dokumente: Friedenbeschlüsse zur Aussen-, Friedens-, und Sicherheitspolitik." In *SPD Parteitag Hamburg, 1977.* Bonn: Vorstand der SPD, 1977.

Für Sicherheit und Frieden: Sicherheitspolitische Informationstagung der SPD-Bundestagsfraktion, Bremen, May 19–20, 1979. Bonn: SPD-Bundestagsfraktion, 1979.

Grundsatz Programm: Beschlossen vom Ausserordentlichen Parteitag der SPD, Bad Godesberg, November 13–15, 1959. Bonn: Vorstand der SPD, 1959.
"Materialen: Sicherheitspolitik im Rahmen der Friedenspolitik." In *Leitantrag des Parteivorstands für den Parteitag in Berlin*. Bonn: Vorstand der SPD, 1979.
Sicherheit für Deutschland: Wahlprogramm 1980. Bonn: Vorstand der SPD, 1980.
"Unkorrigiertes Protokoll 9–10." In *SPD Wahlparteitag, Essen 1980*. Bonn: Vorstand der SPD, 1980.

Christian Democratic Union/Christian Social Union
"Aussenpolitische Fachtagung, March 4–5, 1980." In *Frieden in Freiheit sichern*. Bonn: CDU, 1980.
"CDU Bundesparteitag, Ludwigshafen, Okt. 23–25, 1978." In *Grundsatzprogramm der Christliche Demokratische Union Deutschlands*. Bonn: CDU-Bundesgeschaftsstelle, 1978.
"Freiheit durch Sicherheit: Unsere Verantwortung für die Zukunft." In *CDU/ CSU sicherheitspolitischer Kongress, Januar 11–12, 1980*. Bonn: CDU/ CSU, 1980.
"Rede vor dem CSU-Parteitag an 29 September 1979." In *Franz Josef Strauss: Mit aller Kraft für Deutschland*. Bonn: CSU, 1979.

The Greens and the Peace Movement
Die Grünen: Bundesprogramm. Bonn: Die Grünen, 1980.
Paktfreiheit für beide Deutsche Staaten, oder, Bis, das der Tod uns eint? Berlin: Arbeitsgruppe Berlin- und Deutschlandpolitik, Alternative Liste, 1981.
The Preservation, Promotion, and Renewal of Peace: A Memorandum of the Evangelical Church in Germany. Frankfurt: Evangelical Church in Germany, 1981.
20 Jahre: Deutsche Friedens-Union. Cologne: Deutsche Friedens-Union, 1980.

U.S. Government Publications

Congressional Budget Office. *The Theater Nuclear Forces*. Washington, D.C.: U.S. Government Printing Office, 1977.
Congressional Research Service. *Authority to Order the Use of Nuclear Weapons*. Washington, D.C.: Library of Congress, 1975.
Treaty between the USA and USSR on Elimination of Their Intermediate-Range and Shorter-Range Missiles, December 8, 1987. Reprinted in *Survival*, March/ April 1988, pp. 163–180.
U.S. Congress, House, Committee on Armed Services. *Status of the MBFR Negotiations*. Washington, D.C.: U.S. Government Printing Office, 1978.
—— Committee on Foreign Affairs. *Soviet Diplomacy and Negotiating Behavior*. Washington, D.C.: U.S. Government Printing Office, 1979.

——, ——, Subcommittee on Europe and the Middle East. *The Modernization of NATO's Long-Range Theater Nuclear Forces.* Washington, D.C.: U.S. Government Printing Office, 1980.

U.S. Congress, Senate, Committee on Foreign Relations. *Documents on Germany: 1944–1961.* Washington, D.C.: U.S. Government Printing Office, 1961.

——, ——, Subcommittee on European Affairs. *SALT and the NATO Allies.* Washington, D.C.: U.S. Government Printing Office, 1979.

U.S. Department of Defense. *Annual Report.* Washington, D.C.: U.S. Government Printing Office, 1975–1990.

North Atlantic Treaty Organization Documents

Conventional Forces in Europe: The Facts. Brussels: NATO Press Service, 1988.

General Report on the Security of the Alliance—The Role of Nuclear Weapons. Klaas de Vries (Holland), rapporteur, Military Committee, North Atlantic Assembly. Brussels: NATO, 1979)

Interim Report of the Special Committee on Nuclear Weapons in Europe. John Cartwright (U.K.) and Julian Critchley (U.K.) co-rapporteurs, for the International Secretariat, North Atlantic Assembly. Brussels: NATO, 1981.

Index